# PUBLIC PROCUREMENT RULES OF THE ROAD

## NEGOTIATING PUBLIC TENDERING IN IRELAND AND NORTHERN IRELAND

### A €90 BILLION MARKET

**Peter Brennan and Joanne Gillen**

**Disclaimer**

While the authors provide guidance throughout, the book's suppliers and buyers should not rely exclusively on this material when making commercial decisions. They need to exercise their own judgement at all times. Furthermore, no legal advice is offered, nor should anything be construed as legal advice. In all situations where an interpretation of the law is involved, you should consult a lawyer.

This edition first published 2016 by Carrowmore Publishing
50 City Quay
Dublin 2
www.carrowmore.ie

The moral right of the authors has been asserted in accordance with the Copyright And Related Rights Act, 2000.

ISBN: 978-0-9931716-7-3

**Acknowledgements**

Many thanks to Francis Carroll of Public Procurement Services and Tonia Spollen who reviewed draft material. We are most grateful for the improvements and clarifications that were suggested.

## About the Authors

**Dr Peter Brennan** is co-owner and chairman of Bid Management Services (BMS), the largest bid and tender management consultancy on the island of Ireland. Peter spent the first part of his career working for the Departments of Foreign Affairs and Industry and Commerce, including two postings to Brussels. During his middle career (1986–2001), he was a director of the Irish Business and Employer's Confederation (IBEC) and was responsible for the Irish Business Bureau; IBEC's Brussels office. He has a public policy and research consultancy (EPS Consulting) and is a founder of the Public Policy Advisors Network. He is a director of two state organisations: the Dún Laoghaire Harbour Company and the Sustainable Energy Authority of Ireland. He was chairman of the Climate Change Research Group at the Institute of International and European Affairs from 2007 to 2015. His EU and policy experience has helped BMS develop and expand since it was set up in 2008. He served as a trainer, mentor and presenter on the much-acclaimed InterTradeIreland Go-2-Tender programme. He also advises many public sector buyers. His unique combination of career experiences over forty years in the public and private sectors at national and EU level, as evidenced by his 150+ tender bid wins, means he is one of the most pre-eminent experts in tendering and procurement on the island of Ireland. He has a PhD in EU policy and is a fellow of the Institute of Management Consultants Association and a member of the Association of Proposal Management Professionals (APMP), which sets the global standards of excellence for bid managers. He is the author of Behind Closed Doors: The EU Negotiations That Shaped Modern Ireland (2008) and Ireland's Green Opportunity: Driving Investment in a Low-Carbon Economy (2012).

**Joanne Gillen** CPP APMP Fellow, co-owner and managing director of Bid Management Services, has worked as an extremely successful bid manager on behalf of her clients and has won contracts valued at over €500m across a multitude of sectors in the goods and services spectrum. She is the most highly accredited member of the APMP on the island of Ireland. Furthermore, Joanne is Project Management Institute PMP™ and PRINCE 2™ certified for project management. Joanne was a key driving force behind the accreditation of Bid Management Services to the ISO9001:2008 standard since July 2010 for the company's bid management, public procurement and training processes, making Bid Management Services the only company in Europe to hold such certification. Joanne, as a fellow of the Irish Institute of Training and Development, is also an experienced training provider. Joanne constantly strives to achieve excellence in the preparation of tender documents and this has been reflected in the 80 per cent win rate for Bid Management Services' clients since retaining her services. As managing director, Joanne has been the keystone of Bid Management Services becoming Ireland's largest and most successful bid management consultancy in a few short years.

## List of Abbreviations

| | |
|---|---|
| APMP | Association of Proposal Management Professionals |
| BAFO | Best and Final Offer |
| BQPR | Best Quality Price Ratio |
| BMS | Bid Management Services |
| CAN | Contract Award Notice |
| CCPC | Competition and Consumer Protection Commission |
| CCS | Crown Commercial Service |
| CIPS | Chartered Institute of Procurement and Supply |
| CWMF | Capital Works Management Framework |
| COPE | Centre of Procurement Excellence |
| CPD | Central Procurement Directorate |
| CPV | Common Procurement Vocabulary |
| CV | Curriculum Vitae |
| DCC | Dublin City Council |
| DPER | Department of Public Expenditure and Reform |
| DPS | Dynamic Purchasing System |
| ECJ | European Court of Justice |
| EPA | Environmental Protection Agency |
| ESPD | European Single Procurement Document |
| FOI | Freedom of Information |
| GHG | Greenhouse Gas |
| GN | Guidance Note |
| GPP | Green Public Procurement |
| GTM | Go To Market |
| HBS | Health Business Service |
| HSE | Health Service Executive |
| IBEC | Irish Business and Employer's Confederation |
| IIPMM | Irish Institute of Purchasing and Materials Management |
| ISO | International Standards Organisation |
| ITT | Invitation to Tender |
| LCC | Life Cycle Costs |
| LGOPC | Local Government Operational Procurement Centre |
| LTR | Light Touch Regime |
| MEAT | Most Economically Advantageous Tender |
| NAO | National Audit Office |

| | |
|---|---|
| NASF | Notification to Activate Services Form |
| NDPB | Non-Departmental Public Body |
| NI | Northern Ireland |
| OGP | Office of Government Procurement |
| OJEU | Official Journal of the European Union |
| PIN | Prior Information Notice |
| PIP | Project Implementation Plan |
| PO | Purchase Order |
| PPAN | Public Policy Advisors Network |
| PPP | Public Private Partnership |
| PQQ | Pre-Qualification Questionnaire |
| PSCS | Project Supervisor for the Construction Stage |
| PSDP | Project Supervisor for the Design Stage |
| PSR | Procurement Resource Requirement |
| RFI | Request for Information |
| RFQ | Request for Quotation |
| RFT | Request for Tender |
| SLA | Service Level Agreement |
| SME | Small and Medium Enterprise |
| SRFT | Supplementary Request for Tender |
| TAS | Tender Advisory Service |
| TED | Tenders Electronic Daily |
| TUPE | Transfer of Undertakings and Protection of Employees |
| TRD | Tender Response Document |
| TWD | Total Weighted Discount |
| USP | Unique Selling Proposition |
| WLCC | Whole Life Cycle Costs |

# Contents

# Foreword

The purpose of this book is to help companies (suppliers) on the island of Ireland to sell to public and private buyers by way of competitive tendering and in so doing to win more business.

Given that there are broadly common procurement rules in Ireland and Northern Ireland (NI) – with some notable nuances – we have deliberately sought to inform suppliers in both jurisdictions about the best bid management techniques and persuasive writing skills needed to win public tenders.

The book is aimed at bid managers and senior management who need to be aware of the latest market developments and trends in the field of procurement.

In addition, the material will also be of interest to those new to tendering or those suppliers with limited experience as we cover all the basics in a structured, iterative manner.

Buyers too will be interested as they will get a better understanding of the huge task facing suppliers when they respond to a tender competition. This book will provide buyers with a measure of understanding about their suppliers and the challenges they face as they grapple with complex procurement rules and procedures.

We know from experience that many people struggle to write a tender response and consider this task as a chore. Having read this book you should have the confidence to enjoy writing winning bid responses as much as we do.

Why is a book of this nature relevant and timely?

Firstly, with over €90 billion in government contracts to be awarded on the island of Ireland over the next five years, there is plenty of business to be won.

Secondly, significant reform is taking place; there is a trend towards the use of public contracts with a higher value (using what are called framework agreements); there is huge competition in the marketplace; more suppliers are collaborating through bid consortiums; and there is pressure on pricing as the Irish government seeks to use procurement as a policy tool to save Exchequer spending.

Finally, the procurement rules have been updated to take account of the implementation in Ireland and NI of the EU's new Procurement Directives. This book includes a detailed description and assessment of these new arrangements.

The book is structured in such a manner that each chapter is self-contained, so the reader can easily focus on one particular aspect of tendering and/or procurement.

There is a logical structure, as follows:

Part I begins with the roles and responsibilities of the principal procurement authorities, i.e. the OGP in Ireland and the Central Procurement Directorate (CPD) in NI. We then set out recommended sources of information and an assessment of the market for public goods, services and works in Ireland, NI and other jurisdictions.

Part II introduces and assesses the new EU Procurement Directives. It then explains how procurement competitions should be run (and draws on prevailing government guidance) and the steps which buyers are required to follow. Emerging issues, such as green procurement and the use of innovation partnerships, are also covered. Given their importance, the use of framework agreements is highlighted. The option of setting up a bid consortium is assessed and this section concludes with a chapter on works contracts.

Part III covers the development of your bid strategy using a bid/no-bid methodology and other techniques. The elements of the bid strategy, including pricing, and use of a bid management plan are detailed. We also highlight the need to conduct competitor research to inform your unique selling propositions (USP); to make the best use of sub-contractors; to leverage your bid library; and to produce a bid response that is not only compliant but clearly at a level of quality and content above the competition. The final chapter in this section explains how bids are assessed and marks awarded.

Part IV deals with writing in a persuasive, positive and compelling manner and making the best use of an executive summary. It also highlights the importance of using graphics and photography and provides guidance about the design and layout of the bid response document and how to prepare for a presentation.

Part V covers an area of tendering that is often neglected or under-estimated: contract management. A new procurement option called Dynamic Purchasing System (DPS) is explained as Irish and NI buyers will no doubt make greater use of this flexible arrangement. The subtle but important differences between tendering to the private and public sectors are explained. A summary of the top tender tips concludes Public Procurement: Rules of the Road.

In the past six years we have helped the clients of Bid Management Services win some €1 billion in new business by tendering to the public and private sectors.

We hope the lessons and practical advice embedded in this book will assist you secure a share of the €2,400 billion in public tenders for works, supplies and services that are procured across the EU every year.

# PART I
# The Players, Markets and Information Sources

# Ireland – The Office of Government Procurement

## Introduction

The Office of Government Procurement (OGP) is the executive state agency responsible for procurement in Ireland. It was set up in July 2013 as part of the Irish Government's wider programme for public sector reform and began sourcing operations in 2014.

The OGP, which when fully operational will have a staff complement over 225, reports to the Minister for Public Expenditure and Reform and has its own vote (budget). Its primary aims are to secure some €500 million in savings over three years (2015–2017) across the public sector through efficiencies in public procurement and to achieve better value for money for the taxpayer. As of July 2015, some €100 million in savings had been secured. While the OGP is a non-statutory agency for the present, the intention is that it will be governed by primary legislation.

Suppliers would be well advised to become acquainted with the ongoing reforms in procurement that the OGP is rolling out as they will have a significant impact on suppliers' ability to win tender bids. This reform programme does not affect works contracts (see chapter 9) or procurement by commercial semi-state agencies as they manage their own procurement competitions.

Public procurement is the acquisition, whether under formal contract or not, of works, supplies and services by public bodies. National guidelines governing public procurement must comply with the relevant EU and national legal requirements and obligations. Under EU law, public contracts above a certain value (threshold) must be advertised EU-wide and awarded to the most competitive tender in an open and objective procurement process.

## Capacity and Capability Review

In September 2012, the Department of Public Expenditure and Reform (DPER) published a report commissioned from Accenture, which undertook a capacity and capability review of Ireland's central procurement function.

The report focused on the €6.9 billion of public expenditure made on goods and services, which it considered 'Addressable by Procurement', i.e. the level of spend that could be reduced if procurement reform was introduced in relation to how those goods and services are procured. The report identified annual savings of between €249 million and €637 million that would be achievable if the report's various recommendations were adopted. These recommendations form the basis for the OGP's ongoing reform programme.

## Capacity and Capability Review
## Main Recommendations

1. A hybrid centralised procurement operating model should be set up in a single location in Dublin.

2. Under this model, a new Chief Procurement Officer would be appointed, accountable for national procurement strategy policy implementation and effective compliance. The Chief Procurement Officer would sit at the head of a new agency – the New Procurement Office (subsequently called the OGP),

under the aegis of the Department of Public Expenditure and Reform. The National Procurement Service, National Public Procurement Policy Unit and Centre for Management and Organisation Development would all transition across to the new agency.

3. A new Minister of State for Procurement position would be established within the Department of Public Expenditure and Reform and the Chief Procurement Officer would report to the Minister of State.

4. The OGP's functions would have three primary headings: Policy and Compliance, Strategic Sourcing and Category Management and Procurement Operations.

5. The OGP's Procurement Board would comprise representatives from each of the key procuring Departments at Assistant Secretary General level, to include the (then) Departments of the Environment, Community and Local Government, Defence, Justice and Equality, Education and Skills, Health, as well as representatives from the Department of Public Expenditure and Reform and the Chief Procurement Officer and a representative from the Minister of State for Procurement.

6. The OGP would be responsible for managing all strategic spend for common categories of goods and services. Certain experienced resources from individual procurement teams within the sectors of health, education, etc., would transition to the OGP.

7. A Procurement Officer within each sector would be appointed on a full-time basis to be responsible for procurement across relevant departments and agencies within that sector.

8. In order to enable savings, delivery and compliance, a centralised spend analytics IT system should be introduced to capture all state spend by type, location and seller.

9. Targets would be established, both in respect of spend and

savings, and monthly reports would be provided to the Chief Procurement Officer by each relevant government department.

10. A transition plan would need to be undertaken as new organisational capability is built up over time.

## OGP's Vision and Strategy

OGP's vision is 'to deliver sustainable procurement savings for the taxpayer by optimising value for money across the public service'. Its corresponding mission is that 'customers will have easy access to high quality procurement services that they have confidence in and procurement staff are proud to provide'.

The OGP's strategy, which derives from the Government's acceptance of the Accenture report, is to:

- Centralise procurement expertise.

- Enable consistency and standardisation of approach.

- Align policy with operations.

- Professionalise and modernise public service procurement.

- Deliver better value for the taxpayer.

- Speak with one voice to the market.

- Deliver broader goals in a consistent fashion.

## Table 1.1 – Drivers for Change

| PREVIOUS | REFORMED |
|---|---|
| Highly fragmented | Increasingly centralised |
| Variable procurement expertise | Increased expertise |
| Significant duplication | Predictable procurements |
| Increasing risk | Lower risk |
| Reactive approach | Proactive approach |
| Limited engagement with suppliers | Regular market soundings |
| Poor systems | Investment in systems |
| Incapable of delivering savings | OGP structured for success |

| Low leverage | High levels of leverage |
|---|---|
| Limited sharing of knowhow | Best practice sharing |
| No career opportunities | Professional career path |

Source: OGP (2015)

The proposed reform will result in sharp differences in approach compared to the traditional manner of procurement. The new model is demonstrated in the following diagram.

## Figure 1.1 – New OGP Model

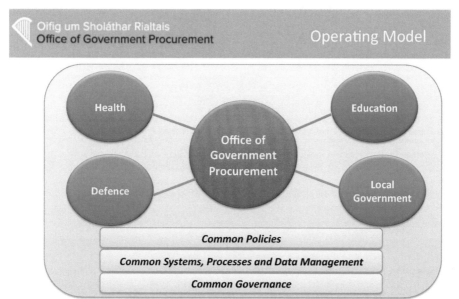

Source: OGP (2016)

The key feature of the new model is that some 3,319 contracting authorities that previously procured goods and services will fulfil the vast majority (60 per cent) of their ongoing requirements through the OGP and four sector-led groups. Thus common goods and services will be sourced from one office, formed from procurement personnel drawn from across the civil service and the wider public sector.

It is important to note that the OGP will not be responsible for contract management as this is the responsibility of individual buyers (see chapter 21).

This is a significant platform of procurement reform that will take several years to implement in full.

## OGP Structure

The vast majority of the OGP's target recruitment headcount is now in place, with many specialist buyers recruited from the private sector. The OGP has offices in Dublin, Cork, Trim, Limerick and Sligo.

The following is the OGP's organisation chart. This is, of course, subject to change.

## Table 1.2 – OGP Organisation Chart

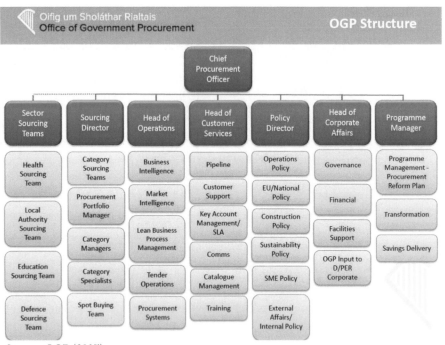

Source: OGP (2015)

## OGP Category Councils

A fundamental change in procurement is the setting-up of OGP-led category councils that are responsible for most of government spending on goods and services in the sub-sectors that comprise the council's remit. The role of each category council is to advise on sourcing strategies for goods and services. Each council comprises members who are nominated by the departments and agencies that are the main users of the category.

The sourcing organisations, with input from the category councils decide:

- Whether the public sector should approach the market in one or more lots;

- What specifications can/should be harmonised;

- How demand can be controlled; and

- Market considerations.

- The following table lists the main category councils and, more importantly, the sub-categories falling within the remit of each council.

## Table 1.3 – OGP Category Councils

| CATEGORY COUNCIL | SUB-CATEGORIES |
|---|---|
| Professional Services | Actuarial, Advisory, Architect, Audit, Banking, Communications, Financial, Insurance, Legal, Quantity Surveying, and Research |
| Facilities Management, Maintenance | Building Maintenance, Catering Equipment, Supplies and Services, Cleaning Equipment, Supplies and Services, Document Management, Fitting and Furnishings, Health and Safety, Laundry, Rental, Security, Sports Equipment, Uniforms and Clothing, and Waste Management |
| Utilities | Electricity, Gas, Fuels and Water |
| ICT and Office Equipment | Hardware, Software, Services, Telecoms (Data, Equipment, Mobile and Voice), ICT Professional Services, and Office Equipment |
| Marketing, Print and Stationery | Advertising, Public Relations, Creative Media, Creative Services, Promotional Events, IT Consumables and Peripherals, Marketing, Printing, Office Printing, Office Supplies and Production Printing |

| Travel and HR Services | Car Hire, Employee Assistance Programme, Health and Safety, Hotel and Meetings (Incentives, Conferences, Events, Pension), Pension, Recruitment, Travel Agency and Travel Services, Training, Temporary Staff and Contractors, Transport (Air, Rail, Road), Postage and Couriers |
| --- | --- |
| Fleet and Plant | Equipment, Fuel, Maintenance, Other Plant (Lifts, Generators etc.), Vehicles Purchased, Vehicle Fit Out, Vehicle Rental, Leasing and Fleet Hire |
| Managed Services | Outsourced Services |

Source: OGP (2015)

## Sourcing Teams

A central feature of the OGP and sectoral sourcing is the setting-up of sourcing teams, which are led by professional procurement managers in the new operating model. The sourcing teams are cross-sectoral and are nominated by the category councils. The sourcing teams are responsible for sourcing a specific category and conducting tenders competitions in line with the agreed sourcing strategy.

In particular, the sourcing teams are responsible for:

- Executing individual tender processes.

- Drafting tender specifications (for review by the category council before issue to the market).

- Evaluating tenders and identifying preferred bidders.

- Delivering compliant sourcing strategies.

- Ensuring that the sourcing strategies and specifications meet with customer departments' and agencies' requirements.

- Developing policies and strategies to manage demand.

The portfolio managers for the category councils are as follows (May 2016). Be aware that new appointments will be made over time and individuals will be moved within the OGP, so contact support@ procurement.ie if you are having difficulty making contact with a named individual.

## Table 1.4 – OGP Category Managers

| CATEGORY | DESCRIPTION | CATEGORY MANAGER |
|---|---|---|
| Professional Services | Legal services | Sean Bresnan |
| | Stenography services | Colm Flynn |
| | Merchant banking | Cathal Conneely |
| ICT and Office Equipment | Electrical equipment | Eileen Delaney |
| | Records management | Martin Hughes |
| | Computer devices | Andy Somers |
| | CRM | Andy Somers |
| | Enterprise virtualisation software | Trevor Kerley |
| | Enterprise back-up software | Trevor Kerley |
| | Physical firewalls | Colm O'Cleirigh |
| | Network/communication equipment | Michael Doyle |
| | Security software application reseller | Bernard Looby |
| | Video conferencing equipment | Michael Doyle |
| | Wide area network connectivity | Michael Doyle |
| | Software asset management software | Trevor Kerley |
| | Co-location services | Colm O'Cleirigh |
| | UPS | Colm O'Cleirigh |
| Fleet and Plant | Minibuses | John Rogers |
| | Fleet maintenance | John Rogers |
| | Pick-up trucks | John Rogers |
| | Tools and hardware | John Rogers |
| | Winter servicing | John Rogers |
| | Landscaping equipment | John Rogers |
| | Digging equipment | John Rogers |
| Travel,Transport and HR | Employee Assistance Services | Roisin KIleen |
| | Occupational health services | Roisin Kileen |
| | Towing services | Donal D'Arcy |

| | Car hire/ground transportation | Donal D'Arcy |
|---|---|---|
| | Courier services | Donal D'Arcy |
| | Health and safety training | Mila Sullivan |
| | Freight (HSE distribution) | Randal MacDonnell |
| Facilities Management | Fire alarm maintenance | Eric White |
| | Window cleaning | Berni Murphy |
| | Boiler maintenance | Eric White |
| | Lift maintenance | Eric White |
| | Portable fire safety supplies | Eric White |
| | Security services | Martin Hughes |
| | Catering services and equipment | Eileen Delaney |
| | Standard PPE | Eric White |
| | Meat, fish and eggs | Eileen Delaney |
| | Commercial cleaning services | Berni Murphy |
| | Cleaning products and equipment | Nuala Scannell |
| Utilities | Utilities | Andy Bogie |
| Managed Services | Executive search | Roisin Kileen |
| | Irish language translation | Howard Maguire |
| | Business support services | Howard Maguire |
| | Managed parking services | Howard Maguire |
| | Debt/payment collection services | Howard Maguire |
| Marketing, print and stationery | Media planning and buying | Mark Holland |
| | Events planning | Mark Holland |
| | New office supplies | Treasa Nic Dhiarmada |
| | Managed print services | Treasa Nic Dhiarmada |
| | Creative, marketing and communications | Mark Holland |
| | Pitch specialists and media auditors | Mark Holland |

Source: OGP (2016)

It would be essential for all suppliers to make contact with these decision-makers about forthcoming opportunities.

CONTACT DETAILS
URL: www.procurement.ie
email: firstname.familyname@ogp.gov.ie
Tel: 076 1008000

Public sector representatives from the main buyers across government who need to procure these goods and services sit on the category councils. This cross-sectional team of functional leads is tasked with providing leadership to the public services for a given category of spend.

By way of example, the following table shows how the ICT category structure will be sub-divided.

## Table 1.5 – ICT Category Structure

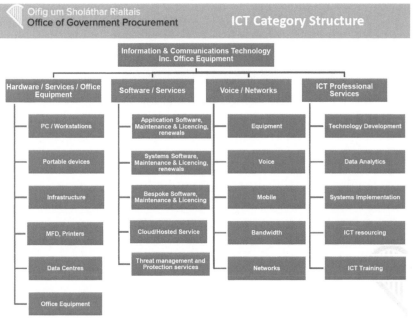

Source: OGP (2016)

The details of the ICT procurement sourcing team are as follows.

## Table 1.6 – ICT Procurement Portfolio

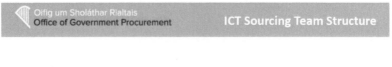

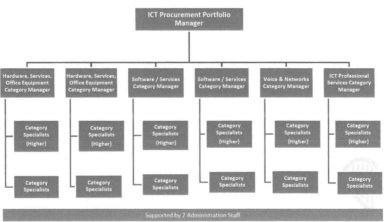

Source: OGP (2016)

## Sourcing Strategies

The role of the category councils is to decide the sourcing strategies for goods and services, taking into account suppliers' requirements, market dynamics and the savings required. The OGP base these strategies on public sector data and intelligence from suppliers. For example, the OGP conducts a thorough investigation of buyers' spending trends and future requirements and seeks to gain a full understanding of the category's market dynamic, including the regulatory environment (where applicable), the degree of competition in the marketplace, the size of the market, the key players and the likely response to the proposed Request for Tender (RFT).

A key element of the strategy is the OGP's approach to lots, i.e. the division of the contract into smaller elements. For example, lots could be divided by reference to geographical location, types of contract (e.g. major complex projects) or subject-matter expertise (e.g. in relation to professional services).

Another aspect of the sourcing strategy is the setting of sub-category-specific selection and award criteria and the factors that should inform the proposed weightings for each award criteria.

The OGP is very much informed by the feedback it gets following its engagement with the market. The OGP's report on legal services is a case to point.

A simplified and standardised sourcing process is being implemented using internal templates.

The following table summarises the ten stages for the OGP sourcing teams that are led by the relevant category manager. It is important for suppliers to realise that a deliberative and iterative effort is now applied to inform the publication of significant RFTs.

## Table 1.7 OGP Sourcing Stages

| PHASE | STAGE NAME | START (DATE) | END (DATE) |
|---|---|---|---|
| Preparation | 1. Item in pipeline | Item received in pipeline | Procurement Service Requirement (PSR) complete with sufficient information received |
| | 1.1 PSR confirmation | PSR complete with sufficient information complete | |
| | 1.2 Project initiation | Procurement lead identified | Project Charter complete |
| | 1.3 Develop sourcing strategy | Internal and external analysis | Tender strategy approved |
| | 1.4 Finalise tender documentation | Tender strategy approved | Tender documentation approved |
| | 1.5 Pre-publication | | |
| Go to Market | 2.1 Conduct Go To Market (GTM) process | RFT published | Tenders received by RFT closing date |

| | 2.2 Evaluation | Tenders received and opened | Evaluation complete and request for contract approval prepared |
| | 2.3 Contract Approval | Contract approval request submitted | Contract approval request approved |
| | 2.4 Standstill | Award notification letters dispatched (including debriefing) | Standstill period (fourteen days) complete |
| Finalise Arrangements | 3.1 Contract Finalisation | Standstill period complete | Contract signed and award notice published |
| | 3.2 Communication of arrangements | Contracts signed and award notice published | Contract drawdown arrangements communicated to buyers via agreed channels |
| | 3.3 Roll-out and mobilisation | Individual buyer requires goods/ services covered by new arrangements | Supplier makes first delivery of goods/services to individual buyer |
| | 3.4 Manage suppliers | Start date of framework/contract | End date of framework/ contract |

Source: OGP (2015)

## Sector-Led Categories

The following sector-led category councils have been set up.

## Table 1.8 – Sector Led Categories

| CATEGORY | COVERAGE |
|---|---|
| Local Government | ■ **Minor Building Works and Civils** (Building, Civil, Electrical, Materials, Mechanical and Roads)<br>■ **Plant Hire** (Plant and Equipment Hire (Driver and Operator)) |

| Health | ■ **Medical Professional Services** (Carers (Disability Care and Senior Care), Care Services, and Locums (Medical Professional)<br>■ **Medical and Diagnostic Equipment and Supplies** (Medical Equipment, Medical Diagnostic Equipment, Medical Diagnostic Services, and Health Information Systems)<br>■ **Medical, Surgical and Pharmaceutical Supplies** (Surgical Equipment and Supplies, Blood and Blood products, Drugs and Medicines, and Medical Gases) |
|---|---|
| Defence | ■ **Defence and Security** (Aircraft and Aircraft Maintenance, Military Equipment and Maintenance, Naval Vessels and Maintenance, Ordinance Equipment, Other Military Supplies, and Military Vehicles and Maintenance. |
| Education | ■ **Veterinary and Agriculture** (Livestock, Feed, Consumables, Equipment, Other Services, Supplies and Veterinary<br>■ **Laboratory, Diagnostics and Equipment** (Laboratory Equipment, Laboratory Diagnostic Systems and Supplies) |

Source: OGP (2016)

The persons in charge of these groups are as follows.

## Table 1.9 - Sector Contact Details

| CATEGORY | CONTACT DETAILS |
|---|---|
| Local Government | Catherine Carmody – 076 1064020 |
| Health | John Swords – 01 6352251 |
| Defence and Security | 01 8046092 (no name designated) |
| Education | Phillip Gurnett – 061 202700 |

Source: OGP (2015)

## Governance

The members of the Procurement Board, who have a mandate to provide oversight to the OGP and leadership on procurement reform, are:

- Chair: The Minister of State at the Department of Public Expenditure and Reform with special responsibility for Public Procurement

- Jim Breslin, Secretary General, Department of Health

- Eileen Creedon, Chief State Solicitor

- Martin Fraser, Secretary General, Department of the Taoiseach

- John McCarthy, Secretary General, Department of Housing, Planning and Local Government

- Niamh O'Donoghue, Secretary General, Department of Social Protection

- Martin Sisk, External Appointee

- Paul Quinn, Chief Procurement Officer, Office of Government Procurement, Department of Public Expenditure and Reform

The following screenshot of procurement.ie – the home page of the OGP – demonstrates the services provided to buyers and suppliers.

## Figure 1.2 – Screenshot of Procurement.ie

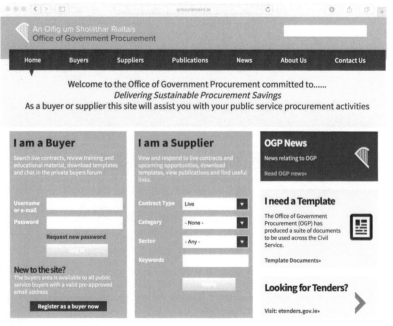

Source: OGP, 2016

Suppliers can search on this site for upcoming opportunities and access the guidance used by buyers in relation to the templates for supplies and services contracts (see chapter 6). In addition, the OGP has supplied information about the expiry dates of all framework agreements.

Both suppliers and buyers need to be registered to get access to key features of the website.

## Tender Advisory Service

The OGP set up a Tender Advisory Service (TAS) for suppliers in February 2015. TAS is an informal service provided free of charge to suppliers to allow them to raise questions in relation to a live tender carried out by the OGP or other public buyers (excluding commercial semi-state bodies).

TAS is available to suppliers with an interest in a specific tender process in the following circumstances:

- The supplier has an enquiry regarding a RFT that has been published.

- The supplier has a registered interest in the specific tender process.

- The supplier has already availed of the clarification process set out in the RFT documentation but is not satisfied with the response(s) received from the buyer.

Suppliers have to complete a Standard Enquiry Form and forward it, and accompanying documentation, to TAS at least six days prior to the tender closing date.

TAS will liaise with buyers on behalf of suppliers to clarify or query tender documentation and, where necessary, will make suggestions to buyers aimed at resolving concerns that have been raised. If an enquiry is judged to be complex, TAS may refer it for review to a member (or members) of the expert panel set up for this purpose.

To avoid delays in the tender process, it is envisaged that enquiries will typically be processed within three working days. In certain instances, clarifications may take longer because of the complexity of the tender process involved.

TAS does not in any way interfere with the statutory rights of individuals under the EU Remedies Directive (see chapter 18) or other relevant legislation, such as Freedom of Information and Data Protection legislation.

Enquiries should in the first instance be made to the OGP Customer Service Desk (tenderadvisoryservice@ogp.gov.ie or phone 01 647 6873), who will advise on the eligibility of your enquiry and the various steps that should be followed to pursue the enquiry through TAS.

The take-up of the TAS has been poor, with the vast majority of queries not appropriate to the service for various reasons; for example, suppliers had not exhausted the RFT clarification process before contacting the TAS.

## Policy Role

The OGP also has a significant policy role, so, for example, it is responsible for the implementation of the new EU Procurement Directives into Irish law (see chapter 5) and the drafting of legislation to put the organisation on a statutory basis. The OGP regularly issues policy guidance to buyers (e.g. Circular 10/14) about initiatives to assist SMEs in public procurement.

## Healthcare Procurement

A new model for health procurement is being implemented in the context of major policy change and reform, including new HSE structures for acute hospitals and community and primary care; Health Business Service (HBS) mobilisation; the setting up of a National Distribution Centre distributing to nine hubs with 6,000 customer delivery points; the development of multi-annual procurement plans (2016–2018); and OGP reform.

HSB Procurement has adopted the following core values:

- Achieving efficiency, effectiveness and best vaue for money in terms of overall life cycle.

- Operating in close partnerships with clinical and technical stakeholders.

- Dealing with quality suppliers, contractors and service providers based on the HSE Supplier Charter.

- Managing risk.

- Operating to the highest ethical standard.

## Table 1.10 - Healthcare Contact Details

| John Swords | Head of Procurement | john.swords@hse.ie | 01 6352251 |
|---|---|---|---|
| Brendan White | Head of Sourcing and Contracts | brendan.white@hse.ie | 052 6191240 |
| Brian Long | Head of Logistics and Investory Management | brian.long1@hse.ie | 061 464074 |
| Siobhan Dunphy | Office of the Head of Procurement Manager | siobhan.dunphy@hse.ie | 01 6352377 |
| Martin Quinlivan | Medical, surgical and pharmaceutical supplies | martin.quinlivan@hse.ie | 052 6125676 |
| Vincent O'Sullivan | Medical and diagnostic equipment and supplies | vincent.osullivan@hse.ie | 021 4928073 |
| Michael Driscoll | Medical professional services | michael.driscoll@hse.ie | 021 4923045 |

Source: HSE (2016)

## Conclusion

The OGP is the central player in procurement in Ireland. As a consequence, suppliers need to foster positive working relationships with the key category council decision-makers.

Many of the OGP's guidelines and policy recommendations are covered in subsequent chapters.

---

### TENDER TIP

Keep up to date with the OGP's news and views.

---

# 2

# Northern Ireland – Central Procurement Directorate

## Introduction

NI's Central Procurement Directorate (CPD) is the government agency responsible for managing procurement competitions and implementing procurement policy. The CPD works closely with nine Centres of Procurement Excellence (COPEs), which govern some 98 per cent of all procurements in Northern Ireland.

Procurement is based on clear policy principles rooted in what are considered to be best practice techniques and operational procedures. As in Ireland, securing value for money is the dominant consideration.

This chapter will introduce the key organisations, decision-makers and policies that shape and influence this small but significant market.

## Central Procurement Directorate

The CPD is part of the Department of Finance and Personnel and provides procurement advisory services to Northern Ireland departments and other public bodies. It publishes guidance for buyers and is also responsible for policy on procurement (see below).

The CPD also directly procures some strategic requirements (such as major IT systems and some capital works) and manages the tender competitions on behalf of many buyers. Its Centre of Expertise for Programme and Project Management provides training and know-how to procurement officers.

The CPD is also implementing an Asset Management Strategy. A key driver is a desire to maximise the potential for aggregation of demand for common goods and services by the practice of category management in the following areas:

- Postal services
- Advertising
- Energy
- Travel
- Facilities management

- Professional services, including banking
- ICT commodities
- Telecoms and networks
- Office supplies

The CPD also carries out pre-market consultations for future procurements in key sectors.

## COPEs

Centres of Procurement Expertise provide expert advice and professional procurement services in the following sectors:

- Education (Education and Library Boards)
- BSO PaLS (Health Estates)
- Housing (NI Housing Executive)
- Roads (Roads Service)
- Transport (Translink)
- Water (NI Water)

The CPD has three COPEs that deal with construction works and services; construction health services; and supplies and services. These COPEs meet the needs of NI departments, their agencies and non-departmental public bodies.

The COPEs help buyers by:

- Helping the client identify their needs and develop a specification.

- Adopting a procurement and contract strategy.

- Incorporating NI Executive policies and sustainability.

- Developing evaluation strategies to ascertain best VfM.

- Carrying out cost analysis.

- Facilitating the tender evaluation.

- Awarding the contract.

- Delivering professional contract management.

A Procurement Practitioners Group, comprising representatives of the CPD and the COPEs, has been set up to inform, test and develop policies and operational issues.

## Table 2.1 – NI Statistics

Spending procured through public sector tendering is valued at some around £2.8 billion a year; some €3.5 billion. Recent reductions in expenditure may see this level fall somewhat in the future.
Nearly 3,000 contracts were awarded in 2014.
Some 80 per cent of all tenders are won by NI suppliers, of which 51 per cent were companies employing less than fifty people.
Micro-businesses win 19 per cent of tenders by value.
An average of 6.4 bids is submitted for every tender.
Leading spenders by department are:
- Health, Social Services and Public Safety (30 per cent)
- Regional Development (27 per cent)
- Education (11 per cent)
- Justice (10 per cent)

Source: CPD (2015)

## Local Authorities

The following District Councils operate independently (from April 2015) and have their own particular arrangements for procurement:

- Antrim and Newtownabbey District Council website

- Armagh, Banbridge and Craigavon District Council website
- Belfast District Council website
- Causeway Coast and Glens District Council website
- Derry and Strabane District Council website
- Fermanagh and Omagh District Council website
- Lisburn and Castlereagh District Council website
- Mid and East Antrim District Council website
- Mid Ulster District Council website
- Newry, Mourne and Down District Council website
- North Down and Ards District Council website

## Meet The Buyer

Meet The Buyer events, organised in collaboration with CPD and the OGP, bring buyers and suppliers together. Over 1,200 suppliers attended the events held in 2015.

## Procurement Board

A Procurement Board has been set up with responsibility for the development, dissemination, and co-ordination of public procurement policy and practice for the NI public service. It is responsible to the NI Executive and is accountable to the NI Assembly.

To emphasise its importance, it is chaired by the Minister for Finance and comprises the Permanent Secretaries General of NI's twelve departments, as well as two external experts.

The Procurement Board, supported by a secretariat provided by the CPD, has policy, evaluation, monitoring and strategic development functions, while leaving operational matters to the COPEs.

## Key Contacts

The following are the contact details for the main NI buyers.

## Table 2.2 - NI Procurement Contacts

| ORGANISATION | CONTACT DETAILS |
|---|---|
| CPD – Supplies and Services | Supplies and Services helpdesk 028 90816031 SSDAdmin.CPD@dfpni.gov.uk |
| CPD – Construction | Construction helpdesk 028 90816555 Construction.Info@dfpni.gov.uk |
| CPD – Health Construction Projects | Health Projects helpdesk 028 90523754 Information.Services@dfpni.gov.uk |
| Health supplies and services (BSO PaLS) | www.hscbusiness.hscni.net/ services/1979.htm |
| NI Education Authority | www.eani.org.uk/about-us/tenders/ |
| NI Housing Executive | www.nihe.gov.uk/index/corporate/ procurement/doing_business_with_ us.htm |
| NI Water | www.niwater.com/tenders/ |
| Translink | www.translink.co.uk/Corporate/ Procurement/Contact-Us/ |
| Transport NI | www.infrastructure-ni.gov.uk/articles/ transportni-current-tenders |

Source: CPD (2016)

## Public Procurement Policy

In Northern Ireland, procurement is seen as a contributor to the delivery of greater equality and social inclusion, along with broader environmental and sustainability goals. The NI Programme for Government includes a commitment to include social clauses in contracts.

In August 2014, the following twelve guiding principles to govern the administration of public procurement were adopted. While there may be a somewhat 'tick box' approach to this list, it is important for suppliers to understand the degree to which senior public servants are committed to this reform and efficiency agenda.

- **Accountability:** Effective mechanisms are to be put in place to enable Departmental Accounting Officers (and their equivalents across the public sector) to discharge their personal responsibility on issues of procurement risk and expenditure.

- **Competitive Supply:** Procurement should be carried out by competition unless there are convincing reasons to the contrary.

- **Consistency:** Suppliers should be able to expect the same general procurement policy across the public sector.

- **Effectiveness:** Buyers should meet the commercial, regulatory and socio-economic goals of government in a balanced manner appropriate to the procurement requirement.

- **Efficiency:** Procurement processes should be carried out as cost-effectively as possible.

- **Fair Dealing:** Suppliers should be treated fairly and without unfair discrimination, including protection of commercial confidentiality where required. Public bodies should not impose unnecessary burdens or constraints on suppliers or potential suppliers.

- **Integration:** Procurement policy should pay due regard to the Executive's other economic, social and environmental policies, rather than cut across them.

- **Integrity:** There should be no corruption or collusion with suppliers or others.

- **Informed Decision-Making:** Buyers need to base decisions on accurate information and to monitor requirements to ensure that they are being met.

- **Legality:** Buyers must conform with EU and other legal requirements.

- **Responsiveness:** Buyers should endeavour to meet the aspirations, expectations and needs of the community served by the procurement.

- **Transparency:** Buyers should ensure that there is openness and clarity on procurement policy and its delivery.

## Guidance Notes

Hereunder are the current guidance notes in place for supplies and services. The current guidance applying to construction works can be found in chapter 9.

**2016**

- Light Touch Regime

**2015**

- Procurement Guidance Note 02/15 – Procurement Pipeline

**2014**

- Procurement Guidance Note 06/14 – Standard Conditions of Contract for Supplies and Services

- Procurement Guidance Note 05/14 – Collaborative Procurement

- Procurement Guidance Note 04/14 – Integrating Sustainable Development into the Procurement of Food and Catering Services

- Procurement Guidance Note 02/14: Implementation of Article 6 of the Energy Efficiency Directive

- Procurement Guidance Note 01/14 – Best Practice in the Management of Property Maintenance Contracts

**2013**

- Procurement Guidance Note 04/13 – Insolvency in the Procurement Process

- Procurement Guidance Note 03/13 – Abnormally Low Tenders

- Procurement Guidance Note 01/13 – Integrating Social Considerations into Contracts

**2012**

- Procurement Guidance Note 06/12 – Helping SMEs Benefit from Subcontracting Opportunities

- Procurement Guidance Note 05/12 – Simplified Approach to Procurement Over £30k and Under Threshold

- Procurement Guidance Note 04/12 – Procurement Control Limits and the Basis for Contract Awards

- Procurement Guidance Note 03/12 – Liability and Insurance in Government Contracts

- Procurement Guidance Note 02/12 – Public Procurement: A Guide for Small and Medium Sized Enterprises (SMEs)

- Procurement Guidance Note 01/12 – Contract Management – Procedures and Principles

**2011**

- Procurement Guidance Note 03/11 – Award of a Contract Without a Competition

- Procurement Guidance Note 02/11 – Helping Small and Medium Sized Enterprises (SMEs) and Social Economy Enterprises (SEEs) access Public Sector contracting opportunities

- Procurement Guidance Note 01/11 – A Guide for Social Economy Enterprises

**2010**

- Procurement Guidance Note 01/10:- Information Disclosure Throughout the Procurement Process and Application of the Rules on the Standstill Period

Suppliers should become familiar with these rules if they are serious about bidding in NI. Of particular significance is the 2012 guidance for SMEs as this sets out how NI buyers should operate tender competitions reflecting EU procurement principles. Thus, in many respects the rules for running tender competitions in both jurisdictions are quite similar. However, the suite of guidance in NI is much more comprehensive in some respects than in Ireland.

All COPEs use standard conditions of contract for the supply of goods and services, which are not negotiable. In common with Ireland, the rules in relation to works contacts are comprehensive and well-developed. There are guidelines in NI about integrating social considerations into contracts. The guidelines also encourage buyers to ensure SMEs are included in the procurement process, possibly as supply-chain partners. It is suggested that successful suppliers should advertise sub-contracting opportunities.

For contracts over £30,000 up to the EU contract value threshold, and where one-off requirements are to be procured, COPEs are to use the open procedure, i.e. a one-stage tender competition with contracts awarded based on the lowest acceptable price. Importantly, NI departments aim to pay at least 90 per cent of valid invoices within ten days. The new EU Procurement Directives were transposed into law in Northern Ireland (and England and Wales) by the Public Contracts Regulations 2015, which came into force on 26 February 2015. See the next chapter for a more detailed briefing about eTendersNI.

## Low-Value contracts

All opportunities with a value in excess of £30,000 are advertised on the eTendersNI website. For contracts below that threshold, a less onerous procurement process applies. Recent guidance (December 2015) has been published about the conduct of procurement competitions for low-value contracts.

## Value for Money

There is a clear definition in NI of what constitutes 'best value for money': 'the most advantageous combination of cost, quality and sustainability to meet customer requirements'. Cost means the whole life-cycle costs; quality means meeting a specification which is fit for purpose and sufficient to meet customer's requirements; and sustainability means economic, social and environmental benefits.

Thus, the NI administration has a much wider understanding of this critical issue for both buyers and suppliers than is the case in Ireland. So much so that every proposed tender in NI must be the subject of a business case at a level of detail proportionate to the value of the contract.

---

TENDER TIP

Do not lose sight of the potential of all-island bidding as a way to gain access to the UK procurement market.

---

## 3

# Sources of Information

## Introduction

This chapter covers essential sources of information that suppliers should be aware of and familiar with when searching for new tendering opportunities.

The Irish portal etenders.gov.ie allows suppliers to register their company details and select the categories of business that they are most interested in. There are some 48,000 suppliers (including companies based outside Ireland) registered on eTenders and some 3,300 active buyers, including public-service bodies, semi-state companies, schools and voluntary and other bodies whose activities/programmes are subsidised 50 per cent or more by a public body.

Once registered on eTenders, suppliers can set up links using the relevant procurement codes and will then automatically receive tender alerts. This 'push' facility is also available on eTendersNI, which is an important source of information about live tenders in Northern Ireland. So too is the UK website Contracts Finder, hosted by the UK government.

We will also introduce you to Sell2Wales.gov.uk, Public Contracts Scotland.gov.uk, Tenders Electronic Daily (TED), the EU procurement portal, and Oppex.com, a global search engine.

Let us start with etenders.gov.ie, which is managed by the OGP.

## eTenders.gov.ie – Overview

It is compulsory for all Irish buyers and organisations in receipt of Exchequer funding to advertise tenders for supplies and services in excess of €25,000 on eTenders. This threshold is based on the full contract value of the tender over its duration and not annual payments. In some recent RFTs, the OGP has reduced the threshold to as low as €12,000 (see below).

In addition, buyers use the website to review the details provided by potential suppliers in order to select a shortlist of suppliers to bid for tenders valued under €25,000. The corresponding threshold for works contracts is €50,000. This service, which is password-protected, is free for all registered users. Several utilities, such as the ESB, use a different 'pay-for-view' portal for some of their contracts. The OGP published some 115 frameworks and 75 contracts (to a value of €1.8 billion) and some 30 PINs in 2015. Non-Irish firms won 11 per cent of contracts awarded.

Figure 3.1 – eTenders

Source: OGP (2016)

## Registration and Email Alerts

OGP encourages suppliers to register with accurate company information on eTenders to ensure maximum exposure to tendering opportunities within their sector.

To register, 'click' on the 'Supplier Company Registration' button. Email alerts are provided to registered suppliers in relation to procurement opportunities arising in their respective areas as determined by the Common Procurement Vocabulary (CPV) codes they have selected for their company profile on eTenders. The CPV is used to define every sub-category of supplies, goods and services, which are the three broad types of tenders that are universally used.

Increasingly, buyers are relying on this database when deciding which suppliers will be selected to tender for below low-value threshold contracts. Therefore registered suppliers should critically analyse the range of CPV codes attaching to their registration to maximise the extent of e-mail tender opportunity alerts and to ensure they are selected as part of a relevant quick quote. The more company information that is entered, the more exposure a supplier may have to opportunities as buyers use eTenders to search for relevant suppliers for quick quotes.

The following largely self-explanatory fields (all sourced from eTenders) should be completed; it will take ten minutes or so to complete the form. It is important that you correctly identify the type of business that you are interested in. Also do not forget to complete the following sections on business alerts; some 50 per cent of suppliers who register on eTenders omit to fill in this part of the form. If you fail to complete this, requirement buyers cannot contact you in relation to tenders below a contract value of €25,000.

## Fig 3.2: eTenders Suppliers' Registration

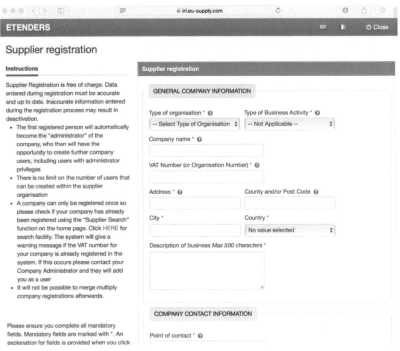

Source: OGP (2016)

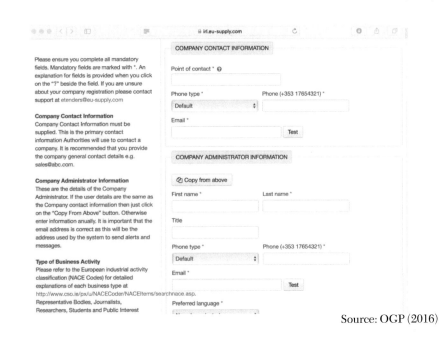

Source: OGP (2016)

## Fig 3.3 eTenders Category Tree

**ETENDERS**

### Category tree

**Instructions**

Search for a category using the free text search, by using keywords or drilling down in the category tree view.

**Please note! If you have selected a higher level of the category, the child categories will not be selected, however, they will be included in any business alert**

Search by category name: [          ] [ Search ]

[ Add selected categories ]

**CPV tree**

- 03000000-1 - Agricultural, farming, fishing, forestry and related products
- 09000000-3 - Petroleum products, fuel, electricity and other sources of energy
- 14000000-1 - Mining, basic metals and related products
- 15000000-8 - Food, beverages, tobacco and related products
- 16000000-5 - Agricultural machinery
- 18000000-9 - Clothing, footwear, luggage articles and accessories
- 19000000-6 - Leather and textile fabrics, plastic and rubber materials

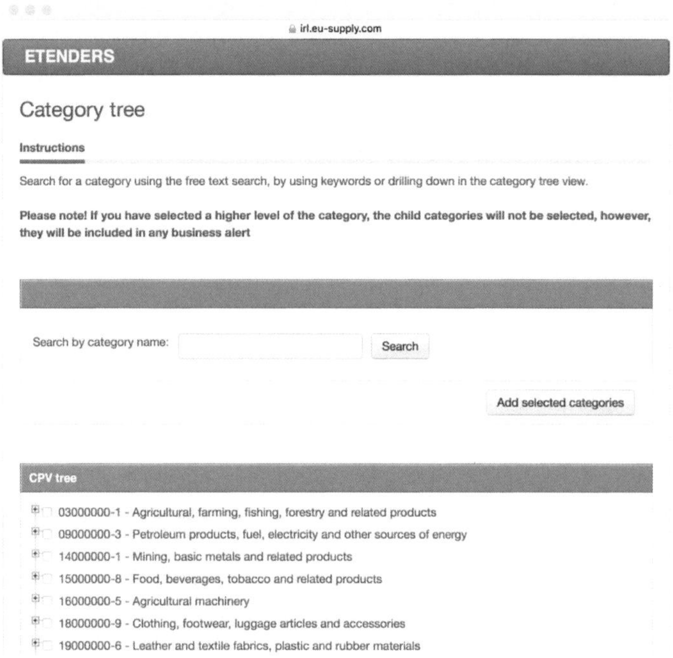

# Searching

There is a powerful search facility on eTenders. Not only can you search for live tender opportunities; using the 'Advanced Category Search' button you can also find all current and past tenders published by every buyer.

In addition, using this advanced search option you will find the names and contact details for the persons responsible for procurement in every buyer organisation registered on eTenders.

If you see a reference to 'OJEU' (Official Journal of the European Union) in a tender notice, this indicates that it has been advertised EU-wide, i.e. the projected value of the contract is above the relevant value threshold for the buyer.

Also note the Contract Awards Notices (CANs) and Prior Information Notices (PINs) that are published, in addition to live opportunities. Hereunder is a screenshot of the search page.

## Figure 3.4 – Screenshot of eTenders Search Page

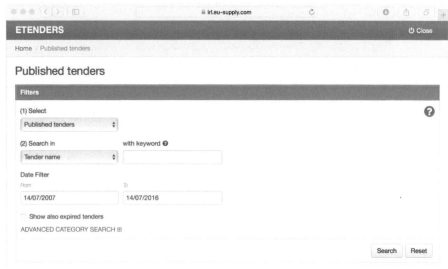

Source: OGP (2016)

# Clarifications

One important feature of the submission section is the following dialogue box, which allows you to submit clarification questions about published RFT.

## Figure 3.5 Screenshot of eTenders Clarifications Page

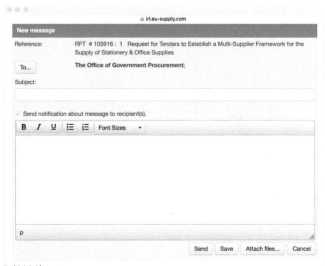

Source: OGP (2016)

## Responding to Tenders

Once you get an alert, you need to express your interest and to do this you should go the supplier home page, which looks like this:

### Figure 3.6 – eTenders Supplier Home Page

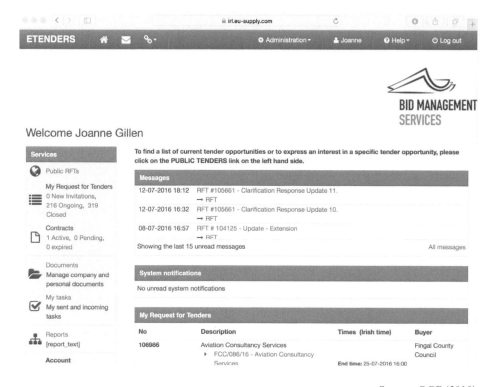

Source: OGP (2016)

Once you have opened the link to the tender documents, click 'Accept' to register your interest. Once this is done, every time there is a message from the buyer, in particular as regards clarification questions, you will automatically receive an email, along with all other suppliers who have registered an interest in this particular opportunity. Clarification questions can be submitted in the 'Messages' section. Type in your questions and press the 'Send' button.

## Help Desk

eTenders operates a Help Desk and can be contacted at etenders@eu-supply.com or on +353 21 243 9277 during office hours.

## Other Features

eTenders also contains the critical guidelines that buyers and suppliers must comply with during a tender competition – RFT templates as well as key source documents. All these documents are reviewed and explained elsewhere in this book.

## ICT Procurement

The DPER has developed procurement arrangements in the areas of ICT, telecoms, and data networking on behalf of non-commercial public sector bodies. In collaboration with a number of cross-sectoral groups, the Department has drawn on expertise across the public sector to leverage volumes and secure benefits from economies of scale. These arrangements deliver value for money, provide goods and services under public-service terms and conditions, and reduce the complexity, cost and time spent on procurement processes.

There are currently three ICT framework agreements in operation. These are listed below.

- Mobile Telephone Framework
- Fixed-Line and VOIP Framework
- Software Asset Management Framework

Government Networks is a private, managed, wide-area network connecting public service agencies on a data, voice and video capable network. A public tender exercise using a 'template RFT' must be undertaken by all buyers who wish to connect to Government Networks.

Non-commercial public buyers that are eligible to use these arrangements include:

- Central government departments, offices and non-commercial organisations which have a formal reporting and legal relationship with these departments.

- Local authorities.

- The Irish health sector.

- The Department of Education and Skills and associated agencies and organisations, third-level institutions, VEC schools, primary and secondary schools.

- The Department of Justice and Equality and agencies and organisations which have a formal reporting and legal relationship with the department.

- The Department of Defence agencies and organisations hich have a formal reporting and legal relationship with the Department.

## Construction (Works) Procurement

Quite separate from eTenders.ie is the government's construction website, which manages tender competitions under the Capital Works Management Framework (CWMF).

This site – see the screenshot below – is used not just for works contracts but for the procurement of construction professionals and advisors, such as engineers, architects and quantity surveyors.

## Figure 3.7 Screenshot of CWMF Home Page

Source: CWMF (2016)

The site contains forms for different types of works and provides templates and procedures that cover all aspects of the delivery process of a public works project, from inception to final project delivery and review. In addition, the site provides detailed guidance on how to complete the relevant forms and also includes template contracts.

These detailed requirements, which have been in force since 2005, are designed to bring cost certainty at tender-award stage; to deliver value for money; and to ensure that public works are managed more efficiently.

It is recalled that all works contracts of a value in excess of €5.225 million must be advertised EU-wide. So if you see a works contract on TED, it is over that value. The local authority group within the OGP is responsible for all 'small' works across the entire public sector.

Chapter 9 covers the CWMF in more detail.

## SupplyGov.ie

SupplyGov.ie (forerly LAQuotes.ie) is a procurement system which facilitates local authorities and other state agencies in procuring goods and services from suppliers and contractors. The website has been developed by the Local Government Operational Procurement Centre (LGOPC) to streamline and manage the procurement process of buyers in respect of the operation of local authority led category councils for plant hire and minor building and civil works.

The LGOPC has a dedicated customer services helpdesk team, which offers support via telephone and email to all users of SupplyGov. ie. The team can be contacted by telephone on 076 1064020 Monday to Friday from 9 p.m. to 5 p.m. (excluding Bank Holidays) or via email at eproc@kerrycoco.ie.

Over the last number of years, the SupplyGov.ie system has been continuously enhanced to accommodate all local authorities as well as state agencies, such as the Office of Public Works, Irish Water and the Health Service Executive (HSE). SupplyGov.ie operates two modules of procuring goods and services through RFTs and Requests for Quotations (RFQs).

## Figure 3.8 – Screenshot of SupplyGov.ie Home Page

Source: SupplyGov.ie (2016)

## eTenders NI

Like eTenders in Ireland, eTendersNI.gov.uk is the essential portal for suppliers interested in bidding in Northern Ireland as tender opportunities valued at over £30,000 are published on this site.

First-time users have to register on the site and can do so by pressing the 'Register' button. The process is a bit time-consuming as quite an amount of company details and other information is required. It will take ten minutes or so to complete. Some 7,335 suppliers are registered on eTendersNI as are 124 contracting authorities.

Once you have entered your company's details using a D-U-N-S number, you can skip a lot of other fields in the registration unless there is a red asterisk, which indicates mandatory information. You must then check your email inbox for your verification email, and activate your registration.

Now log in and use the 'EO Management' option on the left of the screen and 'Edit CPV codes'. Search for the categories that are of interest to your business and save them to your supplier profile.

eTendersNI will then issue an automatic email alert when a relevant tender is published.

Once you have expressed an interest in a particular tender, you can access the published documents by looking in the 'My Correspondence' section. Contact the helpdesk (open during office hours) if you encounter any difficulties. Once registered, you can use the site to monitor new opportunities and the tender competitions you are interested in.

Figure 3.9 – Screenshot of eTendersNI Home Page

Source: eTendersNI (2016)

Once you have expressed an interest in a particular tender you can access the published documents by clicking on the 'View Current Opportunities' button.

On eTendersNI suppliers are referred to as 'economic operators' and buyers are called 'contracting authorities'.

Suppliers are encouraged to check out the current pipeline of tender competitions that cover the CPD's procurement of supplies and services; COPEs' forthcoming requirements; and works contracts.

More details about the capital expenditure pipeline can be found on the Strategic Investment Board's website sibni.org.

In addition, suppliers should be aware of the following categories of collaborative contracts which are in place.

## Table 3.1 - Examples of Collaborative Contracts

| COURIER SERVICES | PHOTOGRAPHY | GRAPHIC DESIGN |
|---|---|---|
| Employee counselling | Office cleaning | Catering services |
| Supply of natural gas | Electricity supply | Vehicle recovery services |
| Office stationery | Laptops | Furniture and flooring |
| HR services | Travel management | Interpretation services |
| Civil engineering works | Recycling collection | Taxi services |

Source: CPD (2015)

For tender opportunities valued below £30,000, buyers will rely on suppliers' registration for specific categories on eTendersNI. For example, if ten suppliers are registered for fire safety training and a buyer wants to send a low-value contract to just five suppliers, then a random selection will be made by eTendersNI to pick the five candidates. Hence the importance of being correctly registered for all the CPV categories that you are interested in.

Clarification questions can be submitted on eTendersNI.

## Contracts Finder

The Contracts Finder website, which is operated by the UK government, provides suppliers with the opportunity to search for current and planned opportunities in excess of a value of £10,000 in Northern Ireland, Scotland, England and Wales. It is a free service.
You enter the category of business you are interested in – for example, 'civil engineering' – and press the 'Search' button.

Every opportunity will appear on screen. What distinguishes Contracts Finder from other procurement portals is that planned procurements are listed. This gives potential consortium partners a good 'heads-up' about the pipeline of work.

In addition, Contracts Finder typically identifies the indicative budget for each opportunity and provides access to tender and contract documentation.

## Sell2Wales

In common with all procurement portals, Sell2Wales allows suppliers to review live opportunities, but registration is required to access the site and express interest in a particular tender competition. Some £4.8 billion in goods and services are procured through this site annually.

Public procurement rules are more or less the same in Wales as in Ireland and other parts of the UK.

There are some 32,700 suppliers registered on Sell2Wales, with 538 buyers also registered. In 2014, some 684 tenders were published, so activity through this website is not as high as on eTenders.ie.

The following screenshot shows the features of the Sell2Wales home page.

Figure 3.10 – Screenshot of Sell2Wales Home Page

Source: Sell2Wales (2016)

The National Procurement Service (Wales), launched in November 2013, provides policy direction and manages the category teams that procure the majority of the country's tenders.

## Public Contracts Scotland

Public sector spending on goods and services across Scotland amounts to over £10 million a year. Suppliers who are interested in this large market can access all live opportunities on the Public Contracts Scotland website.

As in Ireland/NI, there is a political push in Scotland to reform its public procurement environment with a view to generating more Exchequer savings through smarter procurement techniques. The following screenshot shows the features of the Public Contracts Scotland website.

## Figure 3.11 – Screenshot of Public Contracts Scotland

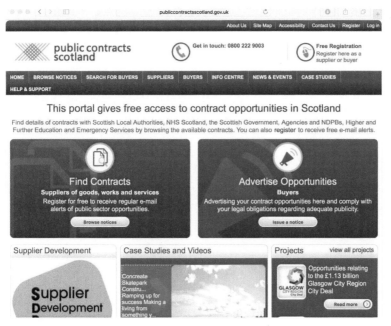

Source: Public Contracts Scotland (2016)

## Tenders Electronic Daily

TED is the online version of the 'Supplement to the Official Journal of the EU' (OJEU)), dedicated to European public procurement. The site provides free access to some 1,500 public procurement notices published across the EU, Norway and Switzerland and beyond every week.

In common with all tender websites, registration is required; not an overly difficult task. Once you are registered, you will get push notifications for all tender (CPV) categories you have selected.

The overall annual value of public works, goods and supplies at EU level is €2,400 billion, or some 19 per cent of the EU's gross domestic product. Tender contracts above the EU value thresholds account for some €425 billion per annum (3.4 per cent of GDP). This is a big market.

Remember that TED is geared for tenders over the EU thresholds and therefore may be of limited interest to some SMEs and of no relevance to sole traders and small owner managers.

## OPPEX

This procurement portal collates all public tenders in the UK, Ireland, and across the world. It is free to register and email alerts are fully customisable. It is also extremely quick to pick up published alerts.

## Conclusions

One of the key principles of the EU Procurement Directives is transparency and this principle is clearly respected on all the tender websites that we have referenced.

If anything, there is too much information to hand. Your job as a supplier is to be forensic about your information needs and to register on and search those sites that are most relevant to your business.

---

### TENDER TIP

Once a week check out Contracts Finder if you are interested in leveraging your tender successes into the £240 billion UK procurement marketplace.

---

# 4

## The Market

### Introduction

The procurement market in Ireland is valued at €14 billion annually. This comprises €8.5 billion spent on goods and services. Included in this overall amount, €2.7 billion of government contracts for supplies and services are not advertised on eTenders as they are valued at below €25,000 (source: TenderScout, 2015).

While €3.6 billion is spent on capital works, the Irish Government's six-year €42-billion capital expenditure programme (see below) will see a sharp increase in the value of works contracts to be procured over the coming period.

Ireland's commercial semi-state companies procure an estimated €2 billion per annum. In Northern Ireland, the value of the procurement market for services, goods and works is €3.5 billion. In the UK, some £240 billion in government spending is tendered every year.

Knowing that contracts to a value of some €90 billion will be procured over the next five years on the island of Ireland is not just an interesting statistic but a clear incentive to suppliers to prepare for what is anticipated to be a record level of tender competitions in the short to medium term.

But the expenditure trends at category level are far more relevant to suppliers. This chapter will delve into expenditure levels at the micro level in order to provide more granular data for suppliers as it is critical that you have an overview of spending patterns within your category.

## Ireland

A Book of Estimates is published by the DPER each year, usually in October, which sets out detailed information about current and capital Exchequer expenditure for all government departments and their agencies. For example, if as a supplier you are interested in the spending under the vote of the Department of Environment, Community and Local Government, then the Book of Estimates will show you the agreed government allocation for every sub-heading (other than pay and pensions) that will be the subject of tender competition. Further insights into expenditure trends can be found in the Comprehensive Expenditure Report (2015–2017) presented to Dáil Eireann on 14 October 2014.

The OGP has published details of the priority contacts and frameworks it intends to procure during 2016. This pipeline is updated quarterly.

Details about the Public Capital Programme 2015–17 were published as part of the 2015 budget. Thus it is possible for potential suppliers to find out about the pipeline of capital works over the coming period. The following table summarises the approved capital envelope for all government departments and their agencies.

## Table 4.1 – Capital Expenditure 2015–2017 (€m)

|  | 2015 | 2016 | 2017 |
|---|---|---|---|
| Agriculture, Food and the Marine | 197 | 200 | 200 |
| Arts, Heritage and the Gaeltacht | 62 | 36 | 36 |
| Children and Youth Affairs | 35 | 17 | 16 |
| Communications, Energy and Natural Resources | 89 | 87 | 87 |
| Defence | 12 | 8 | 8 |

| Education and Skills | 530 | 506 | 555 |
|---|---|---|---|
| Environment, Community and Local Government | 578 | 612 | 700 |
| Finance | 10 | 10 | 10 |
| Foreign Affairs and Trade | 5 | 2 | 2 |
| Health | 382 | 450 | 450 |
| Jobs, Enterprise and Innovation | 450 | 450 | 450 |
| Justice and Equality | 107 | 107 | 110 |
| Public Expenditure and Reform | 130 | 109 | 109 |
| Social Protection | 9 | 7 | 7 |
| Transport, Tourism and Sport | 954 | 1,000 | 1,008 |
| TOTAL | 3,549 | 3,600 | 3,748 |

Source: Budget 2015, Part II. Departments were re-configured in May 2016.

In September 2015, the Irish government published Building on Recovery: Infrastructure and Capital Investment (2016–21), which sets out a €42 billion expenditure programme for works over the six years to 2021. The Exchequer's contribution is estimated at €27 billion. All the projects identified will have to be procured. Further details have been posted on department websites about significant procurements. In addition, NAMA has also published details (December 2015) about its proposed investment of €7.5 billion in residential and commercial properties.

Local authorities have significant procurement requirements and are very transparent about their spending plans, both current and capital. For example, the 2016 budget for Dún Laoghaire Rathdown County Council, like all other local authorities, can be viewed on its website. Again, this data provides suppliers with insights into what each local authority will procure in a given year.

Non-pay spending by the commercial semi-state sector is also significant. The procurement officers of these state companies can provide more details.

## Table 4.2 – Contacts in the Commercial Semi-State Sector

| | DETAILS |
|---|---|
| Dublin Airport Authority Plc. | Paddy.mcmenamin@daa.ie |
| Dublin Bus | info@dublinbus.ie |
| Drogheda Port Company | maritimehouse@droghedaport.ie |
| Dublin Port Company | info@dublinport.ie |
| Dún Laoghaire Harbour Company | +353 1 2801018 |
| EirGrid | +353 1 677 1700 |
| Electricity Supply Board | +353 1 6765831 |
| Galway Harbour | info@galwayharbour.com |
| Irish Aviation Authority | +353 1 671 8655 |
| Irish Greyhound Board | pr@igb.ie |
| Irish National Stud | +353 45 521251 |
| National Lottery | +353 1 8364444 |
| Port of Cork | info@portofcork.ie |
| Irish Water/Ervia | networksinfo@gasnetworks.ie |
| Port of Waterford | info@portofwaterford.com |
| Railway Procurement Agency/TII | +353 1 6463400 |
| Shannon Foynes Port Company | info@sfpc.ie |
| An Post | procurement@anpost.ie |
| Bord na Móna | +353 45 439000 |
| Bus Éireann | info@buseireann.ie |
| CIÉ | info@cie.ie |
| Coillte (Irish Forestry Board) | +353 1 475 1444 |
| Iarnród Éireann | +353 1 7033835 |
| Raidió na Gaeltachta | +353 91 506688 |
| RTÉ | +353 12092820 |
| VHI | 1890 44 44 44 |

Source: EPS Consulting (2016)

By researching the annual reports and strategy statements of these commercial semi-state companies it is possible to find out their procurement pipeline.

Finally, the OGP has published a report, Public Service Spend and Tendering Analysis for 2013 (March 2015), which is based on detailed non-pay expenditure data provided by many large public bodies in the healthcare, education, justice and local authority sectors. While a useful source of information, it should be pointed out that only 63 per cent of total public expenditure of goods and services has been captured in this analysis, i.e. some €3.8 billion gross or €2.7 billion when exclusions such as inter-agency expenditure are taken into account.

## Contact Details

The name and contact details of every senior civil and public servant in Ireland and Northern Ireland can be found in the Institute of Public Administration's Yearbook.

## Category Analysis

Analysing spend by category is the basis of the widely adopted 'category management' approach to procurement. In Ireland, sixteen main categories cover some 97.3 per cent of total procurement spending for goods and services. Eight of these categories are common categories, i.e. categories of goods and services required by most or all sectors and public bodies, with the remaining eight associated with one dominant customer sector.

The following chart sets out spend data by category in 2013. For the sake of completeness, capital spending and spending that is deemed 'uncategorised' is included.

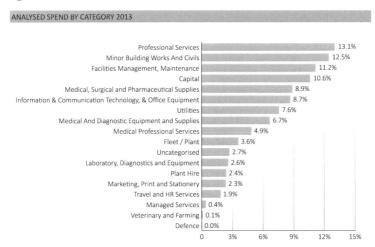

ANALYSED SPEND BY CATEGORY 2013

| Category | Percentage |
|---|---|
| Professional Services | 13.1% |
| Minor Building Works And Civils | 12.5% |
| Facilities Management, Maintenance | 11.2% |
| Capital | 10.6% |
| Medical, Surgical and Pharmaceutical Supplies | 8.9% |
| Information & Communication Technology, & Office Equipment | 8.7% |
| Utilities | 7.6% |
| Medical And Diagnostic Equipment and Supplies | 6.7% |
| Medical Professional Services | 4.9% |
| Fleet / Plant | 3.6% |
| Uncategorised | 2.7% |
| Laboratory, Diagnostics and Equipment | 2.6% |
| Plant Hire | 2.4% |
| Marketing, Print and Stationery | 2.3% |
| Travel and HR Services | 1.9% |
| Managed Services | 0.4% |
| Veterinary and Farming | 0.1% |
| Defence | 0.0% |

Source: OGP (2015)

# Figure 4.1 – Analysed Spend by Category 2013

The following chart shows how much business non-Irish companies have won (bearing in mind the average 'leakage' is 7 per cent).Figure

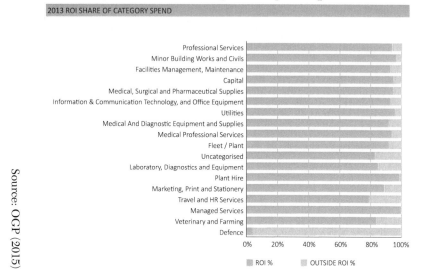

Source: OGP (2015)

## 4.2 – Irish Share of Category Spend

The following chart shows those categories in which SMEs have had the greatest success in securing tenders won by Irish companies.

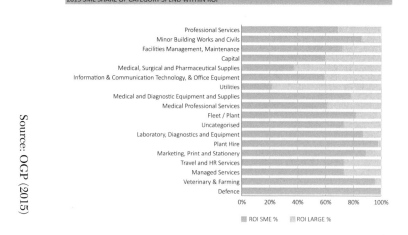

Source: OGP (2015)

# Figure 4.3 – 2013 Spend Profiles by Category

The following chart estimates the average value (and number) of tender awards by category based on eTenders activity in 2013. The data includes expenditure over several future years.

## Figure 4.4 – Average Value of Tender Awards

As can be seen, the construction and civil works category is by far the largest, followed by the ICT and professional services sectors.

While incomplete, suppliers will get a sense of the total potential

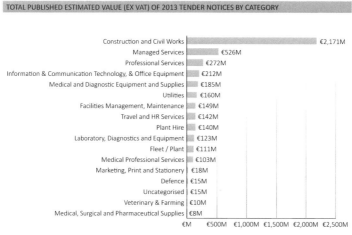

TOTAL PUBLISHED ESTIMATED VALUE (EX VAT) OF 2013 TENDER NOTICES BY CATEGORY

| Category | Value |
|---|---|
| Construction and Civil Works | €2,171M |
| Managed Services | €526M |
| Professional Services | €272M |
| Information & Communication Technology, & Office Equipment | €212M |
| Medical and Diagnostic Equipment and Supplies | €185M |
| Utilities | €160M |
| Facilities Management, Maintenance | €149M |
| Travel and HR Services | €142M |
| Plant Hire | €140M |
| Laboratory, Diagnostics and Equipment | €123M |
| Fleet / Plant | €111M |
| Medical Professional Services | €103M |
| Marketing, Print and Stationery | €18M |
| Defence | €15M |
| Uncategorised | €15M |
| Veterinary & Farming | €10M |
| Medical, Surgical and Pharmaceutical Supplies | €8M |

Source: OGP (2015)

value of their priority category. Remember that when the OGP and other main buyers publish tenders for framework agreements for these categories, and sub-categories, they should provide an indication of possible expenditure over the duration of the agreement, which is typically four years.

## Tendering Activity

The OGP report also assessed buyers' tendering activities in 2013. This data is valuable to suppliers as it is provides clear evidence that the procurement market is dynamic. The OGP report highlighted the following.

- 5,826 tender notices were published in 2014, including some 2,078 from non-public bodies in receipt of public funds.

- 84 per cent of the public sector tender notices (2,600) were for contracts falling below the EU thresholds and these represented just 16 per cent of total estimated value.

- in 2014, 1,279 notices were published for contracts over the EU threshold representing some 84 per cent of the estimated value.

- The average value of an EU notice is some €4 million, while the figure below EU threshold is just €265,200. The large difference is accounted for by the high value of construction contracts.

- Buyers only published CANs in respect of 11 per cent of tenders for supplies and goods falling under the EU threshold; the figure rose to 36 per cent for tenders above the EU threshold.

- There is a pipeline of some 4,500 buyer requirements.

## Suppliers

Over 35,000 suppliers sell to the public sector, with some 48,000 registered on eTenders.

Using the EU definition of a SME as a business employing less than 250, with turnover of less than €50m or a balance sheet of up to €43m, the OGP estimates that some 93 per cent of the value of analysed public spending was won by Irish suppliers, but just two thirds of this amount by volume was secured by SMEs. Irish SMEs were more successful securing tenders outside the jurisdiction, with 78 per cent of SMEs securing exports through tendering.

Other insights about suppliers and their behaviour have been provided by Tender Scout's Cost-Competitiveness-Collaboration report (2015).

22 per cent of suppliers do not request a debrief from buyers.

43 per cent are unlikely to collaborate with other businesses.
The average success rate of a supplier is 29 per cent.
58 per cent do not use competitive intelligence.
€25 million was spent in 2014 by suppliers on bid responses for tenders that were cancelled.
69 per cent of contracts are awarded primarily on price.
57 per cent of suppliers wait for over three months for the results of tender competitions.
70 per cent of suppliers have fewer than fifty employees.

Source: Tender Scout (2015)

## Northern Ireland

The procurement market in NI, while smaller than in Ireland, is proportionally more active given the size of the public sector. The CPD published an assessment of procurement activity for 2012/2013 which gives suppliers a good overview of the dynamics of the local marketplace.

## Table 4.4 – NI Procurement Activity – Highlights

2,966 contracts were awarded, with over 80 per cent won by SMEs by volume.

The value of these contracts was £1.7 billion, with SMEs winning 62 per cent of the contracts by value.

Nearly 80 per cent of all contracts were won by suppliers based in NI, of whom 86 per cent were SMEs.

Over 62 per cent of all contracts were of a value in excess of £3.5m.

Only 4.6 per cent of contracts awarded were valued at less than £30,000.

The total value of the procurement market was £2.7 billion.

Irish suppliers won just 3.6 per cent of NI contracts.

Source: Procurement Activity Report 2012–13, CPD (2014)

The CPD publishes its procurement pipelines on a regular basis.

In addition, the CPD has established the following contracts and agreements which can be used by a number of government departments, agencies and other non-departmental public bodies. These are defined as 'collaborative arrangements'.

- Advertising, design and printing services
- Banking services
- Building materials
- Counselling services

- Courier services
- Energy
- Facilities management
- Financial Services
- Fleet maintenance
- Furniture and Flooring
- Insurance services
- Information and communication echnology
- Personnel and recruitment services
- Office supplies
- Property services
- Protective equipment
- Publications
- Security guarding services
- Training services
- Translation services
- Transportation and storage services
- Travel and taxi services
- Waste recycling management services

---

### TENDER TIP

Keep a close eye on procurement.ie for information about the latest pipeline of proposed contracts and framework agreements.

# PART II
# Procurement
# Rules

## 5

# The 2014 EU Procurement Directives

## Introduction

Ireland's implementation on 18 April 2016 of the new EU Procurement Directives adopted by Member States in February 2014 will not fundamentally change how tender competitions are run; the procurement principles will remain more or less the same. The open and restricted procedures that are used extensively in Ireland and Northern Ireland will not change to any significant extent.

The 2014 EU Procurement Directives replace the Directives in force since 2004, except for the Remedies Directive (see chapter 18). Many issues of interpretation have been clarified; processes have been modernised in light of experience; procurements will be somewhat more SME-friendly; deadlines will be shorter; and some new features and innovations have been added.

The Directives now transposed into Irish legislation are:

- A Directive on public procurement.

- A Directive on the award of concession contracts.

- A Directive on procurement by entities operating in the water, energy, transport and postal services sectors (the new Utilities Directive).

The Government has published the following Statutory Instruments to give effect to these Directives: Public Contracts; Concessions; and Utilities. In October 2014, the OGP sought views from stakeholders about the implementation of the Directives, especially as regards the policy options left to the discretion of the government.

In addition, new template documents to be used in tender competitions for goods and services have also been published for the benefit of both suppliers and buyers.

The Directives were implemented in the UK and Northern Ireland on 26 February 2015 by means of the Public Contract Regulations (No 102) 2005. The UK Government took the decision to fast-track the transposition to take early advantage of the Directive's new flexibilities, improvements and shorter time limits. Cabinet Office guidance has been published. Note that the Regulations do not apply to Northern Ireland buyers with devolved functions. Suppliers bidding in or into Northern Ireland should become familiar with these new rules and procedures.

This chapter addresses the main features of the three new Directives. The following chapter explains how procurements will be conducted under the new arrangements.

## Brexit

There will be no changes until the UK and NI Administration negotiate an exit arrangement with the EU i.e. the current EU procurement rules will apply for at least two years.

If the UK/NI opt for an agreement modelled on what Norway, Iceland and Liechtenstein have with the EU, then the current EU Directives will continue to apply in relation to all contracts over the EU thresholds.

Therefore it is probable that all high value contracts in NI will continue to be advertised EU-wide in a Brexit scenario. The NI Administration will have flexibility to manage tender competitions for sub-threshold contracts. As the current arrangements work well there is arguably a case for continuity. In summary, it is our assessment that Brexit is not going to change the procurement environment in NI.

It is one of the few areas where a status quo can be anticipated.

## Directive on Public Contracts - Introduction

The Directive's main aims are to increase the efficiency of public spending; facilitate the participation of SMEs in public procurement; clarify some key concepts; and incorporate certain aspects of EU case law on procurement.

The following new rules have been introduced to make public procurement procedures more flexible for both buyers and suppliers alike. Some of the more important provisions are explained in more detail hereunder.

## Major Changes in the Public Contracts Directive

1. Buyers will be given additional flexibility to negotiate the terms of contracts with suppliers to obtain the service that best suits their needs; this is called the competitive procedure with negotiation.

2. If submissions are incomplete buyers may ask suppliers for clarity during the evaluation process.

3. The competitive dialogue has been simplified and made more practicable.

4. A new innovation partnership broadens the choice for buyers.

5. Buyers may require that works, services or supplies have a specific label to prove that they comply with environmental, social or other standards set for procurement.

6. Buyers using the open procedure may firstly evaluate the bid responses and then check for grounds of exclusion and the fulfilment of the selection criteria.

7. Suppliers may be excluded from a tender competition if that supplier has shown in the past significant or persistent

deficiencies during the execution of a public contract, e.g. if they have a conviction for failure to pay taxes or social security contributions. Suppliers have the option to 'self-clean' and to start tendering again.

8. In assessing tenders, buyers may take account in the award criteria of the qualification and experience of the staff assigned to performing the contract where this can impact significantly the level of performance.

9. If local authorities publish a PIN at EU level seeking expressions of interest, they may award a contract without further publication of a contract notice.

10. The minimum deadlines for procurement procedures will be much shorter.

11. Contracts can be awarded on the basis of the Most Economically Advantageous Tender (MEAT) using i) price only, ii) cost (using a cost-effectiveness approach), or iii) a 'best price-quality ratio' (BPQR) criteria.

12. Buyers are required to ask suppliers to explain their prices and costs where the tender price appears to be abnormally low.

13. Only the winning supplier will be required to submit all the documentation proving that it qualifies for the contract in question.

14. All suppliers who tender can self-declare that they fulfil the financial and other suitability requirements set out in the tender documentation. The European Single Procurement Document (ESPD), a standard self-declaration form, will facilitate this.

15. The required annual turnover of a supplier should be set by the buyer at no higher than twice the estimated contract value (and not the annual value of the contracts).

16. Buyers are encouraged to divide larger contracts into lots.

17. In some situations buyers may pay sub-contractors directly.

## Contracts Outside Scope

The Directive does not apply to contracts with an estimated value below a determined threshold (see chapter 6) net of VAT. In calculating the value of the contract, buyers must include costs that might be incurred should the term or requirements of the contract be extended. Splitting contracts into lots to avoid this legal requirement is expressly prohibited.

The Directive does not apply to contracts entered into between buyers – so-called 'public-public' contracts. Two scenarios may arise. There may be vertical co-operation, e.g. whereby a local authority exercises significant influence and control over an undertaking that carries out more than 80 per cent of its business on behalf of that authority. Or there may be a horizontal arrangement, whereby a number of buyers genuinely co-operate with each other to meet a shared legal obligation, e.g. local authorities that collaborate with each other at a regional level to collect waste. However, the public buyers may only perform less than 20 per cent of the activities on the open market.

Defence and security contracts and design contests involving or containing classified information are also out of scope.

The Directive does not apply to the beneficiaries of public subsidies where in relation to services contracts the amount is less than 50 per cent of the estimated value and less than €209,000. The corresponding threshold for civil engineering and works is €5.225 million. This is important as many private and voluntary bodies that get Exchequer support over these limits are required to comply with national and EU procurement rules. Therefore contracts awarded by a private entity that is subsidised by 50 per cent or more by a public body must be awarded in accordance with the principles of the EU Procurement Directives and government procurement guidelines. It is the responsibility of the subsidised buyer to ensure that this legal requirement is observed.

The Directive does not apply to service or works concession

contracts or to utilities as these contracts are legislated for in separate Directives (see below).

There are specific exclusions for public contracts and design contests in the field of electronic communications and for public contracts and design contests organised pursuant to international rules.

Service contracts awarded on the basis of an exclusive right are out of scope as are some R&D services.

Importantly, the following service contracts can be awarded without the application of EU procurement rules.

| EXCLUSIONS UNDER OLD RULES | ADDITIONAL EXCLUSIONS |
|---|---|
| • Purchase or rent of existing buildings<br>• Certain audio-visual media services<br>• Arbitration and conciliation services<br>• Certain financial services, including central bank services<br>• Employment contracts<br>• Services awarded on the basis of exclusive rights | • Legal representation<br>• Public loans<br>• Certain civil defence, civil protection provided by non-profit organisations<br>• Public passenger services by rail or metro<br>• Political campaign services during election campaigns |

## Market Soundings

Buyers are encouraged to conduct preliminary market consultations prior to the publication of a tender competition with a view to preparing the procurement documents and informing potential suppliers of their plans and requirements. All market sounding exercises that inform buyer-sourcing strategies should be conducted in a manner that does not distort competition, nor should they result in a violation of the principles of non-discrimination and transparency. Thus buyers will have to be careful to engage with a wide range of stakeholders and not just a selected number of potential suppliers.

As buyers are now expected to engage with the market prior to the launch of a procurement competition, many of the minimum time limits for the submission of tender responses have been reduced (see below).

## Prior Information Notices (PINs)

Buyers should communicate long-term purchasing plans to the market as early as possible by publishing PINs on the eTenders websites.

The OGP recognises that communicating long-term procurement plans to the market gives the market time to react and develop solutions. This is particularly important in the case of large and complex contracts for which SMEs might need time to find partners for joint or consortia bidding.

Specifically, the OGP has told buyers with an aggregated procurement requirement in excess of €750,000 for any product area of supplies or category of services to publish an annual PIN. The PIN is normally submitted by the buyer at the start of the budgetary year and sets out the categories of products and services likely to be procured during the year.

Buyers are also encouraged to publish 'buyer profiles' on their websites with general information on their procurement requirements and to publicise the existence of these profiles in a PIN. Insertion of a PIN does not commit buyers to purchasing or proceeding with a project if circumstances change. It is intended as an aid to transparency and is for the benefit of suppliers. Publication of a PIN permits a buyer to reduce the minimum time for tendering if the PIN has been published in the OJEU within twelve months of publication of the contract notice.

An innovation under the Public Contracts Directive is that a PIN may be used as a call for a tender competition instead of using a Contract Notice. In such a scenario, the PIN should refer specifically to the goods, services or works which are covered; invite suppliers to express an interest; and provide additional specified information about the requirement and the intended procurement process. Only suppliers who respond to the PIN will be invited by the buyer to participate in the subsequent procurement process. The use of the PIN as a call for competition may only be used for the restricted procedure and competitive procedure with negotiation (which can include the setting up of framework agreements and DPS).

> **THE JARGON**
> PQQ = Pre-Qualification Questionnaire
> RFI = Request for Information
> EOI = Expression of Interest
> RFT = Request for Tender
> ITT = Invitation to Tender
> RFP = Request for Proposals
> CAN = Contract Award Notice

## Mixed Contracts

In some situations, contracts to be awarded may contain elements that are covered by one or all three of the new Directives. The general rule is that the type of procurement rules to apply will be determined by the characteristics of the main subject of the tender. For example, if a works contract involves the employment of construction professionals and they represent a small portion of the total value of the contract, then the procurement rules for works and not services should be used. On the other hand, buyers have the flexibility in some cases to procure works, services and supplies by way of separate tender competitions.

## European Single Procurement Document

The European Single Procurement Document (ESPD) is a SME-friendly initiative as it allows suppliers to self-declare their compliance under selection criteria and to edit and reuse this information in subsequent tender submissions. The ESPD consists of a formal statement by the supplier that the relevant grounds for exclusion (see below) do not apply and/or that the relevant selection criteria is fulfilled and on contract award that the relevant information requested by the buyer will be provided. Buyers across the EU are required to use the ESPD template and not to request supporting documents when this evidence can be found on a national database. The ESPD is included as Appendix 4 in the revised RFT templates for the procurement of goods and supplies.

The ESPD should be completed by the primary contractor and, as appropriate, by all sub-contractors or members of a bid consortium.

## E-Procurement

The Public Contracts Directive provides that over time the electronic submission of tenders and procurement notices will become mandatory. This involves publishing contract notices on line (e-notification); publishing all documents for a call for tenders online (e-access); and suppliers submitting offers to buyers electronically (e-submission).

By March 2017, the electronic submission of bid submissions will become compulsory for the OGP/CPD. By October 2018, the electronic submission of bid submissions will be mandatory for all other buyers. The Commission has published a Regulation (November 2015) about the forms and notices that buyers are required to submit and publish. The presentation of the forms is the most noticeable change. The information requested remains largely the same except there are now more mandatory fields which cannot be left blank.

The tools and devices used for communicating electronically will have to be non-discriminatory, generally available and interoperable. The Directive also mandates safeguards on interoperability and data integrity. Electronic signatures can be used in public procurement to certify that the supplier which sent the bid response is indeed the company it claims to be. E-Certis is a free online information system that will assist suppliers in identifying the documents and certificates typically requested in tender competitions in any Member State, Turkey, Iceland, Norway and Liechtenstein.

Dynamic Purchasing Systems are electronic systems allowing buyers to consult suppliers of standardised ('off-the-shelf') works, supplies or services, whose capabilities have already been verified. See chapter 20 for a detailed description of this innovative form of procurement that has many attractions for both buyers and suppliers.

The rules for the use of electronic auctions have been clarified and updated. Buyers can seek tenders by way of an electronic catalogue; a new electronic procurement tool.

## Light Touch Regime and Reserved Contracts

The Public Contracts Directive provides for a new 'light touch regime' (LTR) for health, social, cultural, educational, hotel and restaurant and certain legal services with a value below €750,000. The rationale is that there is very limited inter-EU competition or interest in these services and as such they should not be subject to the full rigours of the EU procurement rules.

For contracts under this value, national rules will apply and contract notices will not need to be published EU-wide. There are no procedural rules (including the absence of rules on the use of award criteria) apart from the obligation to treat bidders equally. These LTR procurements will be subject to the publication of contract notices or PINs and any time limits should be reasonable and proportionate.

In addition, it will be possible to reserve certain contracts for health, social and cultural services to organisations with a public-service mission linked to the provision of these services provided these organisations are based on employee ownership or other participatory principles and the contract duration is no longer than three years.

In addition, the Directive allows certain LTR contracts to be reserved for organisations meeting certain criteria such as public service mutuals and social enterprises (as defined at EU level) working for the inclusion of disadvantaged people. To participate in such reserved procurement procedures, 30 per cent of the employees at the company must be disadvantaged. This arrangement is also available for a three-year period. The rationale is to give these bodies experience of delivering government contracts before being exposed to full EU-wide competition. This provision is in addition to the rule in relation to reserving contracts for sheltered workshops.

As regard the flexibilities allowed under the LTR, the CPD (but not the OGP) has issued guidance covering these procurement categories.

## Dividing Contracts into Lots

The Directive gives buyers the option to award a contract in the form of separate lots and to determine the size and subject matter of such lots. OGP guidance is that buyers should consider breaking contracts into lots. In any event, the RFT must specify the number of lots and may limit the number of lots to be awarded to one tenderer.

If a lotting strategy is not used the buyer must explain why, either in the RFT or at the end of the procurement process. For example, a buyer could reasonably decide not to use lots where the sourcing strategy made a clear recommendation that this would restrict competition or risk making the execution of the contract excessively technical difficult or expensive.

Significant issues will arise in evaluating lots if different suppliers bid for different combination of lots. For example, a buyer may decide the maximum number of lots that any one supplier is allowed to win, even if one supplier submits the best bid (against the award criteria) for more than the maximum number. In that situation, the buyer must specify in the procurement documents the method by which it will decide which lots to award to that supplier.

## Social Aspects

A new cross-cutting 'social clause' has been introduced. Suppliers will be required to comply with the employment obligations in force at the place where the work is carried out or where the service is provided. Any company failing to meet this requirement may be excluded from public procurement competitions. Buyers will be required to exclude any abnormally low-priced tenders if these result from failure to comply with social and labour law (and environmental) obligations under EU or national rules, collective agreements or international law.

Another option available to buyers is that they may decide to award a contract to the supplier that intends to employ the greatest number of disadvantaged people, such as the long-term unemployed. Buyers may also consider the specific working conditions of the employees concerned.

Buyers will also be responsible for ensuring that sub-contractors comply with social and labour law obligations.

## Directive on Utilities

This Directive covers water, energy, transport and postal services. Activities related to oil and natural gas exploration, as well as certain services related to postal services (financial, logistic, electronic and stamping services) are excluded under the new EU Utilities Directive on the grounds that there is sufficient competition in these markets.

Contracts between two public utilities are also exempt from the application of the procurement rules.

The utilities sectors, both public and private, are covered by separate and more flexible procurement rules. Private bodies are covered where they enjoy special or exclusive rights to carry out utility activities. Rights are not special or exclusive rights when granted by means of a procedure involving adequate publicity where the rights were granted on the basis of objective criteria.

## Main Features of the Utilities Directive

■ The revised rules in the EU Procurement Directive are to a great extent included in the Utilities Directive, e.g. as regards the use of the negotiated procedure, the concepts of 'public undertaking' and the provisions applicable to tenders from third countries.

■ Buyers will remain free to choose either to award several contracts to various small businesses or to award a single contract to one large company.

■ The Directive applies to contracts to be entered into by an energy supplier for infrastructure maintenance of the building of a power plant; to the purchase of cars for staff maintaining the water distribution network; and the purchase of buses or computers for the offices of a transport service manager.

■ Private entities which have obtained the exclusive or special right to operate in a utility sector are covered by the scope of the Directive. When these rights have been granted on the basis of a transparent procedure based on objective criteria, the private operator is then exempted from applying EU rules when awarding contracts.

■ Provided a sector is open to competition, a Member State can request that the Commission exempt a particular sector from the application of the Directive.

■ A simplified procedure applies for social, cultural and health services if the value of the contract is below €1 million.

■ With a few exceptions, the maximum duration of framework agreements is eight years (in contrast to four years for other buyers).

The Utilities Directive was implemented in Ireland by way of a statutory instrument.

## Directive on Concessions

The Concessions Directive has not been implemented in Ireland. Concessions are partnerships between buyers and suppliers, where the latter exclusively operate, maintain and carry out the development of infrastructure (ports, water distribution, parking garages, toll roads, etc.) or provide services of a general economic interest (e.g. energy and waste disposal).

Concession contracts are seen as important instruments in the development of infrastructure and strategic public services. The absence of clear EU rules until now was seen as an obstacle to the free provision of services at EU level.

Concessions are the most common form of Public Private Partnership (PPP); although PPPs have never been defined in EU public procurement legislation. The Directive does not deal with the requirement for PPPs to take the legal form of either a public contract under the Public Contracts Directive or a concession subject to the Concessions Directive.

Because Member States adopted a different approach to the award of service concession contracts, including direct award with tendering in some cases, it was decided to legislate at EU level to harmonise the essential rules of procurement to avoid ambiguity and to provide legal certainty. Furthermore, concessions have specific features compared to public contracts which justify a more flexible set of rules for their award. For example, concessions often involve high-value, complex contracts of long duration requiring a degree of flexibility during their implementation.

The Concessions Directive will apply, for instance, to the outsourcing of public services in Ireland/NI to the private sector, to gambling services (other than lottery services awarded on the basis of a prior exclusive right) and to many PPP-type contracts.

On the other hand, the Concessions Directive does not apply to licences as this type of activity is covered by the Public Contracts Directive. Rent/lease agreements will not be considered as concessions if the consideration for using land or infrastructure by a private operator does not encompass the provision of specific works of service.

There are subtle differences between a concession and a public contract. A concession involves a supplier that is remunerated mostly through being permitted to run and exploit the work or service and is exposed to a potential loss on its investment. A public contract involves a payment to a supplier for completing the required work or service.

The Concessions Directive does not apply to concessions awarded by buyers in relation to water services, including the disposal or treatment of sewage, nor to hydraulic engineering projects, irrigation or land drainage in some circumstance, nor to the management of electricity distribution (again subject to some conditions) or to ambulance services if they are provided by non-profit operators. Concessions related to services of general economic interest in the area of public passenger rail and road transport are also out of its scope. Also excluded are concessions awarded to a supplier on the basis of an exclusive right, air-transport services and concessions awarded in the fields of defence and security.

Importantly, the Concessions Directive does not apply to existing concession contracts or concessions provided by one buyer to another.

## Main Features of the Concessions Directive

- Covers works and services concessions in all sectors, including the utilities sector.

- All works concessions valued in excess of €5,225,000 have to be advertised at EU level by way of a concession notice.

- Flexibility is built in when 'substantial modification' of a contract arises during the term of the contract.

- Specific (and simpler) rules are set for the selection and award criteria.

- The criterion of lowest price does not apply.

- Negotiations always possible with shortlisted bidders.

- The EU Remedies Directive applies.

- The principles of public procurement apply to tenders for concessions falling below the EU threshold.

- The permissible duration of concession contracts will be set by reference to the period of time necessary for the concessionaire to recoup its investment in the works or service.

- The minimum time limit for the receipt of applications is thirty days from the date the concession notice is published.

- It is left to Member States to define the applicable procedures for the award of concessions.

In the case of mixed contracts, buyers may award separate concessions for the separate parts of the mixed contract. Thus a concession that has as its subject both works and services should be awarded in accordance with the provisions applicable to works concessions if the works element characterises the main subject matter of the contract, and vice versa.

When estimating a concession's value, the buyer must take the potential concession's total turnover (net of VAT) generated over the duration of the contract into account. In addition, the value of all the supplies and services that are made available to the concessionaire by a buyer should be used to determine the threshold.

Buyers are required to provide in the RFT the most accurate estimate possible of the concession's value but not its actual value.

The Directive provides that the duration of a concession should be limited in time but does not lay down a maximum duration. EU guidance suggests the term should be no more than five years and should not exceed the time in which a concessionaire could reasonably be expected to recoup its expenditure, including investments made to achieve certain specific contractual objectives.

The concession contract award criteria are similar to those set under the Public Contracts Directive. The published criteria must be linked to the subject matter of the concession and cannot be framed so as to give 'satisfaction to the contracting authority'. Buyers will have to ensure equal treatment of all participants and respect the EU Treaty principle of non-discrimination.

As procurement procedures were not set down in the Concession Directive, the OGP will determine how buyers should structure their requirements. The first thing they will need to do is to publish a concession notice in the OJEU that describes the concession and discloses the conditions for participating in the concession award procedure, e.g. the minimum turnover, the availability of specific equipment, and experience with similar concessions. Minimum requirements will be provided (for example, frequency of bus services, size of tunnels, etc.) in the concession document, which should also include the fees to be paid by users. Buyers should also indicate the duration of the concession agreement. Mandatory exclusion criteria will apply (as they do in other procurement competitions). The rules for the selection of candidates generally correspond to the requirements under the Public Contracts Directive.

The award of a concession contract without prior publication of a notice is permitted in limited circumstances. In common with procurements under the Public Contracts Directive, it will be possible to modify the contract during its term subject to certain conditions. The Concessions Directive also allows sub-contracting, which is similar to the provisions of the Public Contracts Directive. The buyer is allowed to negotiate with candidates once bids are to hand but cannot change the concession's subject matter or the award criteria.

An interesting feature is that the buyer must record all meetings (including the use of video recording) with potential concessionaires.

The cost of bidding for concession contracts will be somewhat higher for suppliers as they seek to become familiar with the new arrangements. It is also to be anticipated that buyers will get more competitive bids for concession contracts and this will have the effect of reducing suppliers' margins. On the other hand, given that EU-wide rules exist for the first time, Irish/NI suppliers will have a much better prospect of winning concession contracts in other Member States, which are valued at some €10 billion a year. As the Concessions Directive has never been used in Ireland, it will take some time before buyers and suppliers become familiar with it.

## Confidentiality

The Directives allow buyers to impose requirements on suppliers about the use of confidential information they get access to as part of a tender competition. For their part, suppliers may declare elements of their tender response documents to be of a commercially sensitive nature and in such an event buyers are not allowed to release this material. These provisions will have to be consistent with the Freedom of Information Act 2014.

## Conflicts of Interest

The OGP/CPD are required by the directives to implement internal procedures to ensure that the personnel employed by buyers do not have a financial, economic or other personal interest which might be perceived to compromise their impartiality and independence in assessing tender responses. Thus measures will be put in place to effectively prevent, identify and remedy any internal conflicts or potential conflicts of interest.

---

### TENDER TIP

Read and assess the guidance on the new EU Procurement Directives published by OGP/CPD.

---

# Tender Competitions
# Goods and Services

## Introduction

Public procurement involves the acquisition, whether under formal contract or not, of works, supplies and services by public bodies, as well as other organisations in receipt of public funding. It ranges from the purchase of routine supplies or services to formal tendering and placing contracts for large infrastructural projects by a wide and diverse range of contracting authorities (buyers).

> **What Does Procurement Cover?**
> Works – buildings and civil engineering contracts
> Supplies – purchasing of goods and supplies
> Services – all of the most commonly procured services, including professional services, advertising, property management, cleaning, management consultancy and ICT-related services

Some 61 per cent of all contacts (by volume) are for services; 30 per cent for supplies; and, 9 per cent for works.

All procurements are now subject to the rules of the 2014 Procurement Directives (as was explained in the previous chapter). To this end, a suite of guidelines on the award of public sector contracts in Ireland and measures to support SMEs will be published by the OGP. As explained in chapter 2, the CPD has published comprehensive guidance about the new procurement rules.

The OGP has published template RFTs and associated contracts for supplies and services which buyers are encouraged to use in most circumstances. Information (and commentary) about the template for framework agreements can be found in chapter 7. Chapter 19 deals with contract management issues.

The focus of this chapter is on the tender processes used by buyers, i.e. all contracting authorities/bodies, public and private, in receipt of Exchequer funding. As will be explained later, Irish contracts with a value of less than €25,000 (excluding VAT) have to be procured with reference to national rules but the procedures are not as onerous; the corresponding 'low-value' threshold in NI is £30,000.

Chapter 9 covers separate guidance for the procurement of works and construction-related services.

Prevailing guidance about the evaluation of tenders and post-contract award is covered in chapter 14.

> The OGP's guidance is not based on primary legislation. These policy documents do not give rise to legally enforceable rights, but could form grounds for an application for judicial review (where it is necessary to show a buyer acted *ultra vires* or in a manner that was obviously unreasonable or irrational). Hence, some buyers, being aware that the guidance is not legally binding (and being so advised by their lawyers) in relation to tender competitions below the EU thresholds, chose to ignore key recommendations; not providing debriefings to unsuccessful suppliers, for example.

## The Key Principles of Procurement

A competitive tendering process should be carried out in an open, objective and transparent manner that can achieve the best value for money. This is in line with EU Treaty principles and the EU's Directives on public procurement.

Essential EU principles to be observed in conducting the procurement function include non-discrimination, equal treatment, transparency, mutual recognition, proportionality, freedom to provide services and goods, and freedom of establishment.

Buyers are not allowed to design or artificially narrow the scope of a procurement with the intention of unduly favouring or disadvantaging a supplier(s). For their part, all suppliers must comply with prevailing legislation in relation to the fields of the environment, social and labour law, including collective agreements.

OGP advises buyers it is important that the public procurement function is discharged honestly, fairly and in a manner that secures the best value for public money. Accordingly, buyers must be cost-effective and efficient in the use of resources while upholding the highest standards of probity and integrity.

Procurement practices are subject to audit and scrutiny under the Comptroller and Auditor General (Amendment) Act 1993 and Accountable Officers (department Secretaries General and state bodies' CEOs, for example) are publicly accountable for expenditure incurred. Management in government departments, local authorities and offices has been told to ensure that there is an appropriate focus on good practice in purchasing and where there is a significant procurement function that procedures are put in place to ensure compliance with all relevant guidelines.

## The Procurement Procedures

The Public Contracts Directive permits six tendering procedures as follows. Therefore the first task facing a buyer is to select the procurement procedure that is most suited to its requirements. What is significantly different compared to the arrangements under the

2004 Procurement Directives is a general recognition that the option of availing of negotiations can help deliver better value for money outcomes in some circumstances.

## OPEN

Under this single-phase procedure, all interested parties may submit tenders. Information on a supplier's capacity and expertise may be sought and only the tenders of those deemed to meet minimum levels of technical and financial capacity and expertise are evaluated. If there are minimum requirements, it is important that they be made clear in the notice or the RFT to avoid unqualified bidders incurring the expense of preparing and submitting tenders.

The OGP has told all buyers that the use of the open procedure should be the default option, i.e. it should be used in all situations unless otherwise justified.

## RESTRICTED

This is a two-stage process where only those suppliers who meet minimum requirements with regard to professional or technical capability, experience and expertise and financial capacity to carry out a project are invited to tender.

The requirements of the buyer are set out through a contract notice published in the OJEU and expressions of interest are invited from potential suppliers. The second step involves issuing the complete specifications and tender documents (RFT) with an invitation to submit tenders only to those who possess the requisite level of professional, technical and financial expertise and capacity.

It is important to note that, as a basis for pre-qualifying suppliers, only the criteria relating to the personal situation, financial capacity, technical capacity, relevant experience, expertise and competency of candidates are permissible. Buyers may opt to shortlist qualified candidates if this intention is indicated in the contract notice. Shortlisting of suppliers who meet the minimum qualification criteria must be carried out by non-discriminatory and transparent rules and criteria made known to the suppliers. A number of candidates sufficient to ensure an adequate competition are invited to submit bids. A minimum of five (provided there is at least this number of suppliers who meet the qualification criteria) is required.

OGP guidance (Circular 10/10) recommends that the restricted procedure should only be used for contacts above the EU threshold.

## COMPETITIVE DIALOGUE

This is a procedure designed to provide more flexibility in the tendering process for more complex contracts, e.g. public private partnerships (PPPs) involving major transport infrastructure projects, large computer networks or projects involving complex and structured financing. This procedure should not be used in a situation where off-the-shelf supplies or services can be provided by many suppliers.

## COMPETITIVE DIALOGUE CONTD.

Buyers must advertise their requirements and enter into dialogue with suppliers who are pre-qualified on the same basis as for restricted procedure described above.

Through the process of dialogue with a range of candidates, a buyer may identify arrangements or solutions which meet its requirements. Provided its intention is indicated in the contract notice or in descriptive documents supplied to suppliers, a buyer may provide for the procedure to take place in successive stages in order to reduce the number of solutions or proposals being discussed. The shortlisting must be achieved by reference to the award criteria for the contract.

The competitive dialogue (and the competitive dialogue with negotiation) should only be used where:

- Needs cannot be met without the adaptation of readily available solutions.
- The contract includes design or innovative solutions.
- The requirement is complex in nature as regards its legal and financial make-up or because of its risks.
- The technical specifications cannot be established with sufficient precision

In conducting the dialogue, which must be time-limited, buyers must also ensure equality of treatment and respect for the intellectual property rights of all candidates. When satisfied about the best means of meeting its requirements, the buyer must specify them and invite at least three candidates to submit tenders. The most economically advantageous tender will then be selected. Aspects of tenders may be clarified or fine-tuned, provided that there is no distortion of competition or discrimination against any supplier. In fact, following the submission of Best and Final Offers (BAFO), buyers may seek additional clarifications and negotiate with the winning supplier to confirm the proposed financial commitments or other commercial terms contained in the contract.

## COMPETITIVE PROCEDURE WITH NEGOTIATION

A new procedure called the 'Competitive Procedure with Negotiation' may be used in certain circumstances, e.g. where the buyer needs something that is not readily available; where design or innovation is needed; where there is a requirement to negotiate due to the complexity of the contract; and where the open or restricted procedures have failed.

Suppliers should anticipate that buyers will make great use of this procedure as it allows them to negotiate on all aspects of the contract, other than the minimum requirements such as quality, quantities, commercial clauses, social, environmental and innovative aspects. Suppliers will be eliminated by applying the award criteria.

## COMPETITIVE PROCEDURE WITH NEGOTIATION CONTD.

Several safeguards, as follows, will apply:

- Buyers cannot seek to change the minimum requirements by negotiation.
- Nor is it possible to change or vary the award criteria.
- Any changes to the technical specifications must be communicated in writing.
- Confidential information held by a supplier will not be made available to other suppliers.
- All stages of the negotiation should be fully documented.
- The additional submissions by suppliers must be in writing.

Buyers should ensure that the precise circumstances justifying negotiation exist before deciding on the use of this procedure. It should be noted that definitions of 'exceptions' and 'urgency' are strictly interpreted by the European Commission and the courts. Factors giving rise to urgency must be unforeseeable and outside the control of the buyer. Where one of these exemptions is invoked, the buyer must be able to justify the use of the exemption.

As there are similar grounds for using the competitive dialogue and the competitive dialogue with negotiation, buyers will need to consider the respective advantages and disadvantages of both procedures before opting for one. One key differentiator is that the competitive procedure with negotiation does not allow for post-tender negotiations. Initial feedback from NI - where this new procedure has been used - is positive.

## USE OF THE NEGOTIATED PROCEDURE WITHOUT PRIOR PUBLICATION

- No tenders or no suitable tenders were submitted in response to an open or restricted procedure.
- Only one supplier could apply for artistic, technical reasons or because exclusive rights (including intellectual property) had to be protected.
- For reasons of extreme urgency (for example, where immediate remedial works are needed to address flooding or another natural disaster) outside the control of the buyer.
- Where the products involved are for the purpose of research, experimentation, study or development.
- For supplies quoted and purchased on a commodity market.
- For the purchase of supplies from a company in liquidation or in the event of company winding up its business.

## INNOVATION PARTNERSHIP

It is widely accepted that public procurement plays a key role in innovation in areas that are the preserve of the public sector.

Therefore a new procedure called the Innovation Partnership has been introduced to enable buyers to select supplier partners on a competitive basis and have them develop an innovative solution tailored to their requirements. This new initiative is part of a wider EU strategy to promote innovation using public purchasing power. It is similar to the competitive procedure but covers both the award process and, more importantly, the subsequent contractual relationship.

The competitive phase will take place at the very beginning of the procedure, when the most suitable partner(s) are selected on the basis of their skills, capacity in the field of R&D, abilities and price. These partner(s) will be asked to develop the new solutions, as required, in collaboration with the buyers. This research and development phase can be divided into several stages, during which the number of partners may be gradually reduced, depending on whether they meet certain predetermined criteria. The partner will then provide the final solution (commercial phase).

Payments will be made by agreement, in instalments, with reference to set targets.

In summary, the innovation partnership allows a buyer to engage in several rounds of negotiations with a potential supplier(s).

In implementing this new provision, buyers will need to be careful to treat all partners equally and to protect their intellectual property. In addition, buyers will also have to set intermediate targets and termination rights. In all situations, general competition law will apply to any joint ventures formed as a result of the use of the innovation partnership.

If used in a flexible manner, this could be a SME-friendly procurement medium.

Some 68 per cent of procurements use the open procedure; 14 per cent the restricted procedure; and, 15 percent use the negotiated procedure.

## Thresholds

The current EU thresholds (with effect from 1 January 2016) above which it is compulsory to advertise tenders EU-wide on TED (and e-Tenders) are as follows.

## Table 6.1 – EU Threshold Limits (net of VAT)

| CATEGORY | THRESHOLD | NOTE |
|---|---|---|
| Works | €5,225,000 | Applies to all government departments and offices, local and regional authorities public bodies and utilities |
| Supplies and Services | €135,000 | Applies to all government departments and offices |
| | €209,000 | Applies to local and regional authorities and public bodies not covered by the Utilities Directive |
| | €418,000 | Applies to the utilities sector |
| Light Touch Regime | €750,000 | Applies to social, healthcare, (some) legal and other services (listed in Annex IV of the Public Contracts Directive) |

Source: OGP Guidance (2016)

The total value of a contract net of VAT over a period of years should be used to determine the threshold. Thus for a four-year framework agreement for the supply of goods or services to a government department using several lots the value of all envisaged contracts should be added up. Contracts over the EU threshold have to be advertised EU-wide and the full rigours of the EU Procurement Directives apply.

## Table 6.2 – Choosing the Correct Procurement Procedure

| AMOUNT | TYPE OF CONTRACT | PROCEDURE |
|---|---|---|
| €0 – €4,999 | Supplies or services contracts | Verbal or written quotes from competitive suppliers |
| €5,000 – €24,999 | Supplies or services contracts | Minimum three written quotes; emails are acceptable |
| €0 – €49,999 | Works and works-related services contracts | Quick quote (direct invitation, not published on eTenders); see www.constructionprocurement.gov.ie Construction Works Management Framework (**CWMF**) GN 2.3 Section 3.2; note that low-value works contracts include VAT whereas corresponding contracts for goods and services exclude VAT in the calculation |
| €25,000 – €125,000 €50,000 – €250,000 | Supplies or services contracts Works and works-related services contracts | Open procedure non-OJEU (See Circular 10/14) CWMF GN 2.3 Section 1.2 |
| €125,001 – EU Threshold €250,000 – EU Threshold | Works, supplies or services contracts Works and works-related services contracts | Any non-OJEU procedure but usually open or restricted CWMF GN 2.3 Section 1.2 |
| Above EU Thresholds | Works, supplies or services contracts | Any OJEU procedure but usually open or restricted |

Source: OGP guidance (2015)

While this is current OGP guidance, some of the new framework agreements (see below) have imposed new requirements on buyers procuring goods and services below €12,000 in value.

## Deadlines/Timescales

Minimum time limits are set down for the different stages of the particular contract award procedure chosen. While rules are set for above-EU threshold contracts, for below-EU-threshold contracts adequate time must be allowed to enable suppliers to submit a tender.

In all cases, the times specified in days relate to calendar days. When fixing the timescale for submitting expressions of interest or requests to participate or tenders, buyers should take account of the complexity of the contract and allow sufficient time for submitting the necessary information and preparing tenders.

The minimum time limits are reckoned from the date of dispatching the notice to the OJEU. The following table sets out the minimum time limits for procurements under the Public Contracts Directive.

## Table 6.3 – EU Advertising Time Limits

| NORMAL MINIMUM TIME | IF ELECTRONIC TENDER PERMITTED | IF DEEMED URGENT | WHERE PIN PUBLISHED |
|---|---|---|---|
| **Open procedure** | | | |
| 35 days | 30 days | 15 days | 15 days |
| **Restricted Procedure** | | | |
| 30 days (requests to participate and submission of tenders) | 25 days | 10 days | 10 days |
| **Competitive Procedure with Negotiation/Innovation Partnership** | | | |
| 30 days (requests to participate and submission of tenders) | 25 days | 15 days (for requests to participate) and 10 days for tenders | 30 days (for requests to participate) and 10 days for tenders |
| **Competitive Dialogue** | | | |
| 30 days for requests to participate but no explicit time for submission of initial/subsequent tenders | - | - | - |

Source: Bid Management Services (2016)

Sub-central authorities such as local authorities may use evenshorter minimum time limits for procurements using the restricted procedure.

## Low-Value Tenders

It is a basic principle of public procurement that a competitive process should be used unless there are justifiably exceptional circumstances. The type of competitive process can vary depending on the size and characteristics of the contract to be awarded and the nature of the buyer.

For contracts or purchases below the EU threshold values and not part of a 'drawdown' or framework contract, less formal procedures may be appropriate. For example, supplies or services less than €5,000 in value can be purchased on the basis of (verbal) quotes from up to three competitive suppliers.

Supplies or services contracts between €5,000 and €25,000 in value might be awarded on the basis of responses to specifications sent by email to at least three suppliers or service providers. Buyers have been told that these values and procedures are indicative only and should be adapted as appropriate to suit the type of buyer and the nature and scale of the project.

The reasons for selecting the procurement procedures adopted, including procedures where a competitive process was not deemed appropriate, should be clearly recorded by the buyer.

All contract award procedures should include a verifiable audit trail. While buyers are not required to advertise on eTenders for requirements below €25,000, they are encouraged to do so if the anticipated response would not be disproportionate, having regard to the value of the requirement.

Contracts above €25,000 and up to the value of EU thresholds for advertising in OJEU, not part of a 'drawdown' or framework contract, should normally be advertised as part of a formal tendering process.

Publication on eTenders generally meets national advertising and publicity requirements. Depending on the nature of the requirement, it may be appropriate to supplement national website advertising with advertising in other media, in trade publications and other websites. An abbreviated notice indicating the publication of tender details on eTenders should be considered in such cases. Details of an advertised tendering procedure may be sent directly to suppliers who may be deemed suitably competent to participate.

Alternatively, a process of direct invitation to tender may be used. This may involve: an invitation to firms deemed appropriately qualified for a particular project (this may be appropriate for specialised requirements in markets where there is a limited number of suppliers or service providers); or an invitation to tender (ITT) to firms on a list established on an open and objective basis (normally used by buyers which have a frequent or recurring requirement for supplies or services or those wishing to maintain a well-organised ongoing procurement system).

Where direct invitations are issued, suppliers from which tenders are sought should be a good representative sample of all potential bidders in the market concerned. The number invited to tender should be determined by the size and particular characteristics of the project to be undertaken. The number must be sufficient to ensure adequate competition and should not be restricted for reasons of administrative convenience. At least five suppliers should normally be invited to submit tenders.

Buyers keeping a list of suppliers from which they invite tenders should advertise at appropriate intervals (normally on an annual basis) for the admission of interested parties and should ensure that the lists are open to suitably qualified entrants at all times. Care should be taken to ensure that such lists are used in an open and non-discriminatory manner. Under direct tendering procedures, buyers should ensure that recently established firms, or firms with no previous experience of public contracts, are not excluded from invitations to tender. Buyers should also encourage these suppliers by allowing them to tender for smaller contracts initially and then, subject to satisfactory performance, progressing to larger or more complex contracts. It is in the interest of buyers that the pool of potential suppliers is actively maintained and updated.

If the number of suppliers on a buyer's list is too large to invite all suitable firms to tender, a number of those firms, sufficient to ensure adequate competition, may be selected for inclusion in the competition. Selection from the list can be made in accordance with specified criteria, randomly or by rotation – or by a combination of all three. Selection may be based on factors such as overall suitability to the particular project by reference to experience, technical competence and capability and financial standing. The selection process should have particular regard for the need for equal treatment and reasonable distribution of opportunities.

The methods and criteria for selecting suppliers and for awarding contracts should be documented and should be objective, transparent and proportionate. It should be clearly understood that whether responses are to an advertisement or to a direct invitation, all parties in the process must be treated on the same fair and objective basis. Decisions on the selection process for smaller projects or purchases should be recorded by buyers with a minimum of formality.

## Grounds for Exclusion

Several new grounds for excluding suppliers – both mandatory and discretionary – have been introduced, building on the provisions of the 2004 Directives. For example, and importantly, exclusion may occur at any stage during the procurement procedure.

Any decision taken by buyers must be proportionate and should not go beyond what is necessary. Mandatory exclusion arises where there has been a conviction of specified serious offences, including corruption, bribery, money laundering, terrorism and human trafficking. In addition, breaches of obligations in relation to tax or social security contributions will result in mandatory exclusion; under the 2004 Directive discretionary provisions applied for these instances.

The current rules on discretionary exclusion continue, somewhat revised, in relation to situations of bankruptcy and insolvency, New categories include non-compliance with environmental, social and labour laws, potential distortions of competition, grave professional misconduct, conflicts of interest and, perhaps most important of all, where there is significant or persistent deficiencies in the performance of a substantive requirement under a prior contract which led to the termination of that contract, damages or comparable sanctions.

Exclusion for mandatory grounds lasts for five years and is three years for discretionary grounds.

Suppliers who fall foul of these rules will have the option to self-clean, i.e. to provide evidence to the buyer of remedial measures taken. The declaration about compliance with these criteria appears in Appendix 5 of the RFT template documents for goods and services. This declaration must be submitted prior to contract award by the preferred bidder, any sub-contractor on whom the preferred bidder needs to rely in order to meet the selection criteria and, at the option of the buyer, any other sub-contractors.

## Selection Criteria

Provided a buyer is satisfied that a supplier should not be excluded from the tender process for the above-mentioned reasons, the published selection (qualification) criteria will then be assessed. These may relate to:

1. The suitability to pursue the professional activity.
2. Economic and financial standing.
3. Technical and professional ability.

Selection criteria must be proportionate and relate to the subject matter of the contract. In most cases, the selection criteria are assessed using a 'Pass/Fail' test. So, for example, if you do not complete a self-declaration form as instructed this would be a 'Fail' and in such a scenario the buyer will not proceed to evaluate the tender response document. Some buyers assess the selection criteria with reference to a set of minimum marks. So, for example, if your reference sites do not match the buyer's requirements and you only score 50 out of an available 100 and the 'Pass' mark is 60 marks, then your tender response will also be deemed non-compliant.

Buyers may request up to three relevant reference sites from either public- or private-sector clients. Contracts for supplies and services should have been performed in the last three years; there is a five-year limit for works contracts. Buyers will also seek contact details for each project as they may be asked to verify the information provided. Consortium bids should provide relevant examples of where individual members of the consortium have delivered similar requirements. If this is not possible – for instance, if the consortium was set up just to respond to the RFT – then three separate references should be provided by the principal members of the consortium.

Buyers may ask further project-specific questions relating to the supplier's technical and professional ability as part of the selection criteria. For example, it is reasonable for buyers to seek evidence of membership of the supplier and/or key staff to a designated professional body.

Buyers frequently use the ratio 'company's turnover to contract value' as a measure in deciding whether a business has the financial capacity and strength to perform a contract. In addition, and where it is proportional, suppliers may also be asked for other financial information on their annual accounts, such as the ratio between assets and liabilities. In assessing the financial capacity of a supplier to do a job, buyers, as a matter of general policy, should not for routine (e.g. low-value, high-volume) goods and services competitions set company turnover requirements at more than twice the estimated contract value. However, where justified special risks may be attached to the nature of proposed works, supplies or services a buyer may set a higher turnover figure. The turnover limit for framework agreements should be set in general vis-à-vis the likely size of individual contracts or drawdowns in the framework. For non-routine services and goods competitions, it may be necessary to apply higher turnover requirements. For DPS contracts, the minimum turnover rule should be based on the expected maximum size of the contracts that will be performed. If a requirement is specified about levels of insolvency, you should provide the supporting evidence, e.g. a letter from your auditor. Selection criteria may not be re-inserted as award criteria.

## Award Criteria

Provided a supplier meets (passes) all the selection criteria, then the bid response will be marked against the published award criteria. To this end, some important new rules have been introduced.

To date, some 84 per cent of tenders are awarded on the basis of 'MEAT', the Most Economically Advantageous Tender; 16 per cent are awarded on price only. Under the 2004 Directives, buyers had the option of using MEAT or the lowest price. The new procurement rules require that MEAT be used but its definition has changed significantly.

Henceforth, MEAT has to be identified on the basis of the price or cost, using a cost-effectiveness approach, such as life-cycle costs, and may include the best price-quality ratio (BQPR), which shall be assessed on the basis of criteria including qualitative, environmental and/or 'social aspects' linked to the subject matter of the contract. The use of social aspects is also a new feature. Using BQPR will be particularly important when service quality is paramount.

'Quality' can comprise, for example, technical merit, aesthetic and functional characteristics, accessibility, design for all users, social, environmental and innovative characteristics.

Other criteria could include the organisation, qualification and relevant experience of individual staff assigned to the performance of the contract, where the quality of these personnel can have a significant impact on the level of contract performance. Buyers may set a minimum level for required human resources. This will be important when professional services are being procured. So when including your CVs make the business case why each key resource has been included in the team. Other factors include after-sales service and technical assistance and delivery conditions and processes.

The cost element may take the form of a fixed price or cost on the basis of which suppliers will compete on quality criteria only.

OGP has the option in future guidance of declaring that buyers may not use price only or cost only as the sole award criteria or restrict their use to certain types of contracts. In NI and the UK, it has been decided not to rule out price-only award criteria.

One critical aspect of green public procurement (GPP) (see below) is the issue of life-cycle costs (LCC). LCC covers the costs borne by a buyer, such as costs relating to acquisition; costs of use (such as consumption of energy and other resources); maintenance costs; and end-of-life costs (such as collection and recycling costs). In addition, LCC also covers costs imputed to environmental externalities provided a monetary value can be determined and verified. Such costs include the cost of GHG emissions and other pollution emissions and other climate-change mitigation costs. Importantly, the Directive states that the LCC methodology as provided for in Article 6 of the Clean and Efficient Vehicles Directive (2009/33/EU) must be used. Thus suppliers should rely on this methodology and not on the EPA guidance when asked to present LCC as part of a tender's award criteria. The OGP recommends, where appropriate, buyers should seek whole life-cycle costing solutions in their tender documents. However, no detailed national guidance exists about the calculation of LCC.

Buyers are required to seek explanations from suppliers about abnormally low-priced or low-costed tenders before taking action to reject a tender. In particular, buyers are allowed to disregard tender responses with abnormally low prices because they are in breach of international environmental, social or labour law provisions. Buyers may therefore ask suppliers for details about the economics of a manufacturing process, of the services provided or of the construction method or in relation to the technical solutions chosen.

Every tender must indicate the relative weightings for each award criteria chosen so as to determine the MEAT; the one exception is where price only is the sole criteria. Buyers have the option to express weightings within a range or in decreasing order of importance.

New or amended criteria, including sub-criteria, cannot be introduced after bids are submitted or in the course of the evaluation process. If this happens there may be legal grounds to have the competition re-advertised under the EU Remedies Directive.

The evaluation and award process must be demonstrably objective and transparent and based solely on the published criteria. In all cases, tenders which do not comply with the RFT's instructions and requirements will be rejected. The guidelines and practical issues relating to the evaluation of bid responses are covered in chapter 14.

## Other Changes to the Contract

Any special conditions set by the buyer now form part of the contract. In addition, it will no longer be necessary to physically attach the RFT and the successful bidder's tender in the schedules to the contract at the signing stage. These documents are automatically incorporated into the contract provided they are identified in recitals A and B of the template document. Parties may now seek to settle any dispute by way of independent mediation before having recourse to the courts.

## OGP Templates

Since March 2012, buyers have been strongly encouraged by the OGP to use standard RFT and contract templates for the procurement of supplies and services where low- and medium-risk requirements arise. Thus the templates are not recommended for procurements involving ICT equipment.

In addition, the OGP has a template for framework agreements. It is important to note that these RFT templates and associated contracts have been approved by the Chief State Solicitor's Office and will not be re-negotiated under any circumstance.

The template documents were updated to coincide with the implementation of the 2014 EU Procurement Directives. The

OGP took the opportunity to clarify certain provisions; to remove unnecessary duplication; and to update references to legislation.

In signing the Tenderer's Statement enclosed with every RFT, suppliers accept the contract's terms and conditions. The structure of the goods and services RFTs is the same and is divided into four parts:

1. Introduction
2. Instructions to Tenderers
3. Selection and Award Criteria

| | |
|---|---|
| *Appendix 1* | Requirements and Specifications |
| *Appendix 2* | Pricing Schedule |
| *Appendix 3* | Tenderer's Statement |
| *Appendix 4* | European Single Procurement Document |
| *Appendix 5* | Declaration as to Personal Circumstances of Tenderer |
| *Appendix 6* | Contract |
| *Appendix 7* | Confidentiality Agreement |

The buyer only needs to complete the following steps prior to issuing the RFT:

1. Complete the grey shaded text boxes in the RFT.
2. Insert insurance details (if any) at clause 2.21.1 of the RFT.
3. Insert the qualification and award criteria in Part 3 of the RFT.
4. Insert the requirements and specifications into Appendix 1.
5. Insert the pricing schedule at Appendix 2 of the RFT, if required.
6. Complete the text boxes in Schedule A of the contract.
7. If any of the special conditions at Schedule D of the contract are to apply, then in the text box the buyers will mark 'as applies'.

The OGP advises buyers who are planning a procurement competition:

1. To allow sufficient time for planning and completing the competition.
2. To seek, as appropriate, legal, financial or insurance advices at an early stage.

3. To ensure that the RFT's terms and conditions are consistent.
4. To be satisfied that the buyer has the legal power (vires) to enter into the contract.
5. To conduct a risk assessment, the results of which should be reflected in the selection and award criteria.

## RFT Templates – Key Issues

- The requirements should be stated in a concise and consistent manner.
- The tender competition can be cancelled at any time prior to the signature of the contract.
- Every supplier must sign a Tenderer's Statement and other prescribed declarations.
- Special (additional) conditions, such as material changes to the contract, may be added to the standard contract.
- If there is a bid consortium, a primary contractor must be identified.
- Buyers have discretion about the required format of bid response documents.
- The eTenders facility is the recommended medium for clarification questions as an audit trail is required.
- Prices (excluding VAT) are to be fixed for a period set by the buyer.
- The buyer has the option of using a schedule/spreadsheet (Appendix 2) to assist tenderers in the costing of the tender competition.
- Site visits may be facilitated.
- All non-compliant bids will be eliminated from the competition.
- Only compliant bids will be evaluated against selection criteria and tenderers who pass these criteria will be marked against the published award criteria.
- The most careful consideration should be given to the award criteria.
- The minimum standstill period (the period between writing to a preferred bidder and contract award) is fourteen days.

## ESPD

The OGP has started using template tender response documents for its framework agreement tender competitions. These are designed to make it easier for SMEs to respond to RFTs. Chapter 17 provides more details about the new ESPD.

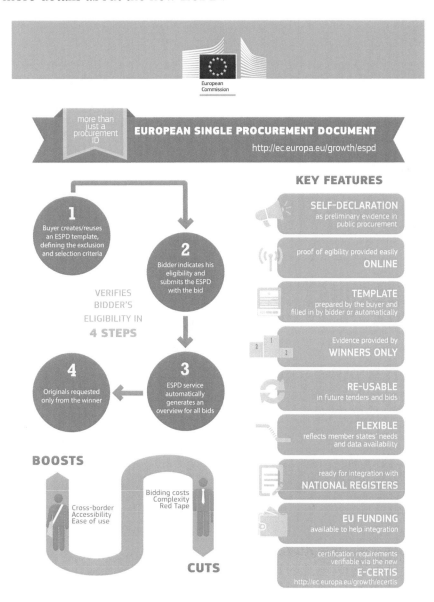

Source: European Commission (2016)

## Flexible Rules to Support SMEs

The OGP published guidance (Circular 10/14 of April 2014) specifically designed to assist SMEs by encouraging buyers to adopt more flexible rules in the running of tender competitions. This policy guidance does not give rise to legally enforceable rights.

The key features of Circular 10/14 are set out hereunder.

### Market Analysis

Buyers should undertake market analysis prior to tendering in order to better understand the range of goods and services on offer, market developments and innovation, what commercial models are available, the competitive landscape, and the specific capabilities of SMEs, etc. To ensure transparency, any information provided by the buyer during this process should be circulated to any potential supplier. Buyers can contact the category council lead (support@ogp.gov.ie) to understand how their needs align to the category council/sourcing team strategy or may be met by an existing framework or contract. The Public Contracts Directive expressly allows buyers to engage with the market prior to the publication of a RFT so long as this does not distort competition. Suppliers can give advice to buyers, for example by suggesting elements of the draft tender documents, again provided this does not distort competition.

### Sub-Dividing Contracts into Lots

The sub-division of contracts into lots facilitates access by SMEs, both quantitatively (the size of the lots may better correspond to the productive capacity of the SME) and qualitatively (the content of the lots may correspond more closely to the specialised sector of the SME). Lots may be also decided on a geographic basis; on a work package basis; and on the basis of internal organisation structure, etc. Buyers should, where reasonable and without compromising efficiency and value for money, consider breaking contracts into lots, thereby enabling smaller businesses to compete for these elements.

## Consortium Bids

SMEs are encouraged by buyers to consider using a bid consortium where they are not of sufficient scale to tender in their own right. The OGP template tender and contract documents allow for a bid consortium to tender for public procurement opportunities. Suppliers considering forming a consortium to bid for public sector opportunities should seek legal advice in relation to the structure and operation of the consortium to ensure that it is fit for purpose and complies with their legal obligations particularly in relation to competition law (see chapter 8).

## Greater Use of 'Open' Tendering

Buyers should use open tendering for contracts below the EU threshold, i.e. €135,000 (exclusive of VAT), in the case of advertised contracts for general goods and services. Above this level, buyers should decide which tendering procedure is most appropriate in each case. This guideline, if fully implemented, will save suppliers and buyers millions of euros in terms of the costs saved by having a single-stage tender competition.

## Capacity Requirements and Previous Experience

Buyers should ensure that any capacity levels set for suppliers are relevant and proportionate to the circumstances of a particular contract. For example, where experience is specified as a selection criteria, it should not be framed in such a way as to unduly narrow a field of eligible suppliers by specifying an exact work type or industry. Buyers may consider the previous experience of individuals who have formed a start-up SME that has yet to establish a track record as a company.

## Documentary Evidence of Financial Capacity

Documentary evidence of financial capacity to undertake a project should not be sought by buyers early on in the procurement process. Instead suppliers should be required in the RFT response to declare that they meet the minimum standards required by the buyer and that they will produce the necessary documentation (e.g. Tax Clearance Certificate, bank statements, audited accounts, proof of professional indemnity, etc.) when provisionally shortlisted in a restricted procedure or when chosen as the preferred bidder in an open procurement competition.

## Insurance

Buyers should only require such types and levels of insurance which are proportionate and reasonable in the context of the particular contract. Factors which may be considered by buyers for the supply of goods and general services should include the risks involved, the value of the contract and the subject matter of the contract. The required insurance coverage will vary from contract to contract, as will the style of insurance cover available to suppliers, particularly in relation to professional indemnity risks. Any requirement for insurance cover should be signalled in the tender documentation. Suppliers should be asked to declare that they can obtain such cover but should not generally be required to have it in place at the time of tendering. Documentary evidence of the insurances to be held will only be required when a candidate has been identified as a successful supplier (a preferred bidder) in a procurement competition. In carrying out tender competitions for the acquisition of routine low-to-medium-risk goods and services buyers should use the following levels as a guide to assessing insurance level requirements.

## Table 6.5 – Insurance Limits

| TYPE OF INSURANCE | INDEMNITY LIMIT |
|---|---|
| Employer's Liability | €12.7 million |
| Public Liability | €6.5 million |
| Environmental Liability | €2 million |
| Professional Indemnity | €50,000 minimum |
| Product Liability | €50,000 minimum |

Source: OGP Circular 10/14 (August 2014)

For bespoke and complex competitions, or if the buyer has concerns with regard to any aspect relating to the subject matter of the procurement, then the buyer should contact the State Claims Agency or their own insurers for assistance in setting appropriate insurance levels. Buyers not covered by the State Claims Agency are asked to contact their risk-management department or relevant insurance advisor to determine the appropriate levels of cover.

## Innovation

Buyers should, where possible and appropriate, encourage new and innovative solutions by indicating in tender documents where they are prepared to accept reasonable variants to the published specifications. Alternatively or in addition, requirements may, for example, be set out in terms of a deliverable which allows suppliers to provide creative and innovative solutions. This output-oriented approach may enable buyers to concentrate on the functional requirements of a product they would like to have but leaves suppliers the freedom to develop new, innovative goods or services which might better correspond to the actual need of the buyer.

# Other Rules

## Issue of Documents

Responses to requests for information, RFT documents and other supporting documentation (if not made available electronically) must be issued without delay and in any event within a maximum of six days of the request. Additional information, requested in good time, must be issued at least six days before the latest date for receipt of tenders. In order to avoid giving unfair advantage, additional information supplied to one party in response to a request should be supplied to all interested parties if it could be significant in the context of preparing a tender.

## Estimation of Contract Value

Estimation of contract values for OJEU publication purposes must be realistic. If a contract, not advertised in the OJEU, attracts tenders in excess of the EU thresholds, there is a risk that the award could be subject to legal challenges. In such an event, a buyer would be required to justify the original estimation. No project or purchase may be sub-divided to prevent it coming within the scope of the EU Procurement Directives. Where a project or purchase involves separate lots the value of all lots must be included in estimating the value of the contract.

## Pilot Projects

Where a procurement process involves a pilot stage, the pilot should be conducted in a manner that allows and encourages the identification of a range of acceptable solutions or options. Buyers have been advised that steps must be taken to avoid the development of relationships with a particular supplier(s) which could hinder a fair and open process or limit competition.

## Sole Suppliers

The OGP suggests that care should be taken by buyers when they face a supplier, service provider or contractor with an exclusive right to provide a particular supply or service in a designated territory. Open-ended arrangements with these exclusive distributors should be avoided where possible. Irish and EU competition law does not prevent an exclusive supplier from providing supplies to customers outside of its designated territory where the exclusive supplier has been requested to do so by that customer. Better value for money can be achieved by seeking tenders from other suppliers, service providers or contractors, outside the region in which there is an exclusive distributor.

## No Charging for Tendering Opportunities

Buyers must not use commercial arrangements which involve suppliers having to pay to access competitions for public contracts. This does not preclude buyers from seeking a deposit for hard copies of tender documents, which is refundable upon receipt of a bona fide tender.

## Receipt and Opening of Tenders

Buyers should ensure that proper procedures are in place for opening tenders (including electronic submissions) to prevent abuse or impropriety at this stage. All tenders should be opened together as soon as possible after the designated latest time and date set for receipt of tenders. The opening of tenders should take place in the presence of at least two officials. The procedure adopted should ensure that, in the case of any dispute, there is a clear and formal, independently vouched report of the tenders received. Tenders received after the closing time for receipt of tenders should not be accepted, unless otherwise stated in the RFT (for example, in situations of force majeure).

## Contract Award Notices

Buyers are required to publish all Contract Award Notices (CAN) over the EU threshold on the eTenders website within forty-eight days of contract award. The CAN should include certain information on contracts awarded (or framework agreements concluded), e.g. the type of contract, the procedure and award criteria used, the number of tenders received, the name of the successful supplier, the value of the contract or the range of tender prices, justification for the negotiated procedure, if used, are published on eTenders as CANs. To date, many Irish buyers have not complied with prevailing guidance on the publication of CANs.

## Green Public Procurement (GPP)

GPP is defined as; 'A process whereby public and semi-public authorities meet their needs for goods, services, works and utilities by choosing solutions that have a reduced impact on the environment throughout their life-cycle, as compared to alternative products or solutions.'

The Environmental Protection Agency (EPA) has published guidance to assist buyers to implement and maintain procedures for GPP. The purpose of the guidance is to provide a practical overview of the issues at stake, best-practice examples and detailed criteria for insertion in tenders for the chosen priority sectors, which account for some 50 per cent of total public spending.

However, to date there is limited evidence that buyers are embracing GPP.

## Table 6.6 – GPP Priority Sectors

| Transport (road vehicles and services) | Energy (electricity, combined heat and power and lighting) | Construction (materials and site management) |
|---|---|---|
| Food | Catering Services | Cleaning products and Services |
| Textiles | Uniforms | IT Equipment (desktops, laptops and displays) |
| Paper | | |

Source: EPA (2014)

At European level, GPP is a voluntary policy, meaning buyers are not obliged to introduce the criteria in their tenders. The Treaty on the Functioning of the European Union states that 'Environmental protection requirements must be integrated into the definition and implementation of the Union's policies and activities, in particular with a view to promoting sustainable development'. There are also a number of areas where EU or national legislation creates specific environmental obligations which must be taken into account in public procurement. These range from the requirement to conduct an environmental impact assessment in advance of certain construction projects; to minimum energy efficiency standards which must be applied when buying office IT equipment; through to rules on the handling of hazardous substances and waste.

Therefore Ireland's GPP initiative is very much based on what is best practice at <u>EU level.</u>

So suppliers should not only become familiar with the EPA guidance but also with what is happening in other jurisdictions as their competitors have far more experience in bidding using GPP criteria.

In addition, suppliers in the GPP priority sectors should be aware that buyers have been advised to require the following evidence to substantiate environmental claims about their products and services, with regard to a growing list of standards, certification schemes and labels which aim to give credibility to such claims.

## Table 6.7 – Verifying GPP Criteria

| PROCUREMENT STAGE | TYPE OF GPP CRITERIA | REQUIRED EVIDENCE |
|---|---|---|
| Selection | Exclusion for conviction for an offence concerning professional conduct, including non-compliance with environmental legislation.<br><br>Ability to apply environmental management measures (all contracts under the new EU Procurement Directives). | Certificate, extract from judicial record or equivalent document. The European Single Procurement Document must be accepted as preliminary evidence of eligibility. However original certificates or documents can be requested at any time.<br>EMAS, ISO 14001 or other equivalent independent third-party schemes. In-house environmental management systems must also be considered and accepted if they demonstrate implementation of the specific environmental management measures required for the contract. If a supplier does not have an externally accredited system, the onus is upon the supplier to prove that this is for reasons not attributable to them. |
| Technical Specification | Environmental standards, production processes, minimum performance requirements (e.g. energy efficiency levels). | Certificates, test reports, technical dossiers or Type I eco-labels. Equivalent evidence must be considered and accepted if it establishes compliance or performance under the specific criteria. |
| Award Criteria | Performance above minimum specified levels, life-cycle costs, added-value environmental characteristics. | If a supplier does not have a third-party label, the onus is upon the supplier to prove that this is for reasons not attributable to them. |
| Contract Performance Clauses | Key performance indicators, incentives, penalties or remedies linked to environmental issues | Eco-labels may be required under the same conditions as above. Other types of evidence are not regulated, but must not amount to a material amendment of the contract as tendered. |

Source: EPA (2014)

## Whole Life-Cycle Costs – Current Guidance

In order to accurately assess the costs of an asset, life-cycle costing should be applied wherever significant costs will arise within the lifetime of the product or service which are not reflected in the purchase price.

WLCC can range from a relatively simple calculation of energy or fuel consumption, time to replacement and end-of-life costs/revenues, through to a more complex assessment including GHG emissions (where a nominal cost is assigned to these).

While a number of different methodologies are available and appropriate for different sectors, the most important considerations are the transparency with which the methodology is presented, the ability of bidders to provide the information requested, and the ability of the buyer to assess and verify it.

WLCC may not be suitable for every contract. However, it is likely to become more widely used following the adoption of the 2014 EU Procurement Directives.

WLCC can be used both at the planning stages of procurement and to compare tendered costs. At planning stages, the methodology should be identified and the period over which costs will be assessed, as well as the discount rate for any future costs (if applicable). This will allow buyers to identify the information which will be needed from bidders during the tender.

For example, in a tender to retrofit a pump for a water treatment works, a buyer included the following in its WLCC calculation:

The award criteria will be lowest life-cycle cost which shall be the sum of the following:

1. kWh/m3 at main duty point of the pump (m3/hour) x expected flow per annum (m3) x Average cost (c/kWh) x assumed life cycle (e.g. 5 years)

Plus

2. kWh/m3 at a secondary duty point of the pump (m3/hour) x expected flow per annum (m3) x Average cost (c/kWh) x assumed life cycle (e.g. 5 years). There may be more than one secondary duty point.

Plus

3. Fixed price lump sum capital cost plus projected energy costs over 5 years

The result was that the pump with the cheapest capital cost became the second most expensive (out of five) when operational costs were taken into account, whereas the second-cheapest pump on capital costs was the least expensive on a whole-life basis, due to its greater efficiency.

Source: EPA (2014) adapting material provided by the Tipperary Energy Agency

While the idea of GPP is to be welcomed, one major omission from the EPA guidance is how implementing GPP can be reconciled with the OGP's instructions to buyers to make procurement competitions more SME-friendly.

## Process Auditor

It is a requirement for a buyer to appoint a process auditor for PPP and capital expenditure projects in excess of €20 million, i.e. where complex and strategically important projects are being procured. This section explains the role of the process auditor and draws on the RFT (March 2016) for the appointment by the Department of Communications, Energy and Natural Resources of a process auditor in relation to the tender competition for the National Broadband Plan.

Having a process auditor in place gives suppliers a high degree of confidence that the tender will be managed in a professional and compliant manner.

### Required Services

A process auditor must be appointed when the buyer has given approval to proceed with the procurement. The following procurement process audit services are usually required.

1. Record that each phase of an approved procurement process checklist has been addressed and given due consideration by the buyer's Project Procurement Board (which is responsible for the strategic direction and overall management of the tender competition).
2. Confirm that the buyer has adhered to the Public Spending Code and the Capital Appraisal Guidelines.
3. Confirm that the operation of the procurement process and decision-making are fair, objective and follow agreed procedures with due process.
4. Directly observe the decision-making process and confirm that decisions are taken in line with the approved procurement process.

5. Review the documentation issued, including the briefing provided to evaluators, to check the fairness and robustness of the procurement process.
6. Attend meetings of the Project Procurement Board and the meetings that evaluate the bid submissions.
7. Liaise directly with the Accountable Officer or the person he designates on matters of material concern.
8. Raise instances where decisions or advices do not appear to have been followed through by the Project Procurement Board.
9. Obtain and retain all relevant documentation relating to the procurement process checklist and the role of process auditor.
10. The post-procurement review stage is outside the remit of the process auditor.
11. The process auditor is not a second layer of project management and should not therefore be involved in decision-making.

## Deliverables

Buyers expect the process auditor to be 'hands-on' and to this end the following are indicative deliverables throughout the procurement cycle; in this case the competitive dialogue was used.

| | PROCESS AUDITOR DELIVERABLES |
|---|---|
| **Pre-Qualification Stage** | |
| Pre-PQQ discussions | Review minutes of meetings |
| Legal advices received about choice of proposed procurement process | Review advices |
| Approval of PQQ | Review of departmental minute |
| Responses issued by way of clarifications to published questionnaire | Review of all responses issued to potential suppliers that expressed an interest |
| Publication of PQQ on etenders and TED | Review of published notices |
| Submission opening | Review minutes |
| **Evaluation Stage** | |
| Guidance issued to Assessment Panel | Review document provided |
| Evaluation review and determination of shortlist | Review minutes of meetings of Assessment Panel |

| | |
|---|---|
| Informing unsuccessful bidders | Review letters issued (and any subsequent correspondence) |
| Conduct four phases of dialogue | Review minutes of all meetings and correspondence with candidates |
| Completion of dialogue phase and determination of shortlist of candidates | Review minutes |
| Informing shortlisted candidates of outcome of dialogue phase and proposed next steps | Review letters issued |
| Report to buyer's management group on outcome of dialogue phase | Review report and departmental minute |
| **RFT Stage** | |
| Approval of business case in line with capital appraisal guidelines/ Public Spending Code | Review of final report and departmental board minute approving the decision to proceed based on the business case |
| Determination of award criteria | Review final report |
| Approval of RFT and contract documentation | Sign off on process |
| Issuing of clarifications to shortlisted candidates | Review of correspondence |
| Tender opening | Review minutes |
| Final report on tender evaluation and selection of preferred bidder | Attend meeting(s) of Assessment Panel Review final report and departmental minute approving the recommendation |
| Issuing of letters to unsuccessful bidders | Review letters |
| Debriefing unsuccessful bidders | Review minutes |
| Conclusion of competition | Preparation of report to Accountable Officer setting out the level of compliance with stated requirements; this report must be agreed before the contract can be signed |
| **Contract Award Stage** | |
| Approval of contract and documentation issued to preferred bidder | Sign off on process |
| Financial close process | Sign off on process |
| Confirm project provides value for money | Review department's assessment |

At any stage during the tender competition, where a point of concern arises the process auditor should inform the person responsible for the competition in writing and the reasons for the concern(s) and other decision-makers should then be informed. The process auditor has to decide if the response provided addresses his concerns.

The bottom line is that the process auditor is required to make a report to the Accountable Officer about the compliance of all aspects of the procurement competition before contract award.

## Procurement Audit Report

Under the EU Procurement Directives, buyers are required to prepare a written report after every tender competition, other than mini-competitions conducted under framework agreements.

- This audit report should contain the following:
- The name of the buyer
- The subject matter and value of the contract
- The results of the pre-qualification process i.e. the names of the successful candidates with reasons provided for selection/non-selection
- Reasons for rejecting abnormally low tenders
- The name of the preferred bidder and the reasons for selecting their tender
- The name(s) of sub-contractors and the share of the contract to be sub-contracted
- Justification, where appropriate, for the use of the competitive dialogue/competitive procedure with negotiation
- Reasons for not awarding a contract or a framework
- An explanation for not using an electronic submission
- Measures taken to address potential conflicts of interest of the evaluators
- Reasons for not using lots

In addition, buyers must maintain records of internal deliberations, records of dialogue or other meetings and details about the preparation of the procurement documents, including the setting of selection and award criteria.

Over time these procurement audits will become an important source of insight for unsuccessful suppliers. These documents may be discoverable under the Freedom of Information Act (see chapter 18).

---

### TENDER TIP

Become fully familiar with the published and prevailing guidance that governs the running of tender competitions. Know the current rules that buyers must respect; their 'Rules of the Road'.

---

## 7

# Framework Agreements

## Introduction

A framework agreement is an arrangement between one or more buyers and one or more suppliers, the purpose of which is to establish the terms governing contracts to be awarded during a given period, in particular with regard to price and, where appropriate, the quantity envisaged.

In other words, a framework agreement is a general phrase for agreements that set out terms and conditions under which specific purchases (call-offs) can be made throughout the term of the agreement. The Public Contracts Directive allows buyers to conclude framework agreements provided they use one of the procedures provided for, e.g. an open, restricted, negotiated or competitive dialogue procedure (see Chapter 6).

The OGP has issued guidance about the use of framework agreements, as has the Crown Commercial Service (CSS) for frameworks in NI. As it is the OGP's intention that the majority of tenders for goods and services in Ireland will be procured under framework agreements, it is essential for suppliers to not only understand what is involved under a framework agreement but to develop their bid and bid-consortium strategies around this default procurement process.

## The Economic Rationale for Frameworks – Demand Aggregation

Aggregation techniques (i.e. techniques used to combine demand for public procurement) – or centralised purchasing – are used across the EU to improve cost savings and the efficiency of procurement. Most Member States, including Ireland, use framework agreements to deliver these savings.

The use of framework agreements has increased in recent years and, according to a report prepared by PWC for the European Commission (February 2014), they now comprise some 25 per cent of the total value of all public contracts awarded above the EU value thresholds, or nearly one in six of all contract awards. In Ireland, the figure is much higher at 36 per cent by value. Centralised purchasing accounts for about 5 per cent of the market in terms of the number of awards and about 20 per cent of total contract awards by value.

The main reason for this trend is the increased pressure on public budgets. One of the preferred solutions was a higher aggregation of demand in the form of centralising procurement to exploit the resulting economies of scale. Another factor driving aggregation is the procurement of goods using common standards.

Perhaps the main driver for buyers is the considerable and tangible reduction in administration and transaction costs associated with the use of framework agreements. For example, PWC found that on average buyers spend eight days of staff time on framework mini-competitions compared to some twenty-two days for a standard procurement. These process cost savings for buyers are considerable. By the same token, suppliers on frameworks do not have to spend a significant amount of time when responding to mini-competitions.

Another trend at EU level is that frameworks are used primarily for routine supplies and commodity purchases.

Accenture's report (August 2012) for the DPER, Capacity and Capability Review of Central Procurement Function, identified €4.3 billion in public spending deemed suitable to be managed by the OGP, with the majority of these procurements to be tendered under framework agreements.

## What the Buyer Should Consider

In considering what type of procurement best suits their requirements, buyers may be tempted to put a framework agreement in place based on competitive tendering because this involves the least amount of work for them over time. However, much more careful consideration needs to given to the launch of a framework tender competition.

Securing value for money will always be a dominant factor in coming to such a decision. But will a framework deliver additional savings? If so, the buyers should try to quantify the net result.

Other issues that should be weighed up include the reduced administrative costs of setting up a framework as subsequent mini-competitions can be managed at a fraction of the time (and effort) compared to a full tender.

Most importantly, the buyer should be satisfied that the same result and benefits cannot be obtained by use of the DPS (see chapter 20). Buyers are also aware from experience that suppliers who are put on a framework panel are likely to reduce the maximum permissible price/fee in subsequent mini-competitions. This is a sure way of saving money.

However tempting a framework agreement might be, the buyer should always conduct market soundings in advance, in particular where the procurement demands delivery nationwide. In particular, the buyer should try to quantify the scope and type of works, goods or services that will need to be called off. OGP guidance is quite clear on the absolute need for market research.

There should be flexibility as regards upgrading the product, service or works required so long as it remains within the scope of the original specification.

At present, several frameworks are in place for the same range of products and services (legal services, for example). Over time it is the OGP's express intention that this level of duplication will be progressively eliminated.

The scale of the tender is another issue. If a framework involves, for example, five suppliers on six panels across four regions, the buyer would need to have the necessary resources to co-ordinate and, more importantly, manage all mini-competitions and contract implementation.

If the requirement is a one-off, or there is a need within a short period, then using a framework would not be at all appropriate, nor is a framework designed for these situations. The open procedure would be the better option.

On the other hand, where several buyers have common and identified needs, for professional services, translation, facilities management, etc., then using frameworks becomes the default option. This is OGP policy.

Finally, buyers need to be mindful that a framework does not breach EU competition rules. For example, where the duration of the contract exceeds four years as this could be deemed as excessive; where the range of products covered is too wide, resulting in the foreclosure of suppliers; where the range of users is too wide, (again) resulting in a foreclosure of suppliers; and where mini-competitions are not run competitively.

## How It Works – EU Rules

1. The Public Contracts Directive sets out the following basic requirements that buyers must adhere to should they decide to procure goods and services through a framework agreement.
2. The term of a framework agreements should not exceed four years, save in exceptional and justified cases. An eight-year framework is permissible in the utilities sector.
3. Where the terms and conditions applying to the framework agreement (contract) are set down in the procurement

documents for the tender competition, a buyer cannot reopen a competition, even for an individual lot, unless the original tender document expressly states this is possible. Here the conditions governing the framework agreement are set in a legally binding manner.

4.  On the other hand, a tender competition using a framework agreement is possible where only some of the terms and conditions are laid down. In such a situation, a framework agreement either does not include critical commercial terms or does not establish in a binding way all the terms necessary so that any subsequent orders can be concluded without any further agreement between the parties. For example, it could be the case that there is no obligation on the buyer to purchase anything. In short, this type of framework is incomplete and a contract is formed only when purchases are called off.

5.  Buyers should for every contract to be awarded consult in writing with the suppliers capable of performing the contract, i.e. all pre-qualified suppliers must be invited to participate in mini-competitions (see below).

6.  The length of a call-off contract is not specified in the Procurement Directives.

7.  A time limit which is sufficiently long should be fixed to allow tenders for each specific contract to be submitted, taking into account factors such as the complexity of the subject matter and the time needed to send in tenders.

8.  Buyers have the option to reserve frameworks to sheltered workshops.

9.  Frameworks can apply to works, supplies or services contracts.

10. For single-supplier framework agreements, call-offs are placed according to the terms and conditions set out in the framework.

11. For multi-supplier frameworks, only two suppliers are needed to be appointed to the panel.

12. For multi-supplier frameworks, buyers have three options, as follows:

    **Direct award without re-opening a competition:** In this scenario, the RFT must set out the terms and conditions. The buyer's choice of a preferred supplier must be based on the objective criteria laid out in the procurement documentation.

    **Mini-competitions:** In this scenario, the RFT does not include all the terms and conditions and as a consequence buyers must organise 'mini-competitions' between the suppliers appointed to the framework. The award criteria for mini-competitions may be different from those applied in the award of the framework agreement.

    **Hybrid:** This option is also open to buyers who, for example, want to make a direct award for low value contracts and mini-competitions for contracts above a determined value. Contract award will be on the basis of the award criteria set out in the procurement documents for the framework agreement.

13. The EU procurement principles of transparency, non-discrimination, fairness and proportionality, etc., apply when buyers launch mini-competitions.

14. While the standstill period applies when a framework agreement is set up, there is no mandatory standstill period for a call-off contract under a framework.

15. Contract Award Notices for call-offs must be published.

## Applying the Rules in Ireland

Guidance provided by the European Commission has been published to inform Irish and NI buyers and those across the EU. In addition, the OGP has current guidance in place (to give effect to sections 33, 34 and 35 of Statutory Instrument 329 of 2006 as it applies to framework agreements).

The 2014 Procurement Directives introduced very minor changes so the rules based on the 2004 Directives will continue to apply. What follows is a commentary on some of the minimum EU requirements and how, in practice, these rules should apply to framework agreements.

**Use of procedures:** To conclude a framework agreement, the open or restricted procedure should be used by the buyer, with the competitive procedure with negotiation and the competitive dialogue only possible in exceptional and justified circumstances.

**Terms and conditions:** Once terms and conditions and award criteria are published at the outset, they cannot be changed subsequently.

**Multiple buyers:** Only the buyers expressly cited in the contract notice, either by naming them directly in the notice itself (e.g. 'all central government departments and all local authorities') or through reference to other documents, may apply the framework. Using a formula such as 'all public bodies' is considered to be unclear and not transparent. In other words, framework agreements constitute a closed system which no one else can enter either as a buyer or supplier. On the other hand, the buyer who leads the procurement on behalf of other buyers does so having secured their agreement about the tendering procedure used and the associated award criteria. In some cases, the OGP will become the 'buyer of buyers' as it is a central purchasing body within the meaning of the EU Procurement Directives.

**Electronic auction:** It is permissible to use an electronic auction under framework agreements but in practice, at least until recently, this option has not been much availed of. OGP (correctly) advises that the use of an electronic auction requires careful preparation.

**Thresholds:** A critical point for both buyers and suppliers is the issue of the threshold above which a framework agreement applies. Buyers often want the continuing flexibility to source local suppliers for low value contracts, i.e. those valued less than €25,000. Small entrepreneurs cannot realistically succeed in winning nationwide frameworks so they tend to focus on local 'below-the-radar' tender opportunities. There is a lacuna here. Some buyers want frameworks to cover all purchases, including those below €5,000, while there is a view that such an approach is not SME user-friendly. As the Public Contracts Directives does not provide guidance about low-value contracts, the choice is essentially political.

**Calculating the value thresholds:** The threshold should be based on the estimated value of all contracts for the duration of the full term of the framework for individual lots or overall if no lots are envisaged and not just a projection of annual expenditure.

**Duration:** While the rule is four years maximum, a longer duration may be justified in order to ensure effective competition for the contract in question if its performance, for example, required investment with a depreciation period of more than four years. There appears to be some uncertainty about the award of contracts – for example, those agreed in year three of the framework – for a period that exceeds four years. OGP guidance is that putting in place an additional contract that extends substantially beyond the published termination date of a framework agreement contract that is due to expire should not be facilitated.

**Lots:** Typically, framework agreements allow for lots, i.e. the division of contracts by region or sub-category, for instance. It is permissible for a buyer to provide that suppliers cannot tender for all lots so as to encourage SME participation.

**Panels/Framework members:** The minimum number of suppliers allowed onto a panel is two, assuming all qualified. In practice, up to twenty suppliers have been shortlisted.

**Individual framework contracts:** This covers, for example, purchase order contracts as part of a wider drawdown arrangement for the supply of goods. In this scenario, the sole supplier is asked to supply goods at a pre-determined fixed price for a quantity set by the buyer as and when a requirement exists.

## Establishing a Framework

Frameworks are advertised using the standard OJEU contract notice for above EU threshold contracts.

Buyers are required to indicate:

1. The intention is to establish a framework.
2. The identity of all the buyers who will be relying on the framework.
3. Whether the framework is for a single supplier or for multi-suppliers, and in the latter case the number of suppliers it intends to include.
4. The duration of the framework; typically no more than four years.
5. An estimate of the total value of the purchases expected to be made by all the buyers covered by the framework.
6. The projected frequency of the proposed call-offs.
7. The procurement procedure being used, e.g. open or restricted, etc.
8. The award criteria (see below).
9. That the mandatory standstill rules apply to the award of the framework but not to subsequent contracts or call-offs.
10. The procedures for mini-competitions.

For a framework involving a single supplier, the buyer should also include the following additional information in the tender notice:

1. How the price is to be determined.
2. Delivery times.
3. Projected quantities.

The price need not be fixed in absolute terms; it is possible that the buyer could set it by reference, for example, to a price index. Where a framework agreement is concluded with a single supplier, call-offs under the framework should be awarded on the basis of the terms laid down in the agreement, refined or supplemented by other terms in the framework agreement but not agreed at that time.

There can be no substantive change to the specification or the terms and conditions agreed at the time that the framework is awarded. In addition, where the terms laid down in the framework agreement are sufficiently precise to cover the buyer's requirement, the buyer can award the call-off without reopening the tender competition, i.e. by direct award.

Similar information is required in relation to multi-supplier frameworks; the only significant additional issue being how the proposed mini-competitions will be operated, the award criteria for such competitions, how suppliers might be rotated, etc. The tender notice must clearly state that the buyer intends to vary some weightings otherwise there is a danger that suppliers would be treated in an unequal manner. New award criteria must clearly be related to (i.e. derived from) the original award criteria. In general, when awarding individual contracts, buyers do not have to go through the full procedural steps required under the EU Procurement Directives; although some Irish buyers do this.

The guidance provided by the OGP is that buyers should use the (single-phase) open procedure when publishing tender notices for framework agreements. While a restricted procedure may be used in some situations, using a negotiated procedure for a framework would be quite exceptional and even inappropriate.

The most critical aspect of a framework agreement is the award criteria set by the buyer. It is recalled that buyers cannot make changes or modifications to award criteria during the operation of the framework. This needs to be borne in mind when buyers launch mini-competitions for the award of contracts. In some cases, buyers may set new award criteria, perhaps with different weightings with regard to their specific requirements. For example, the timeframe for the delivery of a service might be more important in the performance of one contract but less relevant in other cases. In an ideal situation, suppliers would be asked to price the requirement, confirm their availability (and the resources to be deployed) and, where relevant, the proposed methodology to deliver the requirement within the period determined.

**CASE HISTORY**

OGP Framework for Accounting, Audit and Financial Services

On 15 July 2015, the OGP published a RFT under the open procedure to establish nine multi-supplier framework agreements with three lots for the provision of accounting, audit and financial services. The OGP RFT template for services was used, as were the new-style Tender Response Documents (TRD). The framework clients included departments, public bodies under their aegis, non-commercial semi-state companies, local authorities, the HSE and other buyers in the health sector, third-level education institutions, An Garda Síochána, the Irish Prison Service and the Defence Forces. The framework does not cover commercial semi-state companies.

Lot 1 included:

- Accounting (technical and transactions) advisory services
- Business accounting services (bookkeeping, payroll, etc.)
- Financial reporting, compliance and accounts preparation
- Tax compliance and preparation

This lot was divided into three sub-lots with reference to the value of the contracts to be awarded. A maximum of twenty suppliers were selected for contracts valued at less than €25,000; ten for contracts between €25,000 and €200,000; and ten for contracts in excess of €200,000.

Lot 2 (for a maximum of ten suppliers) included:

- Provision of audit services (comprising seven sub-lots)

Lot 3 (for a maximum of ten suppliers) included:

- Appraisal of investment proposals
- Economic analysis and modelling
- Financial strategy
- Project financial management
- Public Private Partnerships
- Tax planning and advisory
- Actuarial services

The first thing to note is that economic consultancy services were covered by Lot 3 but were not explicitly mentioned in the RFT's title. As a consequence, several suppliers did not spot that this type of service was out to tender.

If a sourcing strategy was prepared by the OGP, this was not shared with the professional services covered by the RFT. The projected value of the services (€9 million) over the term of the framework seems very low. The turnover requirement (€100,000 for contracts between a value of €25,000 and €200,000) was not consistent with OGP guidelines. The OGP required evidence of three projects/contracts to a value of at least €87,500, despite the probability than many mini-competitions would be in respect of contracts with a value of less than €25,000.

A long list of clarifications were posted and replied to. Some of the more interesting answers and features of the RFT are as follows (as they set policy and precedent for other frameworks):

1. It was not a requirement that a supplier had to provide every service listed in the lot in order to be included in the framework panel. This meant that for Lot 3, for example, not all the successful suppliers bid for all the lots that were tendered.
2. Separate tenders had to be submitted for each sub-lot, but suppliers could not be appointed to more than two sub-lots under each lot.
3. For lots 1 and 2, suppliers had to self-declare that their organisation was a member of a prescribed accountancy body within the supervisory remit of the Irish Auditing and Accounting Supervisory Authority and that their accountants were members of named bodies. Proof of membership of an equivalent body/ies was not asked for.
4. Blended (average) rates for certain categories of professional services at different levels had to be submitted.
5. Daily rates (on the basis of an eight-hour day) had to include all costs, including travel and subsistence.
6. Cost savings are measured by reference to the prices currently charged to buyers and the tendered price; this assumes there is a difference between the two.
7. Suppliers were required to submit a list of free 'value-added services'.
8. CVs were not required to be included in the response documents. Suppliers would possibly be asked for details of personnel at direct drawdown or mini-competition stage.
9. The framework agreement and the services contract were not open for negotiation.
10. Reference sites could include contracts fulfilled in other countries.

# Ways of Purchasing

## The Cascade Method

If so provided in the contract notice, a buyer may use what is called the cascade method. The supplier ranked first in the tender competition will be given the option of delivering the required works, goods or services, but if this supplier is not capable of or interested in fulfilling the requirement during the framework period, the second placed supplier is given the option to deliver the requirement and if that supplier cannot do what is needed then the third ranked supplier can step in, etc. The OGP has admitted (in the context of their assessment of the market for legal services) that the cascade method is not fit for purpose. We agree with that assessment.

## Mini-Competitions

As requirements arise over the duration of the framework, buyers will contact the appointed framework members in writing and invite them to submit bids, e.g. for the supply of 1,000 units. As all suppliers have been accepted into the framework, they may not need to re-submit material to pre-qualify, or they may have to comply with new award criteria as such criteria may have been set in the original tender notice. However, a refinement of the basic terms may be used, e.g. in relation to particular delivery timescales; additional security needs; invoicing arrangements; inclusion of incidental charges, etc.

The key determinant is usually price and the capacity of the supplier to fulfil the requirement. Suppliers are not usually allowed to submit a bid price in excess of the price provided in their tender response. As a consequence, bid prices usually fall over the duration of the framework.

Furthermore, buyers usually state in the tender notice that they are not obliged to invite all shortlisted suppliers to participate in subsequent mini-competitions. Buyers have to be satisfied in inviting a limited number of suppliers capable of meeting the particular need to bid that this ensures there is adequate competition. Thus a supplier could get onto a framework and not be asked to submit a bid for the duration of the framework.

The following scenario is based on the terms and conditions set out in the RFT for accounting, audit and financial services (see above). Other RFTs published subsequently have used somewhat different rules. Therefore suppliers should examine the rules for their category carefully.

For contracts in excess of €5,000, a buyer will use a mini-competition by issuing a Supplementary Request for Tender (SRFT) that will include details about the scope of the requirements and the deadline for the submission of tenders. Suppliers will have the option of asking clarification questions. All the suppliers on the panel for the sub-lot will be asked to tender on the basis of pre-determined award criteria. To this end, a range of weightings as follows, will be used: cost (25 per cent to 75 per cent); service delivery methodology (10 per cent to 25 per cent); understanding the brief (10 per cent to 25 per cent); and technical merit (10 per cent to 25 per cent). The maximum daily rate for mini-competitions was set at 30 per cent of the overall marks. The term of the contract is two years with the option of having this period extended to four years.

For mini-competitions under the framework for the provision of business, management consultancy and advisory services, the OGP sent a template SRFT response document to all buyers covered by the framework along with guidelines regarding the completion of the document. Framework members will be asked to provide the following details.

| | COMMENT |
|---|---|
| Service levels | Details may be sought about the quality of the supplier's procedures for ensuring an accessible, timely and responsive service; a 24/7, 365-day service; and meeting deadlines and budgets |
| Service Methodology | Details may be sought about the quality of the supplier's understanding of the requirements and the overall approach to the provision of the service. |

| Contract Management | Details may be sought about the quality of the supplier's proposed approach to performance measurement; risk-management and quality-assurance mechanisms; and, issue management and escalation procedures. |
|---|---|
| Quality and Relevance of Resources | A summary CV for each member of the personnel involved in service delivery will be sought, as well as an organisation chart showing resource allocation and management accountability. As appropriate, suppliers may also be assessed on the quality of their procedures for identifying and managing the deployment of subject matter experts to ensure delivery of high-quality successful outputs within the required timescales. |

Buyers have a great deal of discretion in relation to setting the weightings attaching to each award criteria. For example, in relation to costs the weighting can be between 30% to 80%.

While the SRFT response document does not specify a word count limit it should not take an experienced supplier too long to complete.

## Direct Drawdown

Under this arrangement, which should apply to low-value contracts only, the buyer has the option of picking just one of the pre-qualified suppliers. The following scenario is based on the terms and conditions set out in the RFT for accounting, audit and financial services (see above). Other RFTs published subsequently have used somewhat different rules. Therefore suppliers should examine the rules for their category carefully.

A framework client (a buyer) that has a requirement for services valued at less than €5,000 will serve a Notification to Activate Services Form (NASF) on the framework member (supplier) for a call-off contract. Buyers select a supplier based on information contained in a framework members' directory that contains, inter alia, the services provided and the direct drawdown fixed rate tendered; that represented 20 per cent of the marks. If a buyer uses a supplier they may not use the same supplier for a subsequent requirement.

This means that they can revert to the first supplier for their third requirement. If a supplier served with a NASF decides not to tender then the buyer will proceed to issue a NASF on another supplier.

## Northern Ireland

While the rules applying to the award of framework agreements in Northern Ireland derive from the EU Procurement Directives, the CPD has issued (August 2014) its own guidance on collaborative procurement, i.e. the procurement of goods and services which are repetitive and common to multiple organisations. The driver in bringing about a centralisation of purchasing is achieving best value for money in support of the delivery of better government services.

In addition to setting out various operating principles (such as structured stakeholder engagement, benchmarking, use of standardised documents, etc.), the CPD guidance requires buyers to develop a specific procurement strategy for each proposed framework which will take account of the market conditions and the potential impact of SMEs.

| List of Collaborative Procurement Categories | |
| --- | --- |
| • Postal services | • Professional services, including banking |
| • Advertising services | |
| • Energy | • ICT commodities |
| • Travel | • Telecoms and networking |
| • Facilities management | • Fleet |
| | • Office supplies |

The main difference between Ireland and Northern Ireland is that in the latter's case more framework agreements are already in place. The CPD has established contracts and agreements which can be used by a number of government departments, agencies and other non-departmental public bodies; these can be found on the CPD's website. In addition, the scope of the categories to be covered by framework agreements in Northern Ireland is much wider than what is planned by the OGP.

Details are also available (by way of contract award notices and a list on the Department of Finance website) about the companies that have been appointed to the frameworks; the annual value of each contract; the contract start and termination dates; and the duration of possible contract extensions.

## Impact on SMEs

In Northern Ireland, buyers putting a framework agreement in place must consider the impact on SMEs. By their nature, framework agreements tend to be large-scale and have a relatively long (four-year) duration. SMEs have voiced concerns about their perception of being 'locked out' of major tender opportunities for that time period.

Buyers in Northern Ireland are therefore encouraged to do what they can to facilitate SME access to framework agreements – for example, splitting contracts into smaller lots, usually geographically or by the type of service required. SMEs in Northern Ireland are actively encouraged to become sub-contractors or sub-suppliers and to join bid consortia to compete effectively for framework opportunities.

Buyers are also encouraged to hold awareness sessions with SMEs to explain the operational requirements of the framework agreements and the tender process.

As the OGP has yet to fully roll out its programme of framework agreements (see chapter 3), it is too soon to judge whether SMEs will be aversely affected or not. However, in one of the first 'new-style' framework agreements (for business and management consulting) the OGP appointed only one Irish indigenous supplier and six of the eight shortlisted were not SMEs.

---

### TENDER TIP

Due to their scale, many framework agreements are SME unfriendly so consider joining or forming a bid consortium to secure a fair share of this business.

---

# 8

# Bid Consortia/Joint Ventures

## Introduction

It is Government policy in Ireland and Northern Ireland to encourage and support bids submitted by consortia. Collaboration in procurement is becoming increasingly prevalent and will become more commonplace as more tenders for framework agreements are published. However, detailed OGP guidelines for buyers in relation to consortium bids do not exist at present. That said, many suppliers can and do secure business through tendering as a sub-contractor or a sub-supplier as a preferred route to market.

This chapter will explain the types of and structures for collaboration. The perspectives of both buyers and suppliers will provide good insights into this relatively untried form of collaboration. Practical advice is provided about getting started and using a Teaming Agreement as a device to bind the partnership together. Legal and, importantly, competition issues need to be considered prior to parties approaching actual or potential competitors. BS 11000, a business collaboration standard, is recommended for potential partner in large, high-value and complex tenders.

## Types of Collaboration

These include:

- Strategic business partnership
- Consortium bid partnering
- Collaborative supplier relationship
- Joint venture
- Informal alliance
- One-off ad hoc co-operation

## Structures for Collaboration

These include the following.

### Informal

- Include the tasks in the bid response
- All parties sign the RFT

### Semi-Formal

- Sign Teaming Agreement

### Legal

- Set up SPV (rarely required but now a recommendation; see below)

## The Buyer's Perspective

Buyers see the following merits and benefits of consortium delivery:

- Improved and more comprehensive response.
- Better service delivery.
- Scope for new and innovative ideas and solutions.
- Having access to dynamic and specialist sub-contractors.
- More competitively priced bids with delivery by sub-contractors.
- Access to global companies through a local partner.
- One primary contractor taking responsibility for project delivery.

- Engaging multi-disciplinary professionals where complex projects are involved.

- Better value for money as specialist sub-contractors can deliver at lower costs.

Despite a pre-disposition among buyers to encourage bid consortia, a critical first step in any bid response is to clarify from the outset – if no express guidance is set out in the RFT – that buyers will entertain a response from a bid consortium.

Note that a buyer may require the primary contractor to replace a sub-contractor who is subject to one of the grounds for exclusion. In addition, a buyer may require certain elements of a contract to be performed by the primary contractor only.

Buyers could be more proactive in promoting the concept of bid consortia given the proven success of this form of tendering. Furthermore, given the expected introduction of more framework tender competitions where requirements will be divided into lots, buyers will need to be careful as to how bid consortia are managed by primary contractors, e.g. as regards the payment of sub-contractors.

While some buyers use PINs where they expect bid consortia to respond to complex tender competitions, the practice of using PINs to alert bid consortia to upcoming opportunities could be used more systematically.

> 'A large part of the creative ideas for new technologies (and services) comes from SMEs....it is essential that RFTs facilitate joint tendering and be open to consortium bids from SMES.'
> Buying Innovation: The Ten Step Plan
> (Department of Jobs, Enterprise and Innovation, 2011)

## The Supplier's Perspective

### Why Submit a Joint Bid?

Firms taken individually do not have:

- The necessary scale to service the requirements of the contract.

- The necessary previous experience or other technical capacity requirements set by the buyer.

- The necessary geographical reach to service the requirements.

- All of the plant, equipment or other resources required to perform the contract.

- All of the necessary resources, skills or expertise to perform the contract.

- Sufficient turnover/financial capacity to meet the minimum requirements.

Specifically, more suppliers are looking favourably at the option of teaming with partners for the following reasons.

- There is a greater awareness that quite often suppliers on their own do not have the capability or capacity to deliver all elements of a tender.

- Potential access to new procurement opportunities as a sub-supplier.

- Raising the company's profile and credentials with primary contractors and other sub-suppliers.

- Securing valuable reference sites as a result of a team approach.

- Low-cost entry to public contracts given that the work required by sub-contractors in preparing a bid response is usually minimal by comparison to what the primary contractor has to do.

- Gaining know-how and business skills from other companies.

- The opportunity to become a primary contractor having had experience of being a sub-contractor.

## Getting Started

Do not be shy; initiate a bid consortium if it supports your business strategy. In reviewing tender opportunities, think laterally. Can what you produce be included as part of the opportunity as a lead or as a primary sub-supplier? If the new business could have an impact on your profitability then chase it. You do not have to be a primary contractor to start the process of putting a bid consortium together. A junior partner with a unique offering could leverage a larger opportunity as these services could be critical for the success of the proposed service.

If you decide to approach tender opportunities from a partnership perspective then draw up an 'ideal' partner profile. You can do this by making a direct approach to a primary contractor. A cold call might work, provided it is to the right person in the organisation that is targeted. A preferred method is to send a short and personalised email and to follow this up with a call to request a meeting to discuss what you have to offer in relation to a potential tender.

Using market intelligence – eTenders or OJEU contract award notices, for example – you will be able to identify which suppliers in your area of interest are already winning tenders. If there is no obvious company with a public sector track record, then seek out potential partners from your knowledge of the sectors where you have something practical to offer.

In addition, you need to promote your business as a potential sub-contractor. You can best do this while attending trade shows where primary contractors exhibit. Suppliers seeking sub-contractors will typically use business directories unless they are aware of your business and your appetite to work in a collaborative manner. Another approach is to call a competitor who has won a contract and enquire – in a situation where they may have problems scaling up to deliver a new requirement – whether your business could deliver part or all of a work package.

Non-Irish companies that tender in Ireland are aware that their prospects can improve if they collaborate with the right local partner. So if you are tracking a forthcoming tender that is too large for your business or with which you have capability issues, assess whether a global player could be enticed to work with you. One way to find potential international partners in your area of interest is to check out the UK's published list of contract award notices.

## Teaming Agreement

In certain circumstances, the parties to a bid might feel more comfortable if they had the nature of their relationship in responding to a tender opportunity(ies) confirmed by what is called a Teaming Agreement.

The benefits of a Teaming Agreement include:

- The primary contractor avails of specialist capacity which is not available in-house and so can deliver the buyer's requirements.

- Smaller and specialist suppliers get an opportunity to partner with a larger supplier in their niche areas of expertise.

- The parties agree 'best endeavour' terms and conditions and frame their proposed working relationship with this in mind.

- The bid consortium will be perceived as less risky by the buyer if suppliers have concluded a Teaming Agreement.

- The delivery of the buyer's requirements at the most competitive price by using specialist sub-contractors.

- Scope for the parties to introduce and deliver innovative solutions.

- A sharing of the risks.

A Teaming Agreement could cover a specific tender opportunity or indeed a longer-term collaborative effort to secure work by means of tendering. The conclusion of a Teaming Agreement for contracts falling below the EU's procurement thresholds and outside the scope of framework agreements may not be necessary.

## Key Provisions of a Teaming Agreement

1. The company that is the primary contractor must be clearly stated.
2. The parties are usually bound into an exclusive arrangement, i.e. they cannot join another bid consortium.

3. The scope of the work allocated or to be allocated between the parties.
4. A statement that on contract award, the primary contractor will sub-contract defined work packages to defined sub-contractors.
5. All sub-contractors have an absolute duty to deliver their part of the contract.
6. The parties' rights, roles and responsibilities.
7. Payment and invoicing arrangements.
8. Agreement that the Teaming Agreement lapses on contract award (in the event that it is opportunity specific).
9. The law applicable is that of the buyer's jurisdiction.
10. Arbitration and dispute resolution provisions will be used.
11. A clear termination date is set as well as circumstances that might lead to the ending of the Teaming Agreement.

## CASE HISTORY
## The Public Policy Advisors Network

The PPAN was set up in 2012 by five former public servants who had considerable practical and academic credentials in the area of evidenced-based policy research.

While this collaboration worked as the partners shared know-how and business opportunities to good effect, it soon became clear that to get on OGP frameworks the membership of the PPAN would need to be increased.

In May 2015, the PPAN was expanded and now covers fifteen individuals who all have a public-service background; those who have private-sector public policy practices; and recognised leaders in their respective areas of expertise.

The PPAN also has three members based in NI.

This has enabled members of the PPAN to form bid consortia that have tendered for (and been successful) in getting on OGP panels for policy advisors.

The range of policy areas covered includes the following:

| Economics | Planning and Development | Energy | Climate Change |
|---|---|---|---|
| Public Sector Reform | Transport | Local Authorities | Health |
| Organisation Change | Strategy Development and Implementation | Business Case Development | Governance |
| Strategic Procurement | | | |

## When Are Bid Consortia Most Suitable?

It depends on what the buyer is looking for and whether you are approaching the option of partnering from the point of view of a primary contractor or as a sub-supplier.

The following types of tenders suggest that it might be difficult for a single supplier to fulfil all the requirements.

- Framework agreements for goods and services both for single suppliers and where panels of suppliers are to be appointed.

- Construction works.

- Outsourcing of public services.

- Shared service delivery.

- Provision of multi-disciplinary services such as master planning.

- Situations where goods and services have to be delivered at regional level.

- Where bids into other jurisdictions are involved.

## Critical Success Factors

- Make a business case for joint bidding.

- Standalone opportunity or more long-term?

- Does it 'fit' with your business strategy?

- Joint bids can secure more wins and reduce risks when large-value tenders are involved.

- Senior management must be engaged and supportive.

- Ensure it is competition-law compliant.

## Competition Issues

The Competition and Consumer Protection Commission (CCPC) published a guide in December 2014 about the application of competition law to bid consortia in Ireland.

Potential partners must ensure their collaboration does not spill over into the market more generally. It is therefore essential reading prior to a supplier considering the option of a collaborative approach to bidding. Each consortium member is required to consider its position carefully before entering into detailed negotiations with potential bidding partners.

The guidance does not address collusive bidding (i.e. price-fixing, market-sharing and bid-rigging) as this scenario was covered by CCPC guidance dating from 2009. However, the guidance applies to all situations where consortium bids involve non-competitors, including bid responses to private-sector tenders. The CCPC says competition law per se does not forbid consortium bids; the EU Procurement Directives expressly allow suppliers to submit joint bids.

As a general rule, according to the CCPC, consortium members must not be actual (current) or potential competitors. A bid will not cause competition issues if all of the following four factors are met:

- None of the parties could fulfil the requirements on its own.

- No subset of the parties could together fulfil the requirements of the tender competition.

- Only the minimum amount of information strictly necessary for the performance of the contract is shared (i.e. only 'need-to-know' information relevant to the tender).

- Consortium members must ensure they can compete 'vigorously' in all other contexts.

Even if bid does not satisfy all these requirements, it may still be allowed under competition law provided it has 'net positive effects'.

To this end, a self-assessment Competition Consortium Test is now required, i.e. all members of potential consortium must identify the pro-competitive benefits that result from joint bidding and assess whether those pro-competitive benefits outweigh any anti-competitive effects. Even if a positive outcome is determined, suppliers must always ensure that the consortium is not used as a vehicle to facilitate serious anti-competitive collusion between them in relation to other contracts or markets.

The test must demonstrate all of the following four factors:

1. The bid must produce real efficiency gains.
2. Consumers must benefit from those gains.
3. Any restrictions of competition involved in the consortium bid must be indispensible to the achievement of the efficiency gains.
4. Consortium bidding must not substantially eliminate competition either in the particular public procurement market or in other markets.

Buyers too will need to be satisfied that all bid responses are competition-compliant, e.g. where a sub-contractor is in several consortia. The CCPC suggests buyers may wish to impose information-sharing restrictions. How this can be done prior to the submission of bid responses has yet to be clarified. Thus with regard to the CCPC guide, the OGP will need to issue new guidance to buyers and amend the current framework agreement and other RFT templates.

Specifically, the OGP will need to clarify (taking market soundings inputs into account) for each framework competition if the goods/ services being procured are in a market where there is not much competition to start with, i.e. where the full CCPC guidance does not apply. The CCPC notes that in a market with dozens of suppliers two or three of them getting together to form a consortium is likely to leave enough other players in the market to ensure the tender competition can be effective. With this in mind, the CCPC/OGP needs to clarify whether the guidance applies to a category market share above a determined percentage. The CCPC also needs to clarify if the rules apply to NI partners in Irish bids.

The guidance does not apply to 'full function' JVs (which may need to be referred in any event to the CCPC for formal review). The CCPC recommends asking an independent person – a professional bid advisor, for instance – to manage the consortium bid. The CCPC also recommends, on contract award, the setting-up of a separate company, which is contrary to best practice and current OGP guidance.

The CCPC advises: 'if in doubt, you should seek independent legal advice'. Therefore a considerable burden of proof now falls on potential partners in relation to compliance with competition law that will inevitably add to the cost of tendering as legal/economic advices are needed prior to the decision in principle to set up a bid consortium.

As a consequence, the CCPC guidance may be a hindrance rather than a help to many SMEs. The Competition and Markets Authority provides similar guidance for the NI and UK market.

## Other Legal Issues

The standard contracts for service enclosed with the template RFTs published by the OGP have been approved by the Chief State Solicitor and requests to have amendments to same are usually not accepted. On the other hand, the OGP leaves it up to members of bid consortia to decide how they wish to collaborate, on what terms and conditions and the safeguards they might be mindful to put in place.

The most obvious starting point is who is legally responsible for the delivery of the contract. The template RFTs for goods and services clearly states (Schedule A.1):

> *The contractor is deemed to be the prime contractor under this Agreement and the contractor assumes full liability for the discharge of all obligations under this Agreement and shall assume all duties, responsibilities and obligations associated*

*with the position of prime contractor. The contractor as prime
contractor under the submission hereby assumes liability for its
sub-contractors and shall ensure that its sub-contractors shall
comply in all respects with the relevant terms of this Agreement
to the extent that it or they are retained by the supplier.'*

It is not a legal requirement for a bid consortium to set up a company
because upon contract award one member becomes the primary
contractor and assumes the above-mentioned legal obligations.

## The Primary Contractor

- One member becomes the primary contractor.

- Sub-contractors have identified tasks and share the
  consortium's agreed KPIs and contract requirements.

- The primary contractor charges a small fee to cover common
  administration and co-ordination tasks.

- All parties jointly are severally liable.

- The partner's steering (senior management) group takes key
  decisions.

If a buyer accepts a bid consortium tender bid signed by all the parties,
this may in certain situations form a contract.

Companies who win risky high-value tenders should take legal
advice if they are pressed by the buyer to conclude a Joint Venture
Agreement.

While most OGP procurement contracts are standardised, it is
prudent to get legal advice on the setting up of a bid consortium if you
believe this is necessary and certainly in situations where competition
law might arise.

## Setting Up a Bid Consortium

Preparation is critical to business success.

This is all the more so when taking a decision to work in a
collaborative manner to pursue tender opportunities.

**Must-Dos**
- ✓ Parties have clear common strategy
- ✓ Strengths and weaknesses identified
- ✓ Culture of trust paramount
- ✓ Tasks allocated based on competencies and track record
- ✓ Bid/No Bid every opportunity
- ✓ Lead by example
- ✓ Complete due diligence
- ✓ Early engagement with buyers
- ✓ Be competition law compliant

A joint bid will need careful, diligent and professional preparation. Consider the following.

**Strategy:** Does joint working 'fit' with the business strategies of the parties? If so, this rationale might be shared at the outset.

**Competency**: All the parties should openly disclose their respective strengths and weaknesses with reference to previous contracts as they consider the buyer's requirements.

**Passengers:** Bids should not have passengers or parties who are not fully competent to deliver in their identified area of expertise.

**Trust:** Trust and respect are the key attributes of a joint bidding relationship so it is critical that the parties recognise this from the get-go. If trust in particular is dented for whatever reason this should be a major warning signal for all concerned. The primary contractor has a special role to engender trust and to demonstrate this in his dealing with consortium members.

**Due diligence:** For any contract of significance to your business and in the role of primary contractor, it is essential that you conduct due diligence on potential partners. This can best be done by asking a shortlist of sub-contractors by way of a tender to submit the same level of detail about their financial and economic standing and their technical ability and resources. The level of detail should be proportionate to the scale of their involvement in fulfilling the contract. So, for example, where a sub-contractor would be responsible for 40 per cent of the delivery of the overall contract, then it would be essential to get bank references and to check their credit standing.

**Independent facilitator:** Sometimes parties are thrown together who have never worked with each before. Such a scenario would be usual where a non-Irish company decides to joint bid with a local partner(s) and where no prior commercial relationships existed. Careful consideration should be given to the appointment of an independent facilitator with tendering and sectoral experience to act as a chairperson for the collective bid effort.

## Advantages

- Sharing relevant skills, experience and expertise in complementary manner

- Accessing competencies that only a third party has at an affordable cost

- Shared development costs

- Risks associated with delivery shared

- New and innovative ideas emerge

- Dynamic network created

- Can pitch for larger contracts

- Ability to deliver the buyer's requirements

## The Practicalities of Business Collaboration

Partners of a bid consortium involved with complex and high-value contracts might wish to consider applying the standards set out in BS 11000 to the process of business collaboration.

This standard:

- Identifies how relationship management can help achieve business objectives.

- Evaluates the benefits of entering into single or multiple partnerships.

- Selects the right partner to complement your objectives.

- Builds a joint approach based on mutual advantage.

- Develops added value from the relationship.
- Measures and maintain benefits.
- Develops and executes an exit strategy.

# BS 11000 – The Eight-Step Approach

1. **Awareness**: Identify a clearly defined rationale that is consistent with overall business strategy.
2. **Knowledge**: Establish a platform of knowledge on which to develop a programme for building relationships.
3. **Internal Assessment**: Understand your own capabilities and shortcomings first.
4. **Partner selection**: Identify and select suitable partners.
5. **Working together**: Agree a formal foundation for working.
6. **Value creation**: Seek to maximise the value and new ideas resulting from the partnership.
7. **Staying together**: Include dispute resolution, continuous improvement and adherence to quality standards.
8. **Exit strategy**: Define the parameters for an end to the arrangement.

**Primary Contractor's Checklist**
- ✓ Readiness for joint working assessed
- ✓ Partner selection criteria approved
- ✓ Internal skills gap assessment done
- ✓ Create shortlists of potential partners
- ✓ Negotiate with shortlist
- ✓ Invite first choice to become sub-contractors
- ✓ Complete due diligence
- ✓ Complete Consortium Competition Test

---

TENDER TIP
If you can gain more business from being in a bid consortium, then set one up or collaborate with partners.

# Tender Competitions
# Works

## Introduction

This chapter covers the Construction Works Management Framework (CWMF), which is a structure that has been developed to deliver the Irish Government's objectives in relation to public sector construction procurement reform, as well as the current guidelines applying to works contracts in Northern Ireland.

The strategic objectives of the CWMF are to ensure:

- greater cost certainty at contract award stage;

- better value for money at all stages during project delivery, particularly at handover stage; and

- more efficient end-user delivery.

The CWMF consists of a suite of best-practice guidelines, standard contracts and generic template documents that form the following four pillars that support the framework.

- A suite of standard forms of construction contracts and associated model forms, dispute resolution rules, model invitations to tender, forms of tender and schedules.

- The standard conditions of engagement for consultants,

dispute resolution rules, model invitations to tender, forms of tender and schedules.

- Standard templates to record cost planning and control information; and for suitability assessment.

- Extensive guidance notes covering the various activities in a project delivery process.

Provided there is a comprehensive definition of the buyer's requirements in terms of output specifications, and adequate pre-tender detail design input (in the case of traditional contracts), the new public works contracts will enable the key objectives outlined above be achieved. The degree to which output specifications and the pre-tender detailed design input is developed is determined by the following guiding principles, which underpin the new contracts.

- To ensure as far as practicable that the accepted tender prices and the final outturn costs are the same; and

- To allocate risk so that there is optimal transfer of risk to the contractor.

- The achievement of optimal risk transfer is dependent on the public sector client (called the 'employer') providing complete and detailed information, as follows, in the tender documentation.

- For design-and-build projects, the employer must provide detailed output specifications.

- For traditional projects, the employer must provide comprehensive input designs and specifications.

In response to an invitation to tender, prospective consultants and contractors can assess the impact of the risks being transferred and build the costs of such risks into their tender price.

There is a substantial body of legislation that governs construction activities, in particular the Safety, Health and Welfare at Work (Construction) Regulations 2013 and the Building Control Regulations 1997-2014 as these place considerable responsibility not only on contractors but on all those involved in construction projects, including designers, supervisors and individual workers.

## CWMF Review

A December 2014 review of the CWMF has been undertaken by the Government Contracts Committee for Construction and the Report on the Performance of the Public Works Contract sets out recommendations for interim amendments to the contracts and a framework for a medium-term strategy to inform engagement between industry stakeholders.

The revised arrangements – as set out in DPER Circular 01/16 – are aimed at rebalancing risk currently transferred to contractors in recognition of the different economic environment to the one into which the contracts were introduced in 2007 and in particular the different challenges facing both government and the industry in delivering construction projects.

The main changes, as follows, have been implemented.

1.  The Pricing Document is now a Compensation Event to the extent defined in the revised Form of Tender and Schedule, associated with the Employer-designed forms PW-CF1, PW-CF3 and PW-CF5 only.

2.  A procedure for the contracting authority to directly obtain tenders from specialist works sub-contractors who are to be appointed by the contractor (reserved specialists) is introduced in the Employer-designed forms. This is in addition to the existing process of novation which continues to be available on forms PW-CF1-PW-CF5 inclusive

3.  The introduction of a Standing Conciliator under forms PW-CF1- PW-CF4 inclusive. This is mandatory for projects with a value in excess of €10 million and optional for projects between €5 million and €10 million.

4.  A new dispute-management escalation process has been introduced as this will provide an earlier dispute resolution process before conciliation.

Broader engagement on the procurement of public projects will continue with industry stakeholders. They will be invited to contribute to a medium-term strategy, which will encompass procurement and recent developments in the fields of technology and legislation governing the construction industry. Key areas such as performance evaluation, risk management and different contracting strategies will also be considered as part of the strategy with recommendations to be put to government.

## Contracts

A public-works contract consists of a number of interrelated documents. Some of these are entirely standard; some are largely standard, with details added that are specific to the particular project; and some are unique to the project.

There are nine forms of contract for public works, each of which is appropriate in different circumstance.

## TABLE 9.1 – FORMS OF WORKS CONTRACTS

| Code | Contract | Nature of Works | Contract Type |
|---|---|---|---|
| PW-CF1 | Public Works Contract for Building Works designed by the Employer | Building | Traditional |
| PW-CF2 | Public Works Contract for Building Works designed by the Contractor | Building | Design-and-Build |
| PW-CF3 | Public Works Contract for Civil Engineering Works designed by the Employer | Civil Engineering | Traditional |
| PW-CF4 | Public Works Contract for Civil Engineering Works designed by the Contractor | Civil Engineering | Design-and-Build |
| PW-CF5 | Public Works Contract for Minor Building and Civil Engineering Works designed by the Employer | Minor Works, Building and Civil Engineering | Traditional |
| PW-CF6 | Public Works Short Form of Contract | All types of work associated with building and civil engineering | Traditional |

| PW-CF7 | Public Works Investigation Contract | Investigation Work, Building and Civil Engineering above and below ground. | Traditional |
| PW-CF8 | Public Works Short Form of Investigation Contract | Investigation Work , Building and Civil Engineering above and below ground | Traditional |
| PW-CF9 | Public Works Framework Agreement | Any type of work associated with construction | Traditional (for drawdown under Framework Agreement) |

Source: CWMF (2015)

## Model Forms

There are seventeen model forms used under the CWMF. Model Form (MF 1.0) is a compendium of all of the model forms that are available and also includes guidance on how to fill in the forms and when they should be used.

## Table 9.2 – Model Forms Summary

| CODE | DESCRIPTION |
|------|-------------|
| MF 1.1 | **Bid Bond** <br> This is a model of the bid bond that may be used with a public works contract. A bid bond is effectively a contract of guarantee whereby the guarantor or surety (authorised to do guarantee business) undertakes to pay damages to a second party, in this case the employer, when the contractor does not honour his tender. In essence, the guarantor undertakes to be answerable for losses suffered by the employer if the contractor withdraws following a bid. |
| MF 1.2 | **Letter to Apparently Unsuccessful Tenderer** <br> This is a model of the letter sent by the employer to all tenderers other than the tenderer deemed to have submitted the most economically advantageous tender (MEAT). |

| MF 1.3 | **Letter of Intent** |
|---|---|
| | This is a model of the letter sent by employer to the tenderer deemed to have submitted the most economically advantageous tender (MEAT). It indicates that the employer intends awarding the contract to that tenderer, subject to the tenderer meeting listed conditions. |
| MF 1.4 | **Letter of Acceptance** |
| | This is a model of the letter sent by the employer to the successful tenderer (the consultant or contractor) to form the contract. |
| MF 1.5 | **Letter to Tenderers Notifying Award** |
| | This is a model of the letter sent by the employer to the unsuccessful tenderers after the contract has been awarded. |
| MF 1.6 | **Performance Bond** |
| | This is a model of the performance bond that may be used with a public works contract. A performance bond is effectively a contract of guarantee whereby the guarantor or surety (authorised to do guarantee business) undertakes to pay damages to a second party, in this case the employer, arising from a breach of contract, for losses sustained by the employer due to non-performance by the contractor. In essence, the guarantor undertakes to be answerable for losses (up to the limit of the bond) suffered by the employer if the contractor's obligations are not performed in accordance with the contract. |
| MF 1.7 | **Parent Company Guarantee** |
| | This is a model of the parent company guarantee that may be used with a public works contract. A parent company guarantee assures the employer recourse to the parent company's financial standing, technical capability and resources provided the parent company is prepared to underwrite the liabilities of its subsidiary in the competition. For example, such a guarantee should be required if the partners in a joint venture go forward as the contractor in a tender competition having relied on their parent company's financial standing, technical capability or resources to pass the assessment process. |
| MF 1.8 and MF 1.9 | **Novation and Guarantee Agreement / Novation Agreement** |
| | Novation is where the contractor takes over the role and responsibilities of the employer in relation to a contract that the employer has with another party. This arises where an employer enters into a contract with another party with the intention that at some time during that contract the main contractor will replace the employer through a novation arrangement. MF 1.8 is the model of the novation and guarantee agreement that may be used with a public works contract where the contract is being novated to a joint venture company. MF 1.9 is the model of the novation agreement that may be used in all other circumstances. |
| MF 1.10 | **Appointment of Project Supervisor** |
| | This is a model of the form to be used when the contractor is appointed as project supervisor for the construction stage (PSCS) or as project supervisor for the design process (PSDP) and PSCS. It is also used when a contractor's nominee is appointed as PSDP. |

| MF 1.11 | **Professional Indemnity Insurance Certificate** |
|---|---|
| | This is a model of the form used to certify that the contractor has professional indemnity insurance. Where it is requested, the contractor is responsible for maintaining professional indemnity insurance in relation to design negligence. It may be required on traditional contracts where there is a large amount of contractor or specialist design and it is always required on all contractor-designed projects. |
| MF 1.12 | **Collateral Warranty** |
| | This is the model of the form of collateral warranty used to create a contractual link between specialists and the employer. A collateral warranty is a form of deed that seeks to create a contractual link between the employer and specialists contracted to the main works contractor. This can be of value where, for example, the main works contractor becomes bankrupt, as the employer has step-in rights by virtue of the collateral warranty and the employer also has access to the specialists in relation to their design liability. |
| MF 1.13 | **Rates of Pay and Conditions of Employment Certificate** |
| | This is a model of the certificate used to certify that the contractor is compliant with the Industrial Relations Acts 1946 to 2004 and all other relevant legislative requirements. |
| MF 1.14 | **Bond – Unfixed Works Items** |
| | This is the model of the form of bond that the contractor must have in place as a condition of payment for certain unfixed or offsite works items. These are items that have not yet been incorporated into the works. |
| MF 1.15 | **Retention Bond** |
| | This is the model of the form of retention bond that the contractor must give the employer in return for payment that would otherwise be retained until the end of the defects period. |
| MF 1.16 | **Appointment of Conciliator** |
| | This is the model of the form appointing the conciliator who is engaged to assist in the resolution of any dispute between the employer and the contractor. |
| MF 1.17 | **Bond – Conciliator's Recommendation** |
| | If the conciliator recommends that the employer should make a payment to the contractor and the employer does not agree with that recommendation, the employer should issue a notice of dissatisfaction and make the payment subject to the receipt of a bond provided by the contractor for the same amount as the payment. This form is a model for such a bond. The purpose of the bond is to cover the eventuality that the final resolution of the dispute (by arbitration) might reverse the conciliator's recommendation. This provision can also be utilised by the contractor if the contractor has to make a payment to the employer on foot of a conciliators recommendation. |

Source: CWMF (2015)

## Standard Conditions of Engagement

The forms of contract used for consultancy services for work relating to a capital works project and their associated forms of tender and schedules are set out below.

## Table 9.3 – Standard Conditions of Engagement

| CODE | DESCRIPTION |
|------|-------------|
| COE 1 | Standard Conditions of Engagement for Consultancy Services (Technical) This is used for all such contracts with consultants (other than archaeology services) |
| FTS 9 | Form of Tender and Schedule, Consultancy Services (Technical) A schedule (in two parts) that records the details that is specific to the particular engagement together with the form of tender. |
| COE 2 | Standard Conditions of Engagement for Archaeology Services This is to be used for all contracts for archaeological services. |
| FTS 10 | Form of Tender and Schedule, Archaeology Services A schedule (in two parts) that records the details that is specific to the particular archaeology engagement together with the form of tender. |

Source: CWMF (2015)

## Suitability Questionnaires

The suitability assessment procedure involves inviting applicants to submit information (and their named specialists where so requested by the employer) in response to a customised standard questionnaire. The employer uses the information in the responses to determine which applicants (under a restricted procedure) or which tenderers (under an open procedure) meet the suitability standards and which do not. The standard approach to suitability assessment is intended to ensure only those service providers or works contractors that qualify against certain objective and transparent, non-discriminatory, proportionate and fair criteria progress to the next stage of the procurement procedure for publicly funded projects.

The CWMF includes a number of suitability assessment questionnaires that are used in different circumstances, as outlined in the following table.

## Table 9.4 - Suitability Questionnaires

| SUITABILITY ASSESSMENT FOR SERVICE PROVIDERS | |
|---|---|
| QC 1 | Questionnaire: Suitability Assessment for Service Provider: Restricted Procedure |
| QC 2 | Questionnaire: Suitability Assessment for Service Provider: Open Procedure |
| QC 3 | Questionnaire: Suitability Assessment for Service Provider: Independent PSDP |
| QC 4 | Questionnaire: Suitability Assessment for Service Provider: Independent PSCS |
| **SUITABILITY ASSESSMENT FOR WORKS CONTRACTORS** | |
| QW 1 | Questionnaire: Suitability Assessment for Works Contractor, Restricted Procedure |
| QW 2 | Questionnaire: Suitability Assessment for Works Contractor, Open Procedure |
| QW 3 | Questionnaire: Suitability Assessment for Works Specialist for Specialist Area of Work |

Source: CWMF (2015)

## Guidance Notes

The following guidance notes are intended for sponsoring agencies (buyers) embarking on capital works projects, as well as sponsoring authorities (such as government departments) and external consultants appointed in relation to the proposed capital works. It goes without saying that contractors/suppliers need to be fully familiar with these important documents.

## Table 9.5– CWMF Guidance Notes

| REF | SUBJECT |
|---|---|
| GN 1.0 | Introduction to the CWMF: This document presents an overview of the CWMF and its four pillars. |
| GN 1.1 | Project management: Gives an overview of the project-management structures that are required, the processes and procedures that need to be followed, and the contracts and templates to be used in the delivery process of a works project. The main areas covered include the following: <ul><li>The content of the Project Execution Plan, including a sample plan.</li><li>A description of the main project roles and responsibilities involved in the project process, including management, design teams and other technical expert roles</li></ul> |

| | |
|---|---|
| | • An overview of the main project processes and the stages that a project goes through after approval in principle, i.e. planning initial, planning developed, implementation and project review stages.<br>• A description of the risk and value management strategies that may be applied to public works projects. |
| 1.1.1 | Building Control (Amendment) Regulations 2014 – Procurement implications for contracting authorities |
| 1.2 | Project definition and the definitive project brief: This document explains the process that should be used to define precisely the output requirements of a project in the definitive project brief. The project definition is the first exercise undertaken in the planning initial stage. The project definition covers a range of activities that have as their end goal the comprehensive description of all project requirements. These activities are carried out in a systematic, rigorous and formal manner, and lead to definition of the ultimate outcomes in the form of the definitive project brief:<br>Step 1: Preliminary project brief Step 2: Preliminary output specification<br>Step 3: Feasibility study/preliminary report Step 4: Design brief<br>Step 5: Final output specification Step 6: Definitive project brief |
| 1.3 | Budget development: This guidance note explains the structure and format of budget estimates for public works projects. It also covers such issues as the development of a budget for the capital cost of a project and budget costs for other issues associated with the provision of a facility and allocating contingency amounts for inflation and other unquantifiable events. |
| 1.4 | Procurement and contract strategy for public works contracts: This document provides guidance on procurement strategy and on the selection of the most appropriate public works contract to use to deliver a particular project. |
| 1.5 | Public works contracts (more): This guidance note provides practical advice on the operation of the public works contracts. It deals with:<br>• Introducing the Contract: Includes details of the key elements of public works contracts, and the characteristics of the different types of contract.<br>• Managing the Pre-Contract Phase: Outlines the procurement and related issues that employers need to consider in preparing tender documents.<br>• Administering the Contract: Describes how contract-related issues are administered during the course of the construction works. |
| 1.6 | Procurement process for consultancy services (technical): This document provides guidance in relation to the appointment of technical consultants for all stages of the project delivery process, including those for the planning, design and supervision stages of construction projects. It covers:<br>• The procurement procedures available and which one to choose.<br>• The tender process, including how to prepare tender documents, invite submissions and evaluate responses.<br>• Details relating to the standard conditions.<br>• Calculating fee adjustments. |

| GN 1.6.1 | Suitability assessment of construction service providers – restricted procedure: This guidance note deals with suitability assessment under the restricted procedure for pre-qualification of service providers. Topics include: <br>• Key concepts of suitability assessment. <br>• The tasks and forms required to assess service providers. <br>• Determining which criteria to use and how to devise the marking scheme. <br>• How to complete each section of the suitability questionnaire. <br>• Evaluating health and safety competency. <br>• Evaluating the rest of the responses to the questionnaire. |
|---|---|
| GN 1.6.2 | Suitability assessment of construction service providers – open procedure: This note deals with suitability assessment under the open procedure to establish eligibility of service providers to have their tenders evaluated. Topics include: <br>• Key concepts of suitability assessment. <br>• The tasks and forms required to assess service providers. <br>• Determining which criteria to use and how to devise the marking scheme. <br>• How to complete each section of the suitability questionnaire. <br>• Evaluating health and safety competency. <br>• Evaluating the rest of the responses to the questionnaire. |
| GN 1.6.3 | Suitability assessment of construction service providers – minimum standards for suitability criteria |
| GN 1.7 | Standard conditions of engagement, guidance note and sample schedules: This document provides practical advice on how to complete the schedule to the Conditions of Engagement for Consultancy Services (Technical). |
| GN 2.1 | Design development process: This guidance note deals with all events that take place during the design process for both building and civil engineering projects. It deals with the role of design in both traditional (employer-designed) projects and in design-and-build (contractor-designed) projects. In the case of the latter, it highlights that much or all of the design is carried out by the contractor; as a result, the guidance note is less specific about design where the design risk is transferred to the contractor. The guidance note also covers the following topics: <br>• Concepts and considerations during the design process. <br>• Details of how design is to be managed and co-ordinated. <br>• Details of the design activities that take place during the planning initial stage. <br>• Details of the design activities that take place during the planning developed stage. |
| GN 2.2 | Planning and control of capital costs: This document sets out best practice on how to plan and control capital budgets for public works projects, both building and civil engineering, through all stages in the design process. It covers: <br>• The principles of cost planning and cost control of capital budgets. <br>• The practical application of those principles during design development. <br>• Whole-life cost appraisal. <br>• How to manage corrective action and change control. <br>• Risk management tasks in relation to planning and control of costs. |
| GN 2.3 | Procurement processes for works contractors: This guidance note provides advice on the procurement process used for works contractors for both building and civil engineering projects. It covers the following: <br>• Preparing tender documentation. <br>• Inviting tender submissions. <br>• Evaluating tender submissions and awarding the contract. |

| N 2.3.1 | Suitability assessment for works contractors – restricted procedure: This note deals with the restricted procedure to establish suitability of works contractors to be included on a tender list. Topics include:<br>• Key concepts of suitability assessment.<br>• The tasks and forms required to assess main contractors and their specialists.<br>• The tasks and forms required to assess main contractors without specialists.<br>• The tasks and forms required to assess Specialists that are to be proposed in a panel(s) in tender documents.<br>• Determining which criteria to use and how to devise the marking scheme.<br>• How to complete each section of the suitability questionnaire.<br>• Evaluating health and safety competence and compliance.<br>• Evaluating the rest of the responses to the questionnaire. |
|---|---|
| N 2.3.1.1 | Random selection guidance notes |
| N 2.3.1.2 | Suitability criteria for contractors, submission of evidence and procurement thresholds (open and restricted procedure) |
| N .3.2.2.1 | Reconciliation of appendices in GN 2.3.1.2 and QW1, QW2 and QW3 (open and restricted procedures) |
| N 2.3.2 | Suitability assessment for works contractors – open procedure: This document deals with the open procedure to establish the suitability of works contractors to determine which tenders are eligible to be evaluated. Topics include:<br>• Key concepts of suitability assessment.<br>• The tasks and forms required to assess main contractors and their specialists.<br>• Determining which criteria to use and how to devise the marking scheme.<br>• How to complete each section of the suitability questionnaire.<br>• Evaluating health and safety competency and compliance.<br>• Evaluating the rest of the responses to the questionnaire. |
| N 3.1 | Implementation process: This document provides guidance on the Implementation stage of building and civil engineering projects. It covers:<br>• The main roles and responsibilities of the employer and the employer's representative and the contractor.<br>• The management process for administering the public works contract during the construction stage of a project.<br>• How to manage risk during implementation.<br>• Dispute resolution.<br>• Dealing with price variation issues as they arise during the contract.<br>• The project completion and handover process. |
| N 4.1 | Project review: This guidance note gives an overview of the review that is carried out on a project after the facility has been completed and handed over. This is the final stage of the management of a capital works project and it covers a range of activities that have as their end goal the comprehensive collection of project data recorded in an appropriate format so that it can be of benefit on future projects. The following types of material that might be found in a review:<br>• Records of lessons learned from experience during the planning and implementation stages that would be of future benefit.<br>• Exceptional costs incurred during the delivery process that may be of value as reference material.<br>• Performance data in relation to the consultants, the contractor and specialists that could be of benefit on future projects. |
| L 1.0 | Glossary |

Source: CWMF (2015)

The following table summarises where the individual guidance notes fit into the delivery process of a works project. The project stages in the headers of the four columns relate to three of the stages in the Guidelines for the Appraisal and Management of Capital Expenditure Proposals in the Public Sector.

## Table 9.6 – Where the Guidance Notes 'Fit'

| | PROJECT STAGES | | | |
|---|---|---|---|---|
| | 1<br>Planning Initial | 2<br>Planning Developed | 3 | 4<br>Review |
| GN 1 Introduction to the Capital Works Management Framework | | ✓ | ✓ | ✓ |
| GN 1.1 Project Management | ✓ | ✓ | ✓ | ✓ |
| GN 1.2 Project Definition and Development of the Definitive Project Brief | ✓ | ✓ | | |
| GN 1.3 Budget Development | ✓ | ✓ | ✓ | |
| GN 1.4 Procurement and Contract Strategy for Public Works Contracts | ✓ | ✓ | | |
| GN 1.5 Public Works Contracts | ✓ | ✓ | ✓ | |
| GN 1.6 Procurement Process for Consultancy Services. | ✓ | ✓ | | |
| GN 1.6.1 Suitability Assessment of Construction Service Providers, Restricted Procedure | ✓ | ✓ | | |
| GN 1.6.2 Suitability Assessment of Construction Service Providers, Open Procedure | ✓ | ✓ | | |
| GN 1.7 Standard Conditions of Engagement, Guidance Note and Sample Schedule | ✓ | ✓ | ✓ | |
| GN 2.1 Design Development Process | | ✓ | | |
| GN 2.2 Planning and Control of Capital Costs | | ✓ | ✓ | ✓ |
| GN 2.3 Procurement Process for Works Contractors | | ✓ | | |
| GN 2.3.1 Suitability Assessment of Works Contractors, Restricted Procedure | | ✓ | | |

| | | ✓ | | |
|---|---|---|---|---|
| GN 2.3.2　　Suitability Assessment of Works Contractors, Open Procedure | | ✓ | | |
| GN 3.1  Implementation Process | | | ✓ | |
| GN 4.1  Project Review | | | | ✓ |
| GL 1.0　Glossary | | | | ✓ |

Source: CWMF (2015)

## Contact Details

Construction Procurement, Office of Government Procurement, **Email:** construction@per.gov.ie

## Northern Ireland

Hereunder is the current suite of guidance notes in place in relation to works contracts.

### 2016

■ Procurement Guidance Note 01/16 – Licence to Practice Initiative for Electrical Workers

### 2015

■ Procurement Guidance Note 03/15 – Building Information Modelling (BIM)

■ Procurement Guidance Note 01/15: Standardisation of NEC3 Engineering and Construction Contract Z Clauses

### 2014

■ Procurement Guidance Note 07/14: Sub-Economic Tendering in Construction Professional Services Contracts

■ Procurement Guidance Note 03/14 – Construction Works Procurement: Project Bank Accounts (Pilot)

■ Procurement Guidance Note 02/14: Implementation of Article 6 of the Energy Efficiency Directive

### 2013

■ Procurement Guidance Note 03/13 – Abnormally Low Tenders

■ Procurement Guidance Note 02/13 – Construction Procurement: Selection Process Relating to Experience Time Frame

**2012**

- Procurement Guidance Note 01/12 – Contract Management – Procedures and Principles

**2010**

- Procurement Guidance Note 06/10 – Procurement of Construction Works and Services

- Procurement Guidance Note 04/10:- Selection and Pre-Qualification of Contractors

In addition, guidance has been issued in relation to construction works and services contracts, including:

- The Policy Framework for Construction Procurement;

- Tender Arrangements for Construction Works Contracts Up to £4.3m;

- Procurement Processes for Construction Works and Services Contracts Over and Under Threshold; and

- Information about the Buildsafe NI Action Plan.

The CPD has also established contracts and agreements which can be used by a number of government departments, agencies and other non-departmental public bodies (NDPBs). These are defined as collaborative arrangements. The arrangements cover:

- Town planning

- Urban design

- Northern Ireland Fishery Harbour Authority

- Civil engineering works

- Maintenance and minor works

- Integrated consultant team

Contact Details
Construction Helpdesk: (028) 90816555

---

**TENDER TIP**

Procuring works contracts is often far more complicated than the procurement of goods and services so make sure you have a member on your team that has a full grasp of the prevailing guidelines and procedures.

---

# PART III
# Bid
# Strategy

# Developing a Winning Bid Strategy

## Introduction

The Irish public bodies and the Northern Ireland administration publish thousands of tenders for works, goods and services to a value of some €15.5 billion every year. This by any reckoning is a significant market. Those who bid and win are the peers of their business sector. They are considered the most competitive, economically advantageous and the most capable of delivering the publicsector buyers' requirements.

To succeed in winning a public sector tender is not easy and the challenge of preparing a bid response is often off-putting. As a consequence, many suppliers feel frustrated when they fail to pre-qualify and annoyed when they are beaten by the split of one percentage point.

The secret of success in tendering is to bid to win. Going through the motions of bidding is a waste of time and effort. Putting an incomplete bid response together is also a useless endeavour. If you have not identified and addressed the key issues and risks in the most comprehensive manner, your competitors will and they will then score more marks as a consequence. Even if you have a great response ready to go, if it is overpriced by reference to sector benchmarks, at best you will be placed second or further down the line.

The winning bid should be keenly priced to make an acceptable level of profit. All other elements of the bid response should address the qualification and award criteria in detail and at a level that leaves no ambiguity on the page. Your bid should always aim for an A+ grade and the bid team's ambitions must be set at this high level.

All this seems simple – it is if tendering is part of your business DNA. Yet so many suppliers do not get the basics and mindset right and, unless they do, they are doomed to continuous failure. This chapter discusses what you need to do win a tender competition, including the essential research that should be completed before the RFT is published. We also explain the key reasons why bids fail and how to conduct a Bid/No Bid assessment.

## The Basics

Any supplier – sole trader, owner manager, SME, multinational – should at a very minimum have the following in place.

1. **Commitment at CEO/Senior Management Level:** There is nothing worse for a bid manager than to be tasked with the preparation of bids in the knowledge that the senior management – the CEO in particular – is indifferent to this often thankless job. The reason for this level of indifference is often that senior management see bidding as a chore and not as critical a function as sales and marketing, for example. Senior management should listen to feedback from unsuccessful bids. It will soon emerge that a 'tick box' approach to responding to public tenders is not the best approach. Tendering for public sector work is no different than pitching for private client business, yet it is astonishing the number of companies that approach securing new public or private business opportunities from different perspectives. The companies that take tendering seriously at senior-management level; those that invest in their people's tendering skills; those that have a comprehensive

understanding of the process; those that have a clear 'price point', i.e. a price that generates an acceptable profit margin; and those that embed tendering as a core function within the sales and marketing team are more likely to win. If your company is not in this space, then do not be surprised if you continue to get rejection/unsuccessful tender letters. Leadership and motivation from the top is needed; absence of such direction and engagement results in a supplier's bid team wasting a lot of time and effort submitting poor-quality and ill-advised bid responses.

2. **Research capacity:** If a RFT that is critical to your business is published and this comes as a surprise to you, then you have clearly failed to research the buyer's requirements in advance. Situations regularly occur in which incumbents without any prior notice see their existing business re-tendered with just fourteen to twenty calendar days to respond. Every supplier who takes tendering seriously should have a pipeline of prospects under close review. This means that you should know when current contracts fall to be re-tendered and when new opportunities are likely to arise. There is an abundance of information to hand that can assist you in researching new opportunities, including:

   ■ **PINs:** These Prior Information Notices are published by buyers to give suppliers a heads-up about forthcoming opportunities, either a specific tender or a wider range of categories that will be tendered during the year. Once you see a PIN, it is an open invitation to make contact with the key decision-maker in the buyer organisation to find out more about the requirements.

   ■ **Market Sounding:** Sometimes, as part of a PIN, buyers publish expressions of interest to explore the potential interest from the market about a prospective tender opportunity. Again, suppliers are encouraged to engage with buyers to find out more about the opportunity.

- **Meet the Buyer:** InterTradeIreland organises national and sector Meet the Buyer events on a regular basis. These events give suppliers an opportunity to meet buyers on a 'face-to-face' basis, with a view of finding out more about the pipeline of opportunities.

- **Priority Buyers:** Using the 'Advanced Search' function on e-Tenders (see chapter 3), you can find out the contact names and details of all buyers in your region and sector. In addition, we include in chapter 3 the names and contact details of all the OGP portfolio managers. You need to decide which decision-makers are most relevant to your business and then keep in contact with them about their pipeline of work.

- **OGP Work Plan:** The OGP publishes its ongoing pipeline of frameworks and contracts on its website. In most cases, the OGP will conduct a market-sounding exercise in advance of the publication of national framework agreements. It is not only recommended but is essential that you engage in these surveys and keep in touch with the OGP decision-maker.

- **Source Material:** Practically all buyer organisations have published statements of strategy and annual reports which provide valuable insights into their operations. In addition, it is worth searching for the buyer on the Oireachtas website as quite often material not otherwise in the public domain can be found here. Local authorities are very transparent about publishing the minutes of meetings that approve procurements (and their budgets).

- **CANs:** It is a requirement for all above-EU threshold awards that all buyers publish a Contract Award Notice within forty-eight days of the date of contract-signing. The same time limit applies to below-EU threshold awards but the date starts from the tender submission date. The CANs not only provide the name of the winning buyer, but the number of bids and the expected value of the contract. Monitoring CANs in your category will help you build up a picture of the successful bidders and if you have been unsuccessful you can benchmark your company against the trend.

3. **Leverage Your Successes:** No matter how small, winning a public or private tender gives you essential credentials that you should exploit and market in your search for new opportunities. Public sector tender evaluators are sometimes risk-averse. They will almost inevitably go with tried and tested solutions. Therefore it makes sense to take advantage of every public sector win and all comparable bids for equivalent privatesector work.

   In presenting these reference sites to a buyer, spell out their relevance to the opportunity and if at all possible set out your estimate of the proposed cost savings, efficiency gains and/or productivity improvements you would expect to secure if the buyer used your solution. In other words, set out the business case to help the buyer to select your offering above all others.

   If you have a unique solution/process that is working on a pilot basis, try to encourage that buyer to apply it across the organisation and ask the buyer to give you a testimony. If you have persuaded one buyer to use your solution/process, are there others in that space? For example, if one local authority is implementing your solution/process, could other local or regional authorities be persuaded to do likewise?

4. **Knowledge of the Process:** We cover the procurement process elsewhere in the book. The point here is that at least one person within the organisation needs to be totally aware of the procurement equivalent of the rules of the road. So a nominated staff member in the company should be thoroughly familiar with the guidance that buyers have to implement; with the use of template contracts and forms; and ongoing but often nuanced policy changes. Knowing your rights and, as importantly, being aware of the constraints under which tender competitions can be run is essential know-how.

5. **Appoint a Bid Manager:** Depending on the size of the company, it is always helpful to have a person in-house who is responsible for co-ordinating your bid effort. A junior but well-motivated and trained resource is a good option. We will discuss the roles and responsibilities of the ideal bid manager later (chapter 13).

6. **Find an Author:** Many bids lose marks, lots of marks, because they are badly written. It is a sad fact that many professionals are lazy at writing and worse at basic grammar and sentence construction. Unless a bid reads and flows well, the evaluators will struggle to understand what is written and if there are ambiguities marks are inevitably lost. So an in-house author who loves writing is a critical asset to any bid team and should be availed of.

7. **Keep Your Bid Library Updated:** Your bid manager should maintain an electronic bid library so when new bid responses have to be produced all 'commodity-type' documents and materials can be cut and pasted into the bid response and edited to ensure they are fit for purpose. Having a comprehensive bid library also reduces the cost of bidding.

The following documents should be available in a bid library.
- All bid responses
- Feedback from unsuccessful bids
- Executive Summary template
- Corporate/Company information
- CVs (in similar short and long formats)
- Reference sites
- Current Tax Clearance Certificate
- Insurance certificates
- Audited accounts for past three years
- Health and Safety Statement
- Quality management documents
- Photo and graphics materials
- Project Implementation Plan template
- Bid Management Plan template

# The Tender Timeline

There are several distinct stages to a tender competition that are described in the diagram hereunder.

Figure 10.1 - The Tender Timeline

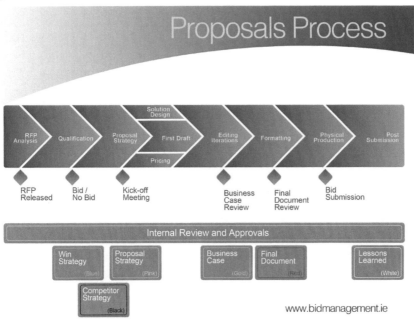

We will now take you through the key stages of a typical tender process and set out what you need to do so that informed decisions are taken in a timely manner throughout the process. In chapter 15, we cover the practicalities of writing, designing and producing the bid response document.

# Pre-Market Research and Preparation

Many suppliers make the mistake of believing that the most important consideration when preparing a bid response is how well it is written or how professional it looks. Perhaps the most important prerequisite, and the one that usually gets the least attention, is the essential work that needs to be done before a tender is published. To have a better chance of winning you need to have three tasks completed before the RFT is published.

Firstly, armed with feedback from successful and unsuccessful tender bids and one-to-one debriefings (see chapter 18), you and the key decision-makers within the company/consortium should have completed a constructive but critical assessment of your ability to score more marks. In every area where you scored less than your competitors in previous tender competitions, you must assess what went wrong, why and what needs to be done to rectify identified shortcomings. If, for example, you dropped marks because your quality standards were not certified, then get the appropriate ISO certification and ensure that someone in the business is skilled up in quality control processes. If your approach and methodology was considered to be inadequate, did you write enough about project implementation, for instance? Should one of your personnel be trained to PRINCE2 or a similar project management standard? If your price proposal was too high, what must be done to get you to a price point where you can still make a good profit margin (see chapter 12)?

This self-assessment, if conducted properly and in a systematic and comprehensive manner, will improve your score and move you much nearer to the status of preferred bidder. Secondly, even if you believe you can improve your score, you still need to keep a watchful eye on your competitors and in particular what they are offering to the buyers you have prioritised. You will get some high-level feedback from tender competitions where they have beaten you, as the buyer should have given you not only your marks but those of the preferred bidder and the relative strengths and weaknesses of your bid compared to the winning bidder.

This intelligence should allow you to make some assumptions about the key differentiators between you and your main competitors. You need to keep close to your competitors at trade shows, at speaking events (where there is always the temptation to reveal new products or innovations) and through your mutual membership of business or sector associations.

Also keep up to date with trade and business journals and monitor news about your sector for any suggestions of new product development or new business that your competitors have won. The company that wins more business knows the key decision-makers in their competitors' companies and the likely style and approach they will take to a new tender opportunity. Being able to benchmark what you provide, not just on price, against your competitors and also being able to adapt your proposed solutions by being informed based on what your competitors are likely to offer will score you more marks.

Thirdly, armed with a critical self-analysis of your capacity and capability to compete and having to hand a robust competitor benchmarking will only take you so far in the process. You need to target key buyers and to be ruthless in your pursuit. To do this, you might list all the priority buyers you believe will want your solution and identify those where there is already an incumbent. Monitor tender competitions to identify when buyers will re-tender as contracts come to an end. If one of your main competitors is an incumbent and you have a relationship with the buyer, try to probe where there might be weaknesses and exploit this in selling your alternative solution.

When buyers have not yet tendered but will do so at some stage in the future, build up a relationship with the key decision-makers. Make every effort to meet public buyers at conferences, trade shows and public events. Sponsor events if this will help you get the necessary access at the right level. You need to have a crystal-clear idea of when the buyer will tender and a full understanding of the buyer's technical requirements and desired solutions.

If appropriate, submit a paper to the buyer showing the savings that could result if your solution was procured using a particular technical specification. This advanced intelligence and positioning – coupled with your ongoing efforts to improve your scores – will make a significant difference once the RFT is published. A professional assessment of the buyer's materials (website, annual reports, newsletters, brochures, etc.) will tell you a lot about the prevailing culture. A practised eye will detect conservative, innovative or compliant materials. Is the dominant language that of a modern 'can-do' organisation or one with clear budgetary constraints? Does the buyer use defensive language, or take pride in its achievements? In your dealings with the buyer, is it your view that they are in touch with the marketplace and latest developments or is the organisation more focused on delivering its statutory remit? These insights, used appropriately, will help you shape the bid strategy that best addresses the buyer's unique perspectives and prevailing culture.

What do the majority of suppliers do?

They wait for the RFT to be published and read the RFT with little or no insight into the buyer's real requirements or 'Hot Buttons'. They respond without researching the buyer's rationale for publishing the tender. In effect, they end up interpreting the buyer's requirements rather than having a complete understanding of what is needed. As a consequence, their proposed solution can be wide off the mark. So even if a much cheaper solution is proposed, it is likely that their 'brochure' (generic) solution will not win. Hereunder is a recommended decision tree that adds a necessary level of discipline to the decision-making process.

Figure 4.2 – Bid Decision Tree

Source: APMP

In summary, pursue opportunities if they are consistent with your business strategy and if you or your bid consortium has the necessary resources to prepare a compelling and comprehensive tender bid response.

# Bid Response Preparation Process

| 1 | Senior managers review the RFT and highlight the key requirements |
|---|---|
| 2 | Conduct a Bid/No Bid analysis and make a decision in principle to bid or not |
| 3 | Appoint a bid manager with delegated authority to prepare the bid response |
| 4 | The bid manager prepares a bid management plan with all tasks assigned |
| 5 | The bid team (including sub-contractors, if applicable) conducts a detailed review of the RFT |
| 6 | Authors are appointed to draft all sections of bid response |
| 7 | Graphics and photography are sourced and generated |
| 8 | Decisions are taken on the design of the bid response document |
| 9 | Complete full business case on the opportunity and confirm decision to bid |
| 10 | Approve iterations of draft sections (including executive summary) |
| 11 | Submit for internal approval |
| 12 | Format, produce and submit the bid response document |
| 13 | Conduct a post-bid review and capture 'lessons learned' |

# When the RFT Is Published

A member of staff in everyone's business should be mandated to monitor the eTenders/eTendersNI daily push feeds for new opportunities in your category. Ideally, the company's nominated bid manager should assume this responsibility.

Your bid communications protocol should require that all relevant decision-makers, including the CEO/CFO where appropriate, get a copy of the RFT notice (and supporting documents), with the bid manager providing a short commentary about the opportunity.

A Bid/No Bid meeting should then be convened within forty-eight hours for every new opportunity, even if the new tender is not too different from previously bid opportunities (see below).

# Reading the RFT

For every RFT, you need to identify all the requirements, including explicit and implicit requirements.

To do this effectively, use two coloured highlighters. In your first review, highlight all the documents that need to be included in the bid response document. Then re-read the RFT with another coloured marker and highlight all the buyer's requirements. So for every 'should' or 'shall' mark the relevant section/sentence. If there are options – defined by 'may' and 'could' – assume these are implicit requirements and highlight them accordingly.

Ideally, two people, including the bid manager, should conduct this scanning exercise. On completion, notes should be compared and the data should then be captured using the following template. The list of evidentiary documents to be sourced should be included in the bid management plan (see chapter 13).

## Table 10.1 – Sample RFT Checklist Template

| RFT REQUIREMENTS | PAGE | EMPHASIS | COMMENT |
|---|---|---|---|
| Three reference sites to be supplied | 15 | Medium | Need to select the most relevant to this opportunity |
| Project Director to be appointed | 23 | High | Preferred internal resource tied up on other client work |
| Samples to be submitted | 24 | Low | Bespoke samples will need to be designed and produced |
| Annual accounts | 3 | High | Current accounts not held in the bid library |
| ISO Certificate | 9 | Medium | Expires in three months |
| Tax Clearance Certificate | 12 | High | TCC is out of date |

This preliminary analysis of the RFT should deliver six outcomes as follows:

1. The main problems and requirements that you must address will be defined.
2. The resources needed to deliver the contract will be identified.
3. The key elements of the bid response will be agreed.
4. The person responsible for each of the work packages required to fufil the contract will be appointed.
5. The buyer's special needs will be highlighted.
6. Potential risks will be pinpointed.

## Bid/No Bid Assessment

For every opportunity, even ones where the published RFT is well signposted, it is global best practice to carry out a structured Bid/No Bid evaluation at the earliest possible opportunity, i.e. within forty-eight hours of the RFT being published. The bid manager should convene this meeting; invite all the key people who will be contributing to the writing of the bid document, including sub-contractors; chair the session; and record the findings.

At its most basic – a model suited for low-value and less complicated tenders – the main reasons to bid and, more importantly, not to bid should be discussed at length with the key decision-makers within the company/consortium. Hereunder are some elements that typically arise in Bid/No Bid assessments. You will note that in some cases a reason to bid or not to bid can be more or less the same depending on one's judgement of the RFT's requirements.

## Table 10.2 – Bid/ No Bid Conclusions

| BID | NO BID |
|---|---|
| We will make a good profit | Profit margin too low |
| Four-year contract term | Technical specifications unclear |
| Will get a reference site for proof of concept | We do not have the financial capacity |
| Need the cash/contribution to fixed costs | No track record; we lack relevant experience |
| Have good relationship with the buyer | We need to find sub-contractors |

| | |
|---|---|
| Have extensive bid library in place | Total guesswork on price; not possible to calculate our margin |
| Cost of preparing bid will be low | Weighting on price too high at 80 per cent |
| We have a fundamental understanding of the client's requirements | Too many risks that cannot be mitigated without increasing costs |
| We have sub-contractors lined up | Award criteria are unclear |
| We know our price point/profit margin | Current sub-contractor has not performed |
| We have the necessary standards/ certificates | Buyer's budget not approved |
| The delivery team has won awards for similar projects | First time bidding into NI/UK market |
| We can leverage our success with other buyers and into export markets if we win | Potential disruptive effect on wider business if we win |
| We have excellent insights about the client's requirements | Currency exchange risk |
| We are the incumbent | Buyer has set very demanding requirements |
| Our bid has clear distinct features | Payment terms unclear |
| We can deliver measurable benefits and savings | Incumbent has advantage |
| We can introduce (free) value-added proposals | Competitors have won similar tenders |
| Our bid consortium has won similar tenders | We are only going through the motions as the CEO wants us to bid regardless |
| We have the capacity and capability to deliver the contract requirements | Reputation will be affected if we do not win |
| Complete 'fit' with our business strategy | No insights about client's requirements |
| We have excellent writing skills | We do not meet selection criteria on turnover/insurances |
| Our reference sites are relevant and convincing | We are too busy doing other work |
| Feedback from previous tenders suggests we can win this one | Delivery will be difficult as buyer responsible for too many critical issues |
| It is a framework tender | Submission deadline too tight |
| Predictable cash flow over long period | Cannot provide full geographical cover |
| It is not a fixed-price contract | TUPE complications |

Consider the following.

| BID TO WIN IF ... | DO NOT BID IF ... |
|---|---|
| • The opportunity 'fits' with your business strategy<br>• Buyer is aware of your credentials<br>• Price is not a key success factor<br>• You have (and communicate!) a comprehensive understanding of the client's requirements<br>• All potential risks have been assessed<br>• Gaps in skills and expertise are identified<br>• You can deliver VfM<br>• You have compelling USPs | • You are going through the motions<br>• Risks are too high<br>• You cannot fulfil all the requirements<br>• Cannot price the requirements<br>• No relevant experience<br>• Disruptive effective on other parts of the business<br>• Lack the scale or skills required<br>• No partners in place<br>• The timescale to bid is too short<br>• The incumbent is too strong |

For more complex and larger bids it would be helpful to put a score of 1 to 5 against all the Bid/No Bid factors and if the higher total score suggests a bid then go for it. These findings should inform your bid strategy.

Remember that no buyer expects you to respond to a RFT; whether you do or not is your choice. If you have a particularly close working relationship with a buyer who asks you to bid (for low-value contracts), always reply explaining why you have decided not to bid. For example, you could say 'We have other commitments at this time and do not have the necessary resources and/or capacity to deliver the contract. We are, of course, interested in being asked to bid for other opportunities at a later date.'

> To win ...
> Invest in market research
> Invest in relationships with priority buyers
> Invest in cross-border opportunities
> Invest in your team's tendering skills
> Invest in tender bids
> ... if not your scene, then bow out.

Our rule of thumb is that we never bid unless we believe we have a better than 50/50 chance of winning: '... *at least 60% of proposals submitted should never have been written.*' TenderScout (2015)

## The Hard Questions

The most critical issues that need to be assessed in detail in almost every situation – the hard questions – are as follows.

Profit: If you will not make a pre-determined profit at an acceptable level to the business then do not bid unless you have good strategic reasons for submitting a below-cost, at-cost or low-priced bid. If you cannot price the work packages of the bid you will not be able to assess your margin. Guesswork will be expensive, especially if a fixed-price contract is involved. In all situations, include the cost of bid preparation in your calculations.

Risks: The delivery of all contracts, regardless of size, involves some element of risk. These risks need to be fully stress-tested, mitigated where possible and managed. The more complex the project and the more partners that are involved, the higher the level of potential risk. A bid response that does not factor in the impact of inherent risks associated with project delivery and implementation, and the costs associated with remedying problems, will inevitably cost the supplier during contract delivery. Under-providing for a risk could wipe out your forecast profit margin.

Capability: Can you alone provide exactly what the buyer wants and to the required standards? Even if you can, can this be done without disrupting the business, to the detriment of other clients? If you have capacity issues, then find partners who can complement the resources that you have in-house.

Insights: Do you have a fully informed and well-researched assessment of the buyer's real needs and worry issues or 'hot buttons'? What are your competitors' likely solutions and general approach? Can this fundamental understanding of the buyer's requirements and competitor analysis be translated into the provision of a solution that will deliver tangible benefits and savings?

**Unique Selling Propositions:** What clear differentiators can be developed, with supporting evidence, to convince the buyer that you have true and genuine USPs that set you apart from your competitors.

**TUPE:** If you have to accept the incumbent supplier's staff, make sure you know what you are taking on. While the TUPE rules are complex (see chapter 19 for more details), it is a supplier's task to master these provisions and to quantify and cost the implications of any personnel that may be transferred with the contract. It is the buyer's responsibility to provide adequate information so as to enable a potential supplier to make an informed decision on whether to bid or not.

# Clarifications

One output of the Bid/No Bid session is a list of issues that need to be clarified. Buyers strongly recommend that suppliers always ask questions about the published RFT. Buyers are fully aware that suppliers cannot respond – or indeed decide in principle to respond – unless they have the full facts and a complete understanding of the brief.

Therefore it is essential, using eTenders/eTendersNI, to put questions to the buyer during the period provided for, which is typically a week before the submission date. Bear in mind that the replies will be copied to everyone who expresses an interest in the RFT. So do not reveal any element of your proposed bid strategy or unique bid offerings and ideas.

It is important to keep abreast of responses from the buyer to queries submitted by suppliers as these clarifications may affect the technical specification or the selection and award criteria. Often when many suppliers query the same aspects of the RFT, e.g. the precise meaning of a technical specification (in relation to quality control, for instance), the buyer is then alerted that the RFT is not sufficiently precise and may clarify and indeed change the specification. In some cases, buyers will even adjust award criteria if there is a body of evidence from many suppliers that some aspects of the RFT are unbalanced or if they fail to meet the key EU procurement principles.

Following the initial analysis of the RFT, you will have a better appreciation of the key issues where you have a complete, partial or no understanding. You need as a priority to bid on the basis of the full facts. Hereunder are some questions that you might wish to submit to the buyer to complete your knowledge gap.

## Table 10.3 – Clarification Questions

| How will the price be calculated? |
| Are there any sub-award criteria and if there are, could please publish them? |
| How much was spent on this service/supply in each of the last three years? |
| Has a budget for the contract been approved? |
| What certification/standards (or equivalent) are acceptable? |
| Is there an incumbent and if so could you please provide the supplier's name and those of all sub-contractors? |
| Has the incumbent had access to any documents or insights not published in the RFT? |
| Are the insurance requirements proportionate to the contract risk? |

Armed with answers, you should be able to decide to bid – or not, as may be the case – and to write in a more informed manner about a particular award sub-criterion.

If suppliers argue that tender specifications are unclear, the courts will look at whether the supplier used the opportunity to raise queries during the tender process.

## Storyboarding

Another way to identify clarifications and to define the outline of your bid strategy is to 'storyboard' the opportunity. This is a technique used by film directors to plan scenes they intend to shoot. In talking through various options and approaches, they narrow down their preferences and what actually works, thereby saving time and money.

In the context of a live bid, storyboarding involves the bid team taking each award criterion or sub-criterion, one by one, and talking through how you will respond. Using a flip chart, the lead author of the section's response then notes comments, ideas and proposals made by everyone in the room. Soon post-its, scribbles, notes and bullet points populate the flip chart, all designed to record ideas, proposals, issues, clarifications and, above all, the response that best 'fits' the award criteria.

Once the first award criteria is done, then another lead author takes the next section and so on. The power of storyboarding – best used for more complex bids – is the energy you will get as the entire team strives to get to grips with the RFT and to provide mutual help to scope out key messages and your USPs.

Once this exercise is complete, and informed by the Bid/No Bid decision, the lead authors can start writing with a clear agenda and an even clearer bid strategy in mind.

## The Business Case

For below-EU threshold tenders, it is usually quite sufficient to decide to bid or not based on the outcome of the Bid/No Bid assessment.

However, for larger opportunities, and certainly bids involving multiple partners, it would be advisable to conduct a full business review of the opportunity.

The outcome of the Bid/No Bid assessment will inform you, on balance, whether to bid or not. That decision will trigger several actions, as follows, that need to be carried out in parallel if at all possible.

1. All risks should be identified and proposed mitigation measures agreed and costed.
2. The finance team (or you and your accountant) start assembling the elements that will determine the cost proposal.
3. A series of clarification questions are submitted to the buyer to probe, e.g., apparent shortcomings in the RFT.
4. Your capacity and capability to deliver is assessed in fine detail with regard to current and projected commitments to other clients.

As soon as the outcomes of these exercises are to hand, the bid manager, with the company's senior management, should make a final decision on whether to bid or not. This assessment should be driven by the finance function, with the bid manager responsible for inputting non-financial data.

In practical terms, it often happens that a decision is made to bid based at the outset on the basis of the team's assessment of the RFT, but additional factors (risks, for instance) or facts (clarifications to the technical specifications) emerge as the RFT is considered in detail. If the balance of argument moves in the direction of a 'No Bid' then stop work on the bid response.

For large-scale opportunities, a full business case review should be completed no later than halfway through the timescale for submitting a bid, as set out in the RFT. Once you have gone through the rigour of conducting a business case, the acceptable pricing point will emerge. This will be a key consideration in all subsequent Bid/No Bid decisions.

## Lessons Learned

The final part of the bid response production process is the carrying out of a post-bid submission review with the full bid team. The bid manager should facilitate this review as soon as is feasible after the bid response is submitted. This will ensure that memories are fresh before the team moves on to other work.

You will need to find out what worked (for example, new VfM proposals); what did not (for example, sections that were submitted while still incomplete); and what should have worked better (for example, earlier engagement by the finance team). The bid manager should take careful notes of the lessons learned in preparing the bid response document as all constructive comments will help with the next bid and, importantly, with a possible presentation to the buyer, where any shortcomings will need to be covered off.

A post-bid review should also assess the quality and general responsiveness of the designated authors. To this end, pay particular attention to your sub-contractors. If a partner company fell short in providing usable and required inputs to defined standards, this might suggest a below average commitment to the bid consortium.

It is rare that a bid response document is prepared without a glitch or two. Being aware of what to look out for will make the writing and preparation of subsequent bids a bit less stressful.

> ### TENDER TIP
>
> Do not bid unless you believe you have a better than 50/50 chance of winning.

# The Elements of a
# Bid Strategy

## Introduction

This chapter will cover the key elements of a typical bid strategy. These include knowing the buyer's Hot Buttons; defining your solution and the most appropriate level of compliance; finding partners; determining your cost strategy; and setting out your unique selling propositions.

We also cover the situation facing incumbents and those seeking to displace them. While each bid is unique, all bid responses should address the core elements of a bid strategy as set out hereunder.

## Key Elements of the Bid Strategy

The following graphic captures the key elements of a typical bid strategy.

Once all available information, insights and competitor research is to hand, you will be in a position to begin developing your bid strategy.

While no two bids are the same, the following issues could be considered in most bids.

## Hot Buttons

What are the buyer's real needs, as distinct from stated problems?

Quite frequently, these 'Hot Buttons' are not explicitly stated. You should therefore read in between the lines of the RFT to assess what is left unsaid. These elements are almost always psychologically oriented and process-oriented.

Addressing these Hot Buttons is important in selling your goods and services because your acknowledgement and communication of these issues behind the rationale for the tender competition helps you build trust, empathy and chemistry with the buyer.

Using the example of the Irish Rugby Football Union's RFT for bid advisors (for the 2023 Rugby World Cup), one could capture the IRFU's Hot Buttons as follows.

## Table 11.1 - IRFU'S Hot Buttons

| HOT BUTTON | HOW ADDRESSED IN BID RESPONSE | BENEFITS TO IRFU |
|---|---|---|
| Prefer to work with known partner | Include current IRFU advisors in bid consortium | They will deal with preferred partners |
| Require solid evidence of comparable track record | Global leader in sports events tendering leads the bid | Reliance on an advisor with a proven relevant track record |
| Need to neutralise potential competitors | Instruct global communications company with significant experience | Insights and intelligence secured about other nations submitting bids |
| Secure wide stakeholder engagement | Extensive use of digital media techniques | Real-time influencing of disparate stakeholder groups |
| Robust project management in place throughout bid process | Appoint a full-time and widely experienced project director | An integrated and co-ordinated strategy is delivered |

Source: Bid Management Services (2016)

Suppliers who invest in pre-RFT research will be best positioned to not only identify a buyer's Hot Buttons but to integrate these insights into their bid strategy.

In summary, a Hot Button is a process-related desire or concern of a buyer that will have a significant effect on yours sales strategy; on project management; and on your general approach and proposed methodology.

## Defining Your Solutions

Before you start work on the definition of your solution, you will have completed: an assessment of what your competitors are likely to offer; a full review of the technical specifications; and an approximate quantification of the benefits of your solution.

A comprehensive understanding of the RFT requirements is fundamental to the definition of the solution (as may be clarified by way of responses to your questions). In addition, you will need to know the likely response of the buyer to whatever you propose.

There are three options.

You may opt to deliver a solution that is fully compliant with the RFT. In this scenario, you communicate that what you are proposing matches point by point all the specifications as set out in the RFT. Anything that falls short of full compliance will lose marks so submitting a fully compliant bid is the minimum expectation.

For many buyers this is all they want. From your pre-RFT research, you will have determined the prevailing culture towards risk and contract fulfilment. For example, if a buyer wants 100,000 units delivered every month then all you need to do is to persuade the evaluators that you have the capacity and capability to fulfil the contract.

Other buyers may set clear technical specifications, but in reality want innovation and value for money options. In this scenario – beyond compliance – suppliers will need to think through and cost additional features that may be deemed to be innovative.

If you are offering innovative and/or VfM solutions, make sure you convince the buyer that you can deliver. As the evaluators are generally risk-averse, it would be critical to provide evidence as to where the proposed solutions have worked in comparable situations. The best way to do this would be to provide a detailed financial benefit using benchmarking data. Thus if your proposed software for monitoring wellness has driven absenteeism rates down by 8 per cent for one public buyer, what is your best estimate of the savings for the current opportunity? In so doing, you will be able, with reference to your track record, to demonstrate quantified benefits, operational efficiencies and/or productivity gains.

The third option is to offer variations to what is in the RFT. Many suppliers do this because what they offer does not exactly match the RFT's technical specifications. This is a big mistake. Evaluators need to be able to compare like-for-like solutions so if you stray beyond the brief your bid may be deemed non-compliant. Most RFTs make it clear that variations to the RFT requirements are not acceptable.

On the other hand, some RFTs may expressly look for costed variations. If this is allowed, then respond accordingly. For example, the RFT may look for volume discounts or seek phased solutions.

In large, complex tenders, usually involving new technology, buyers will secure their solutions using the negotiated procedure. The suppliers shortlisted may submit quite different solutions to achieve similar outputs. By negotiating with these suppliers, buyers will narrow down their options and once a revised solution is agreed internally they will ask the suppliers shortlisted to submit their Best and Final Offer (BAFO). This iterative process of defining the most appropriate solution is actively encouraged under the Public Contracts Directive.

## Incumbents

The first obvious question is to find out if there is an incumbent, who it is and how have they performed. So use the opportunity to ask clarification questions.

If you are prioritising an opportunity where there is an incumbent (and well in advance of a RFT being published), you could ask the buyer organisation under the Freedom of Information Acts for specific data; there is no fee for a FOI request. If you make an FOI request after the RFT is published, it is highly likely you will not receive a reply before the tender submission deadline.

Some public servants have a low tolerance to FOI requests, so get one of your professional advisors to make the request, thereby protecting your identity.

Use wording along the following lines:

*Under the Freedom of Information Acts please provide me with all records, documents, reports, and emails between the department and company X, the current supplier of the service to outsource HR management. The information should cover the period 1 January 2014 to date and be provided in electronic format where possible.*

The incumbent will have to give permission for records to be released. Routine and non-confidential information cannot be protected so a FOI request may turn up progress reports, financial data, quality-control issues, patterns of delivery and the identify of the key decision-makers. This type of information, when put to good use, will certainly help you formulate an aggressive response to dislodge the incumbent.

The fact that the incumbent knows a FoI has been responded to will put them on high alert. If this trawl of FOI data throws up issues – for instance, project drift or the use of out-of-date software – then do not be shy of letting the buyer know about your alternative solutions.

Ahead of the publication date of the RFT, there are no legal restrictions on buyers talking to potential new suppliers. The procurement rules are very strict when it comes to the re-tendering of a contract performed by an incumbent; the buyer is required to provide the same information to all potential suppliers. If you are in doubt about whether this rule is being observed, then ask a clarification question.

In all situations, ask the buyer to supply information about the expenditure levels over the previous period as this will give you a good sense of the potential scale of the opportunity. But you need to do much more.

Incumbents typically enjoy a good working relationship with buyers. This can make them a bit complacent and in a re-bid they are often inclined not to challenge the buyer in any way. Incumbents will in many cases bid to preserve the status quo. They may be somewhat reluctant to drop their price as this will raise questions as to whether they have previously been overcharging. Incumbents are less inclined to be innovate.

You, on the other hand, armed with advanced intelligence, know the incumbent's weak points, the quality of service delivery and the risk appetite of the buyer. You can benchmark the benefits of your proposed solution against what the incumbent has been offering. You bid accordingly.

You could also target one of the current sub-contractors by offering them a better deal. Having a disgruntled incumbent sub-contractor on your bid team will give you precious insights. Under 30 per cent of incumbents win their re-bids.

This is a scary statistic for complacent incumbents and an encouraging statistics for suppliers who might otherwise be shy of an attempt to dislodge an incumbent.

## Competitors

It is critical well in advance of preparing a bid that you are monitoring the positioning, profitability and performance of your main competitors and their successes, or otherwise, in winning tenders.

You could use your contacts within companies to explore their modus operandi. Keeping an eye on your competitors at trade shows, conferences and network events will also help you build up a profile of their strengths and weaknesses.

Check out the LinkedIn profiles of competitors and their staff as employees often inadvertently give away what might appear to them to be trivial information, which in your hands helps you build a more comprehensive picture of their commercial approach.

You then need to benchmark your business against whom you believe to be the main rivals for the particular opportunity and in so doing a matrix along the following lines could be prepared based on the published award criteria.

## Table 11.2 – Benchmarking Competitors

| ISSUE | OUR COMPANY | B | C | D |
|---|---|---|---|---|
| Pricing | 85 | 95 | 100 | 95 |
| Experience | 90 | 80 | 85 | 85 |

| Delivery team | 75 | 80 | 80 | 90 |
|---|---|---|---|---|
| Proposed solution | 85 | 85 | 70 | 90 |

Source: Bid Management Services (2016)

This data can be gleaned from feedback on unsuccessful bids, from an assessment of Contract Award Notices and from pure market intelligence.

The key issue that emerges in this scenario is price as other competitors appear to offer lower prices. So can you re-configure your cost base to match your competitors and/or reduce your margin? As all four competitors have somewhat similar scores, what will differentiate your bid proposition? If there is a perception that your delivery team is just average, do you need to recruit or find a better mix within the team? While your proposed solution is clearly 'fit for purpose', how can it be adapted to score the highest mark?

Armed with such forensic insights, you are in a much better position to write a winning bid. Knowledge of one's competitors – and communicating your differentiators – can make the difference between winning and losing a bid. In summary, you should always ask the following two questions.

How can we counter competitors' strengths to exploit their weaknesses? How will these competitors counter our strengths, exploit our weaknesses or redefine the overriding requirement? Companies that do not conduct a competitor assessment win far fewer bids.

## Understanding the Client's Requirement

Assuming the buyer knows what he wants (and often this is not so evident), the RFT should set out the background and then the specific requirement(s). However, in many cases, the buyer stops short, sometimes well short, of setting out a precise list of expected deliverables and Key Performance Indicators (KPIs). If you cannot drill down to this level of detail, how can you decide how to best resource the contract, never mind price it?

Most public buyers of any significance have a website that usually contains their annual reports, statements of strategy, background documents (including research reports) and codes of practice. Local authorities are perhaps the most transparent as they publish full details of their budgets and supporting documents. An expert search of this information usually turns up additional insights. If nothing obvious emerges, then search the buyer on www.oireachtas.ie – the Oireachtas website – as Dáil debates are often a treasure trove of unpublished information. Quite often the reports of the Comptroller and Auditor General will provide an assessment of the buyer's expenditure and you may well find criticisms that would need to be addressed as part of your bid response strategy.

If this trawl fails and you are still puzzled as to what the buyer really wants, then ask a series of clarification questions until you get the answers you need. Misinterpreting a buyer's requirements will result in you losing marks as your solution will not be 'fit for purpose'. Take nothing for granted; you may think something is relevant, but it is the buyer who makes the call. Hence the criticality of always probing the RFT requirements to test them.

## Level of Compliance

For every opportunity, you would be well advised to prepare a detailed checklist of all compliance documents and to list these in your bid management plan (see chapter 13).

The majority of these documents should be in your bid library.

The following is a list of typical compliance documents.

### Compliance Documents

| | |
|---|---|
| • Current Tax Clearance Certificate | • Evidence of standards |
| • Audited accounts | • Organisation chart |
| • Bank reference | • CVs |
| • Insurance certificates | • Reference sites |
| • Quality certificates | |

In addition to requiring suppliers to source documents in order to provide evidence in relation to their economic and financial performance, the RFT will also set out a series of requirements that should be addressed by suppliers in their bid response. Use the same methodology above-mentioned; highlight all the requirements and then list these in a document that should be shared with your bid team. This is more than an academic exercise as failure to address a buyer's requirements will lose you marks.

For more complex tenders, you might wish to prepare a RFT compliance checklist as this will provide you and your team with a clear line of sight about the extent to which your documentation meets the buyer's requirements.

## Table 11.3 – RFT Compliance Checklist Template

| REQUIREMENT | SATISFIES | PARTLY SATISFIES | FAIL | COMMENT |
|---|---|---|---|---|
| Adequate financial capacity | | ✓ | | Tax Clearance Certificate expires in three months |
| ISO Quality Certificate | ✓ | | | To include in section 3.4 |
| CVs | | ✓ | | Sub-contractors have yet to provide CVs |
| Reference sites | | | ✓ | Need to leverage experience of proposed sub-contractor |
| Health and Safety Statement | ✓ | | | To include in section 4.1 |

Source: Bid Management Services (2016)

The bid manager should keep this checklist under close review, especially as the deadline for the bid submission looms. The checklist could also be part of the bid management plan.

# Deciding on Partner(s)

This important consideration was covered in chapter 8 on bid consortia.

# Defining Your Cost Strategy

This issue is covered in the next chapter.

# Your Unique Selling Proposition(s)

When you have completed your initial assessment of the RFT and your competitors and analysed the buyer's requirements in detail, then you should start determining your Unique Selling Propositions (USP), which will show the buyer how you stand out from the competition.

In determining your USP, remember that many companies lose tenders because they focus mainly on what they can provide and fail to set out what precise benefits the buyer will gain if their solution is used. Being able to deliver monetised benefits may be your USP.

One of the outcomes of storyboarding the opportunity is that your key differentiators will be identified.

> **Your USPs**
> Industry leader
> Best benchmarked solution
> Award-winner
> Personnel with above-average sector experience
> ICT adapter
> ISO certification
> Have Teaming Agreements with bid partners
> Proven track record as an innovator
> Capacity to deliver nationwide
> Offer volume and other discounts
> Robust risk management completed
> Testimonials

Once you identify a shortlist of USPs, your particular differentiators should be woven throughout the bid response document.

Bear in mind that USPs can and do vary from bid to bid and do not assume that the buyer knows your USPs.

# Risk Assessment

While a formal Risk Register may not be necessary, e.g. in relation to commodity-type supply contracts or low-value services, it is a foolish supplier that does not consider the risks involved in the delivery of a contract.

An outline Risk Register should be prepared for any project of scale and complexity along with a risk management plan. Some risks may have already been flagged or alluded to in the RFT. While the detailed work will be done after contract award, it is prudent – if not essential – that you have thought through the key risks before you allocate resources and price the bid. Risks almost inevitably increase the more partners that are involved in project delivery.

Chapter 19 deals with risk management as a key element of contract fulfilment. As many buyers are not familiar with risk management techniques, the majority of RFTs do not refer to risk, nor do they allocate marks for risk management. Perhaps because some buyers believe all risks are negative and expensive to sort out, a 'sweep-under-the-carpet' approach is used.

Do not be shy about flagging potential risks and proposed mitigation measures in your bid response; this could be one way for you to differentiate your offer. Thus in the section in the bid response on approach and methodology include material about your approach to risk and your risk-management strategy. Highlight the importance of robust risk management for the buyer.

## How Risky is the Proposed Contract – Key Questions

| |
| --- |
| Do you fully understand every element of the technical specification? |
| Have you allocated the most appropriate level of resources to each work package? |
| Is every element of project delivery in the budget? |
| Do you need to include a contingency reserve? |
| Do you have the financial capacity to deliver given the payment terms? |
| Will the delivery of the contract have a disproportionate negative impact on other client work? |
| Is there a risk of reputational damage should problems arise? |

Risk permeates most aspects of project delivery, so beware and be prepared.

## Quality Control and Quality Assurance

Practically every RFT demands a response in relation to quality control (and sometimes quality assurance), yet it is astonishing how so few suppliers actually have certifiable processes in place.

It is essential that you not only have the relevant ISO certificate/BS standard for your sector – and include a scanned version of the current document in the bid response – but also that you communicate your approach to quality from start to finish, preferably with reference to similar projects. Appoint a named person with responsibility for quality control.

If you have testimony from clients attesting to the quality of your service delivery, then include this in the bid response.

---

### TENDER TIP

Never start writing a bid response until the overall bid strategy is agreed.

---

**12**

# Pricing Strategies

## Introduction

The golden rule is to price to win. It is not possible to provide absolute advice on pricing strategies as markets for goods, supplies and works are quite different and the dynamics will change depending on national economy factors and the size of the contracts tendered. Furthermore, a small supplier will have quite a different perspective to a large multinational where activity-based costing techniques are well developed.

Also suppliers' approach to pricing is quite often based on their business strategy and supporting sales strategy. For example, if a company is determined to grow, it may well decide to price the bid to buy market share. On the other hand, suppliers may decide to offer deep discounts in order to secure a placement of an innovative product or solution with a key buyer.

This does not mean you need to have the lowest price, but what it does involve is a commercial assessment of your price compared to that of your competitors and confidence you will out-score them in the non-pricing part of the award criteria. This chapter starts with the determination of your pricing point, i.e. the price at which you will make an acceptable profit. It also covers value for money propositions and how bid prices are determined by buyers and calculated as part of the published award criteria and the strategies that suppliers should weigh up before they submit their costed proposals. Other issues dealt with include abnormally low tenders; discounts; whole life-cycle costs; e-Auctions; and allocating the correct level of resources to fulfil the RFT's requirements.

## Pricing Point

A critical starting point is knowing your 'pricing point'. For the purpose of illustration, it is assumed you have lost five consecutive bids and you got your marks on price as well as the marks of the winning suppliers. This will tell you in no uncertain manner how far you are off the price required to win.

You have two choices, both quite reasonable: you reduce your costs or you decide not to bid. This assumes you submitted a cost proposal that fully reflected the actual cost of project delivery (including the cost of preparing the bid), to which you added a margin. It would also be reasonable to assume that you have a pre-determined profit margin below which the board/shareholders will not approve proposals.

On the other hand, you might be new to this area of work and have to start from first principles in terms of submitting a price proposal. Whichever way you approach the pricing of a RFT, you must always price to win. Essentially, you need to be fully aware of the balance inherent in being capable of delivering a solution and delivering that solution at a profit.

You also need to know the buyer's budget or to have a good appreciation of its approximate size. If the RFT is for a re-bid you should ask the buyer (using the clarification questions facility) for the amount spent over the previous three years in as great a level of detail as can be provided. Local authority buyers provide transparent details about their budgets (see chapter 3) and this can be a good source. For all framework agreements, the OGP, based on market soundings and category-spend analysis, will usually publish an indicative four-year budget.

If you are the incumbent, there is nearly an automatic assumption that you will reduce your costs in a re-bid situation. To do this, it would be important to conduct an assessment of actual costs against budget to get a clear indication of your ongoing profit margin. Armed with this intelligence, you will be in a much better position to develop a budget for the re-bid.

The most successful suppliers will know to a fine level of detail the prices that their competitors charge. You can get this type of information from trade shows, feedback from CANs and as an unsuccessful bidder, and insights about competitors from their former employees. Your pricing strategy needs to be based on an assessment of this pricing intelligence.

However, bear in mind that at all times you do not have to have the lowest price; just a low price relative to the competition that can be compensated by you scoring the maximum marks in the non-pricing categories.

In determining your pricing proposal, be sure to:
1. Capture all costs fully reflecting the Risk Register.
2. Add a small contingency reserve.
3. Address full lifetime costs (if the RFT so requires).
4. Add a profit margin.

It is also possible to set a lower margin for certain work packages, e.g. those with long duration and/or high expected volumes.

**How Price is Determined**

The most frequently used formula is that the lowest price secures the maximum available mark. The following formula illustrates how this works in practice: where 250 out of an overall total of 1,000 award criteria marks are available and a supplier bids at a price (€1,300) much higher than the lowest bid (€1,000).

Cost = Lowest Total Fixed Fee  X  Number of marks
        TFF under evaluation     available (250)

Cost = €1,000 X 250 = 192.3
      €1,300

In this working example, the higher priced bidder loses 58.3 marks because their bid was 30 per cent more expensive than the low price bid.

# Value for Money

What does Value for Money (VfM) actually mean?

To some ill-informed buyers, it means the lowest price for the poorest quality. VfM is essentially the provision by suppliers of monetised benefits, be they in the form of savings, productivity improvements or efficiency gains.

In Northern Ireland, the following definition of VfM was approved (March 2011) as it relates to procurement: 'The most advantageous combination of cost, quality and sustainability to meet customer requirements'. In this context, cost means consideration of the whole life cycle; quality means meeting a specification which is fit for purpose and sufficient to meet the customer's requirements; and sustainability means the economic, social and environmental benefits considered in the business case on the procurement opportunity.

Given what many suppliers have delivered in the past few years, with poor outcomes and below-standard solutions based on the lowest possible cost, there has been a rethink about VfM among the more strategic buyers. Buyers are becoming responsive to a 'value' selling proposition as distinct from a pure price bid.

VfM should involve you as a supplier providing added value in a qualitative and quantitative sense. So if you are responding to a RFT that requires an element of VfM, consider some of the following issues.

## Table 12.1 – VfM Options

| |
|---|
| • Demonstrate the lessons learned from previous contracts and how they can be applied to the new contract. |
| • Demonstrate how people's individual experience can save the buyer money (and quantify the impact). |
| • Set-up a specific web portal to support project management. |
| • Provide free consultation on campaigns. |
| • Show discounts separately. |
| • Provide free advice on new forms of media/message transfer (digital marketing), potentially through internal briefings, etc., to help buyers do their jobs better. |

- Innovative ideas regarding the form the message may take (e.g. branded memory sticks) or how it could be delivered, e.g. providing all field staff –including those of the buyer – with iPads.
- Partner with a suitable firm to offer conference or event services.
- Offer live sharing of documents (specific web portal for this contract) to allow buyers to view progress and updates.
- Have an emergency procedure for tight deadlines to include innovative use of technology.
- Partner with appropriate organisations to ensure appropriate conversion to Braille, languages, etc.
- Excellent sub-contractor selection and management processes.

Source: Bid Management Services (2016)

If you claim to offer a VfM solution, then explain precisely what you mean with reference to a costed worked example. A credible explanation is needed at all times rather than a generic mention of VfM and its alleged benefits. So quantify the proposed saving, productivity gain or efficiency gain; identify any qualitative elements; estimate the pay-back period; clarify the timing of the cost reductions; and state how the buyer will be able to measure your VfM propositions.

> Price is what you charge for your product/service.
> Value is your customer's perception of what that product/service is worth to them.

If at all possible, compare your VfM proposals with those of your main competitors. If you have prepared your value proposition carefully it should write itself.

In summary, the typical elements of a value proposition include:

- Measurable results that can be identified.

- Clear benefits that are clearly articulated.

- Improved productivity or efficiency gains.

## Savings, Benefits and Efficiencies

The OGP, CPD and other buyers have a remit to achieve savings through the use of smart procurement. They expect and should get as a result your best solution that will result in measurable savings. So, in addition to setting out your proposed solution, go a step further and try to quantify the savings, however small they might be.

For example, if you are supplying cleaning products, you could point out that their strength and characteristics are such that they will last six months longer than cheaper and sub-standard alternatives. Using your products could, for instance, result in the buyer not having to re-supply every six months if inferior (weaker strength) products are procured. Use of your cleaning product therefore could generate a €X,000 saving over the duration of the contract.

Describing how the additional features of your software solution on the monitoring of employee absence, provided at no additional cost, will reduce the absentee rate from X per cent to Y per cent and as a consequence the pay-back period for the proposed solution is just Z months.

Another example could involve a call centre where additional investment in technology above the RFT's requirement would generate measurable cost savings in terms of staff deployment, the quality of the service and the turnaround time of calls answered. These cases seek to demonstrate that it is often quite easy to put a number on the savings that your solution can generate. So instead of selling the solution, sell its bottom-line impact also.

Not all solutions are amenable to the identification of precise savings. If this is the case, you might then communicate how your solution will drive project delivery efficiencies. For example, giving all team members (including those of the buyer) access to secure tablets when on-site is a productive use of basic technology. So too is the setting-up of a secure project extranet where both buyer and supplier can share 24/7 access to all reports, documents, drawings and other project-specific information.

Improving productivity is also an important issue for buyers. So consider, where appropriate, adding features that could improve performance both within the project and indeed outside its parameters. For instance, if you are a training provider, consider including a 'train the trainer' module so that over time the buyer's own staff will be qualified to deliver training without having to procure it on an ongoing basis.

Another idea could be to provide the buyer with unique legacy know-how that you develop as part of the project delivery or indeed based on your wider experience. What these examples seek to demonstrate is that the supplier who wins goes the extra mile and seeks to convince the buyer that their solution is not only fit for purpose but will result in measurable savings, process efficiencies and productivity improvements.

## Table 12.2 - Kinds of Benefits

| TYPE | EXAMPLE |
|------|---------|
| Baseline benefit | Robust Project Implementation Plan |
| Individual buyer benefit | High rate of return on the investment |
| Hot Button benefits | The fast-tracking of contract delivery |
| Theme benefits | Legacy and know how transfer |

Source: Bid Management Services (2016)

Would you give more marks to the supplier who submits a bid that goes beyond pure compliance?

## Presenting Data

Buyers are more impressed with pricing proposals that are fully justified. So if you submit a fixed-fee proposal, also provide a detailed budget breakdown justifying the components of that proposal. In that way, the buyer can see how you intend to allocate your resources.

Communicate that this fully justified budget is presented in order to demonstrate that you have addressed the buyer's requirements and have allocated identified personnel to fulfil each and every requirement.

Err on the side of providing more data rather than less. For instance, in the area of professional advisory services, where several distinct work packages are involved, break down the cost of delivery by package and by person. Thus for work package 1, ten days will be provided by a senior director at a daily rate of €1,000; twenty days will be provided by a manager at a daily rate of €750; and thirty days by a project executive at a daily rate of €500.

You will score more marks by proving a fully justified budget as part of your overall approach and methodology.

If the RFT format allows it, explain your cost assumptions, e.g. if they are based on the costs of delivering a similar project for another buyer. This will give the evaluators confidence that the prices are not only realistic but an accurate reflection of past performance. Set out your assumptions about costs and in so doing make sure they reflect any guidance provided in the RFT, e.g. some buyers will ask suppliers to quote prices exclusive of VAT, travel and all administrative costs associated with project delivery.

An exception is unit cost pricing, for which buyers typically ask for prices of individual items in the form of a schedule.

If at all possible, use graphics to communicate your pricing proposals. Tables, pie charts or bar charts should be used as frequently as is deemed necessary in all your bid responses.

Always include your pricing proposal, in summary form, in the Executive Summary, along the following lines: 'We will deliver this project for a fixed fee (VAT exclusive) of €123,000.'

Finally, bear in mind that in submitting pricing data, all this material is identified as being commercially sensitive and cannot therefore be released under the FOI Acts.

## The Buyer's Perspective

Before addressing your pricing strategy and options, it is important to have a complete understanding of where the buyer is coming from. Unless you can appreciate the buyer's strategy in relation to costs, how can you possibly determine yours?

All RFTs must include price as part of the award criteria. Therefore one of the first tasks that a buyer has to consider is the weighting to be attached to price; the elements comprising the price and how price is to be calculated.

## CASE STUDY
### The Port of Cork RFT for Legal Services

Here is an extract from the Port of Cork's tender for legal services. Note the guidance provided. What the buyer required was a sample of costs at determined levels of experience. The number of hours included in the table was a sample only and did not represent any expectation on the part of the Port of Cork of the number of hours it required for the completion of any services.

This formula allowed suppliers to set hourly rates but they did not have to submit a fixed-fee proposal for particular services. It appears that the buyer was not in a position to issue precise instructions when the RFT was published; hence indicative fee rates were sought.

Each tenderer's fee proposal shall comprise of its tendered hourly rates for the following categories of staff:

* Partner
* Solicitor 5+ years post-qualification experience
* Solicitor 2–5 years PQE
* Solicitor <2 years PQE

The proposed hourly rates shall be listed in a table of hourly rates in the format below.

1. The tendered hourly rates shall include all fees, costs and expenses associated with the carrying out of the services e.g. costs of all labour including secretarial services, travel and subsistence, accommodation, postage, telephone costs, photocopying, other overheads, insurances and liaison with all relevant individuals and authorities.

2. All tendered hourly rates included in a tenderer's fee proposal shall be exclusive of VAT.

3. The tendered hourly rates shall be fixed and free from fluctuations in cost and no price variation shall be allowed for any rise or fall in the cost of labour and, materials. The tendered hourly rates of the successful tenderer are fixed for the duration of the contract. Tenderers shall complete the table set out below in accordance with the above instructions:

| Category of Staff | Hourly Rate (€) | Number of hours | Total fee (€) |
|---|---|---|---|
| Partner | | 500 | |
| Solicitor 5+ years post-qualification experience | | 750 | |
| Solicitor 2–5 years post-qualification experience | | 700 | |
| Total | | | |

# Allocating the Correct Level of Resources

One sure way to reduce your costs is to re-balance the mix of resources allocated against key personnel. As long as the project is delivered to the technical specifications and to a defined quality standard, it is your choice how best to allocate resources to deliver the RFT requirements.

Also beware that some buyers look for a blended rate, i.e. a fee that reflects the inputs from personnel with different levels of experience. As the following examples seek to demonstrate, tweaking the hours or the charge-out rate of the senior (most expensive) staff can get you to a position where you could end up with a lower average cost of delivery. In this case, €2 is the equivalent of a 4 per cent reduction in costs.

## Table 12.3 – Schedule of Hours

|  | LIKELY HOURS | RATE USED | REVENUE |
|---|---|---|---|
| Partner Rate | 400 | €60 | €24,000 |
| Senior Manager Rate | 1000 | €60 | €60,000 |
| Associate Rate | 1600 | €35 | €56,000 |
| Totals | 3000 |  | €140,000 |
| Average Rate |  | €52 |  |

|  | LIKELY HOURS | RATE USED | REVENUE |
|---|---|---|---|
| Partner Rate | 400 | €50 | €20,000 |
| Manager Rate | 1000 | €60 | €60,000 |
| Associate Rate | 1600 | €40 | €64,000 |
| Totals | 3000 |  | **€144,000** |
| Average Rate |  | €50 |  |

Source: Bid Management Services (2016)

# E-Auctions

An electronic auction (e-Auction) is conducted between buyers and suppliers. Suppliers bid 'live' on a secure portal for the goods to be supplied. Note that e-Auctions are rarely held for service contracts.

This option is used when the commodity to be purchased is of sufficiently high value to generate savings with regard to the additional costs involved in running an e-Auction, which can be as high as €10,000. Buyers like e-Auctions as the process drives prices down.

In all situations, the buyer will clarify the rules of the e-Auction in advance. It is also a requirement that the use of an e-Auction is clearly mentioned in the RFT. Therefore it is not possible for a buyer to receive bid submissions and then decide that an e-Auction is to be held.

The most common format is a reverse auction. Here suppliers bid against each other by submitting lower bids with the lowest unique bid winning. The OGP has published underline about e-Auctions, so if you are invited to participate in this type of operation make sure are fully familiar with these rules. For example, buyers are advised on how to convert non-price criteria into a price equivalent for the purposes of shortlisting suppliers who will be invited to bid against each other on price only.

Buyers can use the services of an e-Auction service provider if they do not have the software needed to operate the auction.

Suppliers who are bidding for goods and services that will be determined by an e-Auction will require expert financial advice to work out the price to be submitted in the bid response but more particularly during the live e-Auction itself.

You will need to have a clear bottom line below which you are not prepared to bid.

## Framework Mini-Competitions

Getting shortlisted on a framework is a great achievement. However, you need to be well prepared for the first mini-competition that will involve you submitting a price for a defined drawdown.

The first thing you need to find out is your ranking among the shortlisted companies. Do not assume that the higher you are on the list, the lower your price was as non-price criteria could have secured you a high ranking.nThe rule of most framework mini-competitions is that the price you submit is the maximum permissible when subsequent price proposals are made. Thus when a mini-competition is opened if you had quoted, say, €100 per hour, you are not allowed to bid any higher for the duration (four years) of the framework.

Buyers' experience with mini-competitions is that this form of procurement drives down costs, often quite dramatically, over a relatively short period. No surprise then that buyers opt for frameworks as significant savings in expenditure are guaranteed. What happens is that the shortlisted companies proceed to out-bid each other on price to secure the available work and inevitably the lowest price bid gets the contract as in most cases the weighting attached to non-price criteria are lower than the marks available for the price.

Suppliers need therefore to be mindful that in dropping their price to secure contract work they do not fall below an acceptable net profit margin.

## Use of Directories in Frameworks

Some of the new OGP template framework agreement RFTs include a new arrangement for contracts valued at less than €5,000/€12,000. Taking the framework for accounting and audit services as an example, the OGP will develop what is called a 'framework members' directory'. The data will be based on what the shortlisted suppliers provided in their bid response (as recorded in the tender response document) for each lot and sub-lot.

Suppliers are required to submit a fixed blended rate for a qualified accountant, auditor or consultant. The rate tendered is fixed for all grades of key personnel for all engagements for direct drawdown contacts valued at less than €5,000.When a framework buyer has a requirement for services estimated to be below this amount, a

Notification to Activate Services Form will be sent to some (or all) of the framework members in relation to the required service.

Interestingly, a much higher minimum threshold of €12,000 is being used for the OGP framework for business advisors to the health and healthcare sectors. Suppliers should therefore pay particular attention to how they calculate their blended rate for these low-value direct drawdown contracts.

# Bid Budget

For above-EU threshold proposals, it is recommended that a bid budget be prepared, which could include the following elements:
1. The cost of pre-bid research
2. The cost of personnel time on bid preparation
3. Third-party costs (for example, the costs of external advisors)
4. Development costs (web design for instance)
5. Production costs (printing, folders, graphics, photography)
6. Other costs (travel, etc.)

With experience, companies will know what is affordable and acceptable when a new opportunity arises. It is important that the costs included in the bid budget be taken into account when calculating the opportunity's profit margin. While all bids are different, a rule of thumb is that bid costs should not exceed 5 per cent of the total costs of the contract. This implies you have a system that is capable of recording staff time and third-party costs.

Including the costs of the time of personnel involved in preparing a bid is important as the opportunity cost of skilled personnel should be reflected. Senior management needs to be satisfied that it makes more sense, for example, to have a marketing director working on a live opportunity as distinct from spending his/her time chasing other new business.

# Discounts

You may not be able to offer a discount as many pricing schedules do not allow for this. However, be prepared to offer a discount as part of your pricing strategy.

An informed buyer will always ask for (and will be attracted to) discount proposals; for instance, if a pre-determined volume of spending is exceeded within a set period.

The attraction of a discount from the supplier's perspective is that there is a recognition that for greater effort and/or drawdown, the buyer will continue to spend and use the supplier.

It is therefore not at all unusual for buyers to request percentage reductions in prices over, for example, a contract with an overall value of €100,000 or where 100,000 units are to be supplied.

The buyer's discount implies a reduction in your profit margin unless you manage to restructure the cost components for the delivery of that service. For example, having delivered 100,000 units, you have achieved some economies of scale that may allow you to bulk purchase or manufacture at a lower price per unit.

## CASE STUDY
### OGP RFT for Legal Services

In this RFT, 50 marks out of 1,000 were set aside for discounts based on total volume spend awarded via the framework that was tendered.

The following data had to be completed (and a sample response is included).

| A<br>Volume Spend | B<br>Weighting | C<br>% Discount Offered | D<br>Weighted Discount (CXB) |
|---|---|---|---|
| ≥€100,000 | 3.0 | 5% | 15 |
| ≥€200,000 | 3.0 | 5% | 15 |
| ≥€300,000 | 3.0 | 10% | 30 |
| ≥€400,000 | 3.0 | 10% | 30 |
| ≥€500,000 | 6.0 | 20% | 120 |
| | | Total Weighted Discount | 210 |

The buyer evaluated the Total Weighted Discount (TWD) by reference to the highest TWD offered, with the tenderer offering the highest TWD achieving 100 per cent of the maximum score available with all other TWDs being scored relative to this TWD based on the following formula:

Volume Discount = $\dfrac{\text{TWD under evaluation}}{\text{ScoreHighest TWD}}$ X Number of marks available (50)

In this scenario, the TWD of 210 (the highest) is compared to a TDW of 180.

Score = $\dfrac{180}{210}$ X 50 = 42.86

Thus, by not discounting as deeply as the lowest-priced supplier, this supplier dropped 7.14 marks or 7.14 per cent of the total available marks.

# Abnormally Low Tender Prices

Buyers are required to seek explanations from suppliers about abnormally low-priced/ costed tenders before taking action to reject a tender. In particular, buyers are allowed to disregard tender responses with abnormally low prices because they are in breach of international environmental, social or labour law provisions. Buyers may therefore ask suppliers for details about the economics of a manufacturing process, the services provided or the construction method, or the technical solutions chosen.

Having received these clarifications, buyers should then complete a risk assessment based on the information provided. If the buyer concludes that the performance of the contract would be jeopardised, the tender may be rejected.

A tender which might be regarded as abnormally low may not be rejected without investigation and consideration of the relevant elements that gave rise to a particularly low bid. Such elements might include an innovative technical solution or exceptionally favourable conditions available to the supplier. The supplier should be given the opportunity to explain the cost basis of the tender.

As regards works contracts, the NI Department of Finance and Personnel guidance (June 2013) recommends that abnormally low tenders should be identified on the basis of the adjusted average; where the highest tendered price is ignored. Where a tender received is more than 15 per cent below the adjusted average and outside a proximity margin, it should be considered as an abnormally low tender and the supplier should be so advised. The guidance includes helpful worked examples.

The CWMF also recommends that buyers should seek comprehensive additional written details where there is a suspicion that the tendered lump sum may be abnormally low. For example, a buyer used the following formula in a recent RFT for construction service providers:

> *The contracting authority will base the (price) score for the tendered hours on the basis of the average for all the valid tenders received. On carrying out this assessment the scores will be allocated accordingly. If the tendered sum for the services is less than 20% of the average of all those received then the contracting authority may elect to determine this tender is an abnormally low tender and remove it from the rest of the process.*

## Pricing Schedule

Ensure that any pricing schedules provided in the RFT are completed in the format provided. Failure to do so could result in your bid being deemed non-compliant.

Price should always be evaluated exclusive of VAT.

This rule is especially important in relation to works contracts. One Irish buyer has awarded contracts to construction professional firms not registered in Ireland who quoted on a VAT exclusive basis, while Irish suppliers who were required to include VAT in their price proposal were deemed to be too expensive. The net loss to the Exchequer in terms of revenue lost was ignored by the buyer 'as they had a budget to meet'.

Where price is the sole criterion, the contract should be awarded to the lowest priced bid complying with the specified requirements.

# Variations

Unless expressly permitted to do so in the RFT, do not qualify your price/cost proposal. Adding variations to a bid could disqualify the tender response. If unsure about the buyer's intentions then ask a clarification question.

# Life-Cycle Costs

For some tenders it may be necessary to calculate prices on the basis of LCC. Chapter 6 deals with this complex issue.

---

### TENDER TIP

Only bid if you are satisfied with the projected net profit margin and contract payment terms. Never bid if you cannot price the RFT requirements.

---

# 13

# Bid Management

## Introduction

Bid management consists of:

1. Bid planning
2. Bid co-ordination
3. Overseeing bid writing and editing
4. Ensuring high quality and on-time delivery

For every opportunity, the bid manager should prepare a bespoke Bid Management Plan as a 'roadmap' to guide the bid team through all phases of the bid process. The roles and responsibilities of a bid manager, the person with such a position within a business or the designated person who is tasked with preparing the bid response, are also explained. In this chapter we cover the practicalities of bringing basic project-management techniques to bear to help you and your business work through the logical steps (yes, they are logical!) from the time a tender is published to its submission.

## The Bid Team

For small value bids, the sole trader/owner-manager will take charge of the entire bid response document production process.

As the size and scale of the opportunity increases, it is advisable to put a formal structure in place.

For example, a bid manager should be appointed to oversee the process. The key attributes of this person is an ability to project-manage the bid response process; to motivate the bid team; to provide leadership; and to write and review content.

| THE IDEAL BID MANAGER |
| --- |
| Is a leader and motivator |
| Has project-management skills |
| Has delegated authority to get the job done |
| Is a key member of the bid team |
| Delivers the bid management plan |
| Fosters high levels of quality control |
| Is expert in procurement rules |
| Understands the business |

A bid director should be the most senior decision-maker within the company who has full delegated authority to take the decision to bid based on the business case (that should be prepared in all cases involving bids in excess of the EU threshold). The bid director may in some situations become the nominated account director for the opportunity.

Functional managers/directors should be appointed at the outset to take charge of the agreed work packages. As appropriate, sub-contractors should be required to nominate relevant personnel with the requisite skills and experience. External advisors may also need to be appointed. For example, a copywriter, graphic and design consultants, a photographer, and bid and tender advisors.

Companies should also provide the necessary facilities (including, where appropriate, a secure room and encoded communications in some situations) and administrative support to the bid team.

## Bid Planning

Every bid response situation requires careful planning and thought. Here are some of the key tasks that all bid managers should carry out on behalf of their bid teams.

- Bid/No-Bid decision facilitation
- Analysis of bid specification
- Research into competitive situation and market factors
- Sourcing bid partners
- Chairing and mediating bid meetings
- Submitting clarification questions to the buyer
- Bid resource analysis and availability

In addition, the bid manager should also be responsible for the following:

- Bid team structure
- Bid planning meeting
- Decisions on structure, format and content of bid
- Assignment of writing and editing responsibilities
- Quality planning
- Document management and version control procedure
- Communications planning

## Bid Management Plan

Hereunder is a template Bid Management Plan which should be drawn up immediately after the company decides to bid. Most tender opportunities could use this basic template. Obviously, the Bid Management Plan would be significantly more detailed for a large-scale tender involving multiple parties.

What this Bid Management Plan shows clearly are:

1. The key elements of the RFT
2. The award criteria to be addressed
3. The documentary evidence that needs to be sourced
4. Communication protocols

5. Who does what
6. The required writing style
7. When tasks have to be completed
8. The document production schedule

## Bid Management Plan

| | |
|---|---|
| ...ority ...e | |
| ... Advisor | |
| ...der ...cription | |
| ...ation | |
| ...ing date ...ender ...mission | |
| ...very ...ructions | |
| ...tact person ...queries and ...ing date | |
| .../Fail ...eria | |

| Award criteria | | | |
|---|---|---|---|
| | | | |
| | | | |
| | | | |
| | | | |
| | | | |
| | | | |
| Appendices to be signed as part of the RFT response | | | |
| Allocation of responsibility | | | |

| | |
|---|---|
| T Structure | |
| oposed netable | |
| ocuments quired | |

| | |
|---|---|
| | |
| Questions for buyer | |
| Win theme | . |

The bid manager should keep this plan up to date and under close review as the bid team work in a collaborative manner to contribute to the preparation of content for the bid response. This Bid Management Plan should be saved in the bid library as a template.

## Bid Co-Ordination

A further set of tasks for the bid manager centres around the job of making sure that all aspects of the bid are fully and seamlessly coordinated.

For example, a bid manager should deal with the following:

- Draft schedule of outputs and deliverables
- Finalisation of structure and content of bid
- Definition of bid budget and method overview
- Cost and pricing assumptions for contract
- Contacts and meetings
- Design and layout of bid

- Co-ordination of bid content
- Presentation preparation and rehearsal
- Post-bid review

## Bid Production

The final part of bid management involves producing the bid response document. We cover this and associated tasks in chapter 17.

> TENDER TIP
>
> Use project management techniques to plan, co-ordinate and manage the bid process.

## 14

# How Bids Are Assessed and Scored – The Maths Exam

## Introduction

Tenders are very often won and lost on the split of one percentage point. So if your writing falls short on the most minor of details, you could end up in second place. Knowing how bids are marked (scored) will help you stay on high alert as you and your team respond to the published award criteria.Beware that buyers are trained to eliminate non-compliant bids and to deduct marks when evaluating award criteria where suppliers respond inadequately or incompletely to the guidance provided in the RFT.

It is hugely frustrating to find out that your bid document was never assessed because you forget to include a document that was requested in the RFT under the selection criteria. It is even more annoying to find out that you came second, losing out by less than one percentage point. In this chapter, we will take you through the steps the buyers should go through from the time your bid response is submitted to the end of the process, i.e. when a preferred bidder and unsuccessful suppliers are notified about the outcome of the tender competition.

# Evaluation of Tenders

The OGP's guidance to buyers is that the evaluation of tenders should be carried out by a suitably competent team and that the evaluation and award process must be demonstrably objective and transparent and based solely on the published selection and award criteria. This is best achieved by the use of a scoring system based on all the relevant weighted criteria, indicating a comparative assessment of tenders under each criterion.

For larger projects (€25,000 and above), it should be the normal practice to have the evaluation of tenders carried out by a team with the requisite competency. This may include a competent person from outside the public body directly involved with placing the contract or a person from another comparable buyer organisation. Transparency and objectivity are best demonstrated by the use of a scoring system or marking sheet based on the relevant weighted criteria, including price, indicating a comparative assessment of tenders under each criterion. The evaluation process for tenders above EU thresholds will be similar in many respects to that for below-threshold competitions.

## Evaluation Criteria

All tender competitions require buyers to publish pre-qualification or selection criteria and separate award criteria. It is not allowed to set selection criteria and then include these same selection criteria in the award criteria.Buyers may choose to award contracts on the basis of the lowest priced tender or the BQPR, specifying, in addition to price, various other criteria, including running costs, servicing costs, level of after-sales service, technical assistance.

When a contract is being awarded on the BQPR basis, the notice or the tender documents must state all of the criteria being applied in the award process, giving the relative weightings for each criteria. If it is not technically possible to indicate criteria weightings in advance, they must be listed in descending order of importance. New or amended criteria, including sub-criteria, cannot be introduced after bids are submitted or in the course of the evaluation process. If this happens (as it does in reality) there may be legal grounds to have the competition challenged under the EU Remedies Directive.

Does your bid response document communicate that you have the right solution; that you profoundly understand the buyer's requirements; and that all obvious risks have been comprehensively addressed? In summary, the evaluation and award process must be demonstrably objective and transparent and based solely on the published criteria.

## Selection Criteria

The OGP's RFT templates for supplies and services list the typical selection criteria that appear in most bids.

They are:

- A Form of Tender/Tenderer's Statement to be completed by the primary contractor, i.e. the company that will have the relationship with the buyer. This form is standard and should be signed and, if necessary, witnessed and, in rare situations, a company seal may need to be affixed.

- A self-declaration about the financial and economic standing of the primary contractor, including required insurances, valid Tax Clearance Certificate, audited accounts (and a banker's reference in some situations). A sample self-declaration form (ESPD) can be found in chapter 17. Note that usually a preferred bidder will have to provide the required evidence within ten or so working days from the date it is notified of preferred bidder status.

- Evidence of technical and professional ability, e.g. the provision of short or long CVs; evidence of academic achievements; specific details about required competencies; and the role and responsibility of each team member.

- In addition, some RFTs ask for details about relevant experience, with reference to case histories. In addition to details about contact names, the value of the work done, the duration of the contract and the resources assigned, it is important to state (adding a box if necessary) why you picked the selected reference sites and their relevance to the fulfilment of the RFT's requirements.

■ A declaration about the personal circumstances of the tenderer that deals with situations such as bankruptcy, professional misconduct, fraud and non-payment of taxes. In some cases, this declaration may need to be witnessed by a public notary; see the example in chapter 17. This declaration is an EU requirement, yet the OGP and other buyers require it be completed for all below-EU value threshold tenders.

In most cases, e.g. if the requested documents are not provided or are not completed correctly, a PASS/FAIL rule applies. If you fail even one of ten selection criteria, the evaluation team will not consider the bid response any further and your bid will be deemed non-compliant. You will be informed about this when the results of the competition are communicated to all tenderers at the end of the procurement process.

# Types of Evaluators

There are several types of evaluators, so it is important to know their particular focus and write to address their respective agendas. Keep in mind that while evaluators will be competent in their subject area, they may not be experts on your specific technology and/or proven solution, so explain terms, concepts and processes in an comprehensive, understandable manner.

You should also be aware that buyers often outsource the evaluation of some aspects of complex tender bids to third-party evaluators, including public sector officials from comparable organisations.

# Table 14.1 – Types of Evaluators

| Buyer Type | Focus | Key Question |
|---|---|---|
| Procurement | Compliance with procurement process | Have all the minimum standards been met? |
| Financial | Cost    Budget<br>Savings    Return on investment<br>Payment terms | What measurable benefits will be delivered? |

| User | Adequacy of the proposed approach<br>Effects on the organisation<br>Have all elements of RFT been fully addressed | How will the proposed solution affect my job? |
|---|---|---|
| Technical | Innovation<br>Practical application<br>Standards used | Will the proposed solution work? |
| Decision-maker | Strategic fit<br>VfM | Does this proposal meet our business and political objectives? |

Source: Bid Management Services (2016)

Thus for most bid responses of any significance, you should assume that a team of expert evaluators will cast a critical eye on your bid proposal. Also do not assume that only an internal team from the buyer's organisation will mark your bid document.

## Scoring a RFT Response

Once the evaluators have been given adequate time to review all the bid responses received against the published award criteria, and corresponding guidance, they will be brought together as a group to assess each bid one by one, taking into account their initial assessment. The evaluation team will be provided with a scoring sheet by the buyer's procurement officer or advisor and will use this during the evaluation.

The following scoring methodology is a good indicator of the range of marks available and the justification for the award of marks.

## Table 14.2 - Sample Scoring Methodology

| WEIGHTING RANGE | JUSTIFICATION |
|---|---|
| 90%–100% | Excellent response with very few or no weaknesses that fully meets or exceeds requirements and provides comprehensive, detailed and convincing assurance that the tenderer will deliver to an excellent method. |
| 80%–89% | A very good response that demonstrates real understanding of the requirements and assurance that the tenderer will deliver to a good or high standard. |

| 60%–79% | A satisfactory response which demonstrates a reasonable understanding of requirements and gives reasonable assurance of delivery to an adequate standard but does not provide sufficiently convincing assurance to award a higher mark. |
|---|---|
| 40%–59% | A response which you have reservations about and which have not been addressed by clarification. Lacks full credibility and convincing detail and you feel that there is a significant risk that the response will not be successful. |
| 20%–39% | A response which you have serious reservations about. This may be because, for example, insufficient detail is provided (even post-clarification) and you feel that the response has fundamental flaws or is seriously inadequate or seriously lacks credibility with a high risk of non-delivery. |
| 0–19% | Response completely fails to address the criterion under consideration. |

Source: OGP (2015) RFT for accounting, audit and financial services

The team will usually comprise the key decision-maker (the technical lead), a senior manager, someone responsible for project delivery, the procurement officer and perhaps a subject matter expert from another comparable buyer.

It is best practice for the evaluators to have a general discussion at the outset about the overall standard of the responses received and the key issues that have emerged; for example, about the requirements in relation to quality control. If they have questions of interpretation about the guidance provided to suppliers, these issues should be discussed before each bid response document is individually assessed.

Then the chairperson of the evaluation panel will ask each member for his/her comments on the relative strengths and weaknesses of the bid response under each section and, as appropriate, each sub-section. A discussion then follows as differences of opinion are commonplace. The outcome, by consensus, is the allocation of a mark which is noted by the secretary to the meeting.

Once this is done, the evaluators move to the next section of the bid and allocate an agreed mark and so forth until all the non-price award criteria have been assessed.

The panel then moves onto the second and subsequent bid responses and repeats the same process. When all the bids have been assessed, it is best practice for the evaluation panel to reflect on the provisional marks allocated to make sure, having looked at all responses, that some bids were not marked too harshly, or too generously, comparatively.

Once that is done the marks are then confirmed and recorded. Normally the panel will not have to hand the marks allocated for price as these will be calculated separately by the procurement officer/advisor and this mark ('A' in the case described below) is then added to the non-price marks once the evaluation of all bids is completed.

In the following scenario the following marks were available.

Price (A)        40% Methodology (B)        40%
Innovation (C)        10% Quality (D)        10%

# Table 14.3 – Sample Scoring Sheet

| TENDERER | A | B | C | D | TOTAL | RANKING |
|---|---|---|---|---|---|---|
| A | 36.74 | 25 | 6 | 6 | 73.74 | 8 |
| B | 22.33 | 35 | 8.5 | 8.5 | 74.33 | 7 |
| C | 33.54 | 37 | 9 | 8.5 | 88.04 | 2 |
| D | 40 | 33 | 8 | 8.5 | 89.5 | 1 |
| E | 29.85 | 33 | 8.5 | 8.5 | 79.85 | 4 |
| F | 25.98 | 37 | 8 | 8 | 78.98 | 5 |
| G | 32.63 | 37 | 8 | 8 | 85.63 | 3 |
| H | 25.41 | 35 | 9 | 8.5 | 77.91 | 6 |

Source: Bid Management Services (2016)

As can be seen, the supplier that won had the lowest price by quite a margin. In many situations, suppliers with second- or third-lowest prices win as they excel in some or all of the non-price categories.

The panel will then sign off the final marks as the basis for their recommendation to the buyer's decision-maker. For many tenders, a decision is taken at board level or by the senior management team.

This is a simplistic demonstration as to how scoring is carried out. In more complex bids, buyers will allocate marks out of 10,000 and in so doing will introduce many sub-award criteria.

Under no circumstances can a buyer evaluate a bid using a formula other than the published award criteria, nor can the buyer introduce sub-criteria during the evaluation process that have not been published.

Once the evaluation has been successfully completed and the buyer's decision confirmed, the procurement officer/advisor will then write to the preferred bidder and to the unsuccessful suppliers.

## Scoring – Mini-Competitions

A quite different approach is taken to the scoring of responses under a framework agreement mini-competition. In the vast majority of cases, the buyer will ask the shortlist of suppliers on a panel for a price for the services or goods to be procured. The lowest price will secure the contract. Suppliers are not allowed to bid more than the maximum price set in their original RFT response that secured them a place on the panel.

Experience to date suggests that the widespread use of mini-competitions forces suppliers to drop their prices if they want to win the contract. In exceptional circumstances, buyers may introduce award criteria other than those set in the framework and allocate marks under these award criteria. Do not expect to get feedback after mini-competitions.

Buyers are required to abide by the EU procurement principles in managing mini-competitions.

## Northern Ireland

Tenders are evaluated in a very similar manner in Northern Ireland. Most contracts above the £30,000 ('low-value') threshold are awarded on the basis of MEAT. For supplies and services below the EU threshold, the lowest acceptable price that meets the specification and any mandatory requirements/minimum standards is used. Exceptionally, the best combination of price and quality will determine the award criteria. Buyers are particularly mindful of tender prices for works contracts that might be considered to be abnormally low and guidance has been published to address this issue.

As only electronic submissions are made, most tender responses are assessed by individual evaluators in the first instance. The results are fed into eTendersNI and a meeting of the evaluators is then convened to reach a consensus result under all award criteria. All unsuccessful suppliers get written confirmation of their marks and the comments of the evaluation panel.

## Conclusions

Every word, sentence and paragraph that you write attracts marks or loses marks. Failing to address all the RFT requirements with a sufficient level of detail is the primary reason why marks are lost. So err on the side of providing a more complete and concise description when writing. The next chapter deals with writing styles and, more importantly, writing to win.

> ### TENDER TIP
>
> Your bid should always aim for an A+ mark and the bid team's ambitions must be set at this high level.

# PART IV
# Writing and Producing a Compelling Bid Response

# 15

# Writing and Writing Styles

## Introduction

This chapter is all about writing to win. Writing a successful tender could have a profound impact on your business. Winning several tenders could be transformational. The companies who have invested in writing compelling bids are testimony to what is possible with, let it be said, a relatively small effort compared to securing new business opportunities by other means. Many plcs, professional firms and companies with major ICT brands have fantastic ratings; they are top of the stock market and the media talks about them all the time. But can they write award-winning bids? This is the acid test in tendering.

Many companies have totally compelling business solutions but often fail to communicate the key benefits and customer value when it comes to writing a tender bid. Their emphasis can often be on the solution itself rather than on writing the solution in a way that best captures the target client's interest and imagination. In this chapter, we will address a task that the majority of business people feel awkward about: writing. Not just writing for casual communication but writing in a compelling and positive manner.

Companies spend millions on brand, product development and

intellectual property but take it for granted that they have the in-house skills to write 'word perfect'. The stark reality is that unless you invest in your writers, you will struggle to win bids.

This is especially the case with public sector tenders as all bids are evaluated based on the written word. In contrast, in the private sector a slick PowerPoint presentation may on its own be sufficient to win a contract.

Remember the maxim, 'A hard write is an easy read'.

> 'Do but take care to express yourself in a plain, easy Manner, in well-chosen, significant and decent Terms, and to give a harmonious and pleasing Turn to your Periods: study to explain your Thoughts, and set them in the truest Light, labouring as much as possible, not to leave them dark nor intricate, but clear and intelligible —'
> Cervantes, Preface to *Don Quixote*

# Web of Persuasion

Before you start writing you should have a good sense of the buyer's 'Hot Buttons' (see chapter 10 above); a full understanding of the award criteria; and a good estimation of how your proposed solution compares to that of your competitors. Translating this awareness can best be done by highlighting essential messages throughout the bid response document. The narrative (your story) must be informed, compelling and uniform in terms of look and content.

Your themes should spin a web of persuasion throughout the bid response. The key messages usually relate to:

**Solution:** Given the problems/opportunities set out in the RFT, what is needed?

**Method:** Given that need, how should the solution be delivered?

**Suitability:** Given the proposed methodology, who will deliver and why is this team selected for this task?

**Benefits:** Given these methods and your suitability for the task, what measurable benefits will the client accrue?

These messages should be presented as a coherent proposition – or series of propositions – woven throughout the bid response document.

# Write to the Evaluators

It is important to keep in mind that the people who will read your bid response and allocate the marks have only the page in front of them to judge you; so use their language not yours.

Avoid jargon. Use plain English and keep it simple. Assume the evaluators know absolutely nothing about you and your business. While it will be essential to address technical issues, remember that non-technical staff will be required to read these sections. Therefore adding 'non-technical summaries' is a useful way to keep the generalist on board while the engineers or technicians assess the professional merits of what you are writing.

The writing effort should be in proportion to the award marks. If, for example, 30 per cent is allocated to project approach and methodology then a skimpy section on project management will not score as well as a thirty-page detailed explanation that addresses and interprets every element of the brief.Err on the side of writing more rather than less. You cannot get marks for omitting something but you can get more marks by responding in full and in such a manner that the section to be marked leaves no questions unanswered.

When you finish writing a section of a bid response, ask yourself the question: if I read this as a standalone contribution, are there any issues that the evaluators will think we have not covered and, more importantly, are there parts that have not adequately addressed the buyer's requirements? Therefore review your draft material through the eyes of the evaluators.

# Writing Style

One of the key attributes of a successful bid manager is that he/she can write. If he/she cannot write, then the bid manager will need to source someone who can. Of course, everyone can write but we are talking about a standard that goes well beyond casual communication of the kind exercised on social media, for instance.

The bid manager should set the writing style for the contributors to the bid response and also set out the requirement in the Bid Management Plan (see chapter 13). The RFT may specify the use of a font or font size (or word count/page limits) and if that is the case all writers should be so informed. Different companies have their own preferred font and font size and if such internal protocols exist, in the absence of any client instructions to the contrary, they should be used.

Everyone and every company has a unique writing style and this is to be encouraged. If your business does not have an agreed writing style, then experiment with one. For example, this book is written in New Caledonia, 12pt font size, with single spacing. It would look different if another style (Cambria, 10pt, single spacing) was used, as the following examples illustrate. Which do you prefer? More to the point, which is easier to read?

## Selecting a Font

| | |
|---|---|
| Write about the client and his requirements and how your proposed solution will deliver measurable benefits. Use the executive summary to grab the evaluators' attention about the unique features of your bid response. | Write about the client and his requirements and how your proposed solution will deliver measurable benefits. Use the executive summary to grab the evaluators' attention about the unique features of your bid response. |

What you should always bear in mind is that the tender evaluators are busy people and often have to plough their way through multiple bids of over a hundred pages each. Put yourself in their position. Would you be exhausted having read a hundred pages of a bid response clearly written by several different authors which is full of jargon, spelling and grammatical mistakes and formatting issues? Or would you allocate more marks to a bid response document that flows, is and looks coherent, reads well and has a uniform style?

## Some Basic Rules

Many executive officers in the civil service back in 1970s were 'encouraged' to buy The Complete Plain Words, a writing style guide written by Ernest Gowers. This essential book was first published in 1954 and has never been out of print.

The main purpose of that book was to help public servants write in a clear, jargon-free manner so that those who have to read what they write can better understand the content.

If you are a bid manager, get a copy of the current edition of Sir Ernest Gower's book; it will be your best investment in a long time.

---

**Gower's Recommendations as They Apply to Bids**

Also delete hyperbole from your draft material; drop every 'very', 'best' and 'great'.

Name the client by name in every appropriate instance; do not use the generic term 'client' in what should be a bespoke bid response.

If you use bullet points, never go over one sentence, i.e. two lines.

Use English spelling and not the Americanised version of some words, such as 'program', 'labor', 'check'.

Apply Gower's principles and guidelines.

---

In summary, be consistent; keep it plain and simple; and write in a compelling and convincing manner to score marks. Gower's main principles and guidelines insofar as they relate to bid writing are set out hereunder, with our own titbits added.

## Jargon

A dictionary definition of jargon is 'a word applied contemptuously to the language of scholars, the terminology of a science or art, or the cant of a class, sect, trade or profession'. In other words, the technical terms used which are understood within a business but are unintelligible to outsiders. Also avoid words and terms such as 'big picture'; 'team player'; 'inside track'; 'on the same page'; and 'paradigm shift'.

## Seductive and Other Words (According to Gower)

**Affect** It is a useful word in its place, but not when used from laziness. It may be easier to say 'The progress of the building has been affected by the weather', but it is better to use a more precise word – 'hindered', perhaps, or 'delayed' or 'stopped'.

**Alternative** The use of 'alternative' for such words as 'other', 'new', 'revised' or 'fresh' is rife. 'Alternative' should not be used where the choices are more than two.

**Appropriate** This is an irreproachable word. But so also are 'right', 'suitable', 'fitting' and 'proper'.

**Approximate(ly)** This means very close(ly). An approximate estimate need not be exact, but should be as near as you can conveniently make it. There is no need to use 'approximately' when 'about' or 'roughly' would do as well or even better.

**Decimate** To 'decimate' is to reduce by one-tenth, not to one-tenth.

**Deem** The word is still useful in its technical sense of signifying the constructive or inferential as opposed to the explicit or actual, e.g. 'Everyone is deemed to have intended the natural and probable consequences of his actions.'

**Develop** The proper use of this word is to convey the idea of a gradual unfolding or building-up. Do not use it as a synonym for 'arise', 'occur', 'happen', 'take place', 'come'.

**Dilemma** To be in a dilemma is to be faced with two (and only two) alternative courses of action, each of which is likely to have awkward results.

**Entail** Often some other word such as 'need', 'cause', 'impose', 'necessitate' or 'involve' might be more appropriate.

**Global** The meaning 'spherical' is an archaism. The standard current meaning is 'pertaining to or embracing the totality of a group of items, categories or the like'. Thus the price paid by the state for the coal industry was arrived at by taking a 'global' figure as the value of the industry as a whole, and not an 'aggregate' figure of the values of the separate collieries.

**Implement** This verb means to carry out or fulfil.

**Integrate** This is a useful word in its proper place to describe the process of combining different elements into a whole. It seems now to be the inevitable word for saying that anything has been joined, mixed, combined or amalgamated with anything else.

**Issue (noun)** This word has a very wide range of proper meanings as a noun and should not be made to do any more work – the work, for instance, of 'subject', 'topic', 'consideration' and 'dispute'.

**Issue (verb)** To issue an article of equipment to a soldier is a well-established military phrase and an unexceptionable use of 'issue': the article is issued from store. But the practice has grown up of treating 'issue' as though it meant 'provide', 'supply' or 'grant'.

**Item** It is made to mean almost anything. It is safe to say that any sentence in which this use occurs will be improved either by omitting the word or by substituting a word of more definite meaning.

**Limited** It is pedantry to object to the use of 'limited' in the sense of 'restricted' on the grounds that everything that is not unlimited must be limited. But the word should be used with discretion and should not be allowed to make a writer forget such words as 'few' and 'small'.

**Major** This is a harmless word, unexceptionable in such company as 'major road', 'major war', 'major railway accident'. Do not let major make you forget such words as 'main', 'important', 'chief' or 'principal'.

**Majority** 'The major part' or 'the majority' ought not to be used when a plain 'most' would meet the case.

**Materialise** Do not use this showy word when a simpler one would do as well or better, e.g. 'happen', 'occur', 'come about', 'take place' or even the colloquial 'come off'.

**Optimum** Do not treat 'optimum' as a showy synonym for 'best'.

**Percentage, Proportion, Fraction** Do not use the expression 'a percentage' or 'a proportion' when what you mean is 'some'.

**Realistic** What is realistic is ousting words like 'sensible', 'practical', 'feasible', or 'workmanlike'. Everything nowadays seems to be either academic or realistic.

**Unilateral, Multilateral, Bilateral** These words are not for everyday use. But for ordinary purposes it is best to stick to 'one-sided', 'many-sided' and 'two-sided'.

**Usage and User** These words are increasingly employed where 'use' would be the right word. 'Usage' does not mean 'use'; it means either a manner of use (e.g. rough usage) or a habitual practice creating a standard (e.g. modern English usage). 'User' (in its impersonal sense) is a legal term meaning the enjoyment of a right, and may be left to the lawyers.

**Utilise and Utilisation** These words are rarely needed, for the simple word 'use' will almost always serve.

## Punctuation and Other Rules

The symbols we consider below are the apostrophe, colon, comma, dash, full stop, hyphen, inverted commas, question mark, and semicolon. There are also rules about capital letters, paragraphs, parentheses and sentences.

**And/& (Ampersand)** In general, avoid using '&' in place of 'and'. The exceptions include the formal titles of people or organisations, e.g. Brennan & Sons.

**Apostrophe** The only uses of the apostrophe are: (a) its use to denote the possessive of names ending in 's' and of pronouns ('the client's needs'); (b) its use before a final 's' to show that the 's' is forming the plural of a word or symbol not ordinarily admitting of a plural; and, (c) its use with a defining plural (e.g. 'ten years' imprisonment'). Never use an apostrophe: to create a plural ('books' not 'book's'); to make an acronym plural ('two RFTs' not two 'RFT's'); or when referring to a decade ('2010s' not '2010's'). No apostrophe is required in 'its' when used in the possessive sense of 'belonging to it'. Apostrophes can also be used to indicate missing letters in contraction ('we're' – 'we are').

**Capital Letters** Capital letters are used for the first letter in every sentence, for proper names and the names of the months and days, and the titles of books and newspapers. The only difficulty is with words that are sometimes written with capitals and sometimes not. Many writers overuse capital letters and do not adopt a consistent approach. Use a capital for the particular and a small letter for the general. Thus, for example, 'It is a street leading out of Oxford Street'. Whatever practice you adopt, be consistent throughout any document you are writing. Unless an abbreviation is involved, never use capitals in headings or in the body of a text.

**Colon** A colon is used to mark more sharply than a semicolon would the antithesis between two sentences and to precede an explanation or to introduce a list or series: in the words of Fowler, 'to deliver the goods that have been invoiced in the preceding words'.

**Semicolon** It marks a longer pause, a more definite break in the sense, than the comma; at the same time, it says, 'Here is a clause or sentence too closely related to what has gone before to be cut off by a full stop'. The semicolon is a stronger version of the comma. You should also use a semicolon when a series of bullet points are listed.

**Comma** The correct use of the comma – if there is such a thing as 'correct' use – can only be acquired by common sense, observation and taste. Present practice is markedly different from that of the past in using commas much less freely.

**Contractions** Apostrophes are used to indicate missing letters in contractions, for example:

| | | | |
|---|---|---|---|
| It's | It is | We're | We are |
| Haven't | Have not | You're | You are |

Do not use contractions in bid responses.

**Fada** Public bodies in Ireland are understandably quite fussy about the correct spelling of their title/name in Irish, so use a fada at all times when it is appropriate, e.g. An Bord Pleanála; An Garda Síochána, etc.

**Full Stop** The full stop is an exception to the rule that stops should be few; it should be plentifully used, given that sentences should be short.

**Hyphen** Do not use hyphens unnecessarily. If, for instance, you must use 'overall' as an adjective, write it like that and not 'over-all'. But if you do split a word with a hyphen, make sure you split it at the main break. To prevent ambiguity, a hyphen should be used in a compound adjective (e.g. 'well-written', 'first-class', 'six-inch', 'copper-coloured'). Other common uses of a hyphen include: 'e-business', 'hi-tech' and 'e-submission'.

**Paragraphs** The chief thing to remember is that, although paragraphing loses all point if the paragraphs are excessively long, the paragraph is essentially a unit of thought, not of length. Every paragraph must be homogeneous in subject matter and sequential in the treatment of it. If a single sequence of treatment of a single subject goes on so long as to make an unreasonably long paragraph, it may be divided into more than one.

**Parenthesis** The purpose of a parenthesis is ordinarily to insert an illustration, explanation, definition or additional piece of information of any sort into a sentence that is logically and grammatically complete without it.

**Question** Marks Only direct questions need question marks; indirect ones do not. There must be one at the end of 'Have you made a return of your income?' but not at the end of 'I am writing to ask whether you have made a return of your income'.

## Abbreviations

Be careful how you use abbreviations, especially if you are describing the buyer organisation. An Garda Síochána is not the AGS, but the Sustainable Energy Authority of Ireland uses the abbreviation SEAI, so that use is correct. If you use abbreviations, spell out the words for the first time (e.g. Request for Tender), then abbreviate the words in brackets (RFT). Use abbreviations only when the reader will understand them. GNP (gross national product) and R&D (research and development) are in common use. Add a list of abbreviations after the list of contents where you are working on a long and detailed tender.

## Common Mistakes

An organisation is singular; so the department/government is (not are) a state agency. 'Their [possessive form of the word 'they'] proposal will not be as good if put there [at or in that place]'. Not 'There proposal will not be as good if put their'.

'The effect [a noun] of the weather was to affect [a verb] growth'. The uses of 'effect'/'affect' are often mixed up. As are the uses of advise and advice. 'I advise [verb] you to take advice [noun]'. 'The principal [adjective] reason for stating the principle [noun]' is another example of where similar words should be used correctly.

## Avoid Verbiage

In writing plain English, some words work better than others, as the following table illustrates; take your pick.

# Table 15.1 – Avoid Verbiage

| Acquaint | Inform or tell | Advert | Refer |
|---|---|---|---|
| Ameliorate | Improve | Apprise | Inform |
| Assist | Help | Commence | Begin |
| Consider | Think | Desire | Wish |
| Donate | Give | Evince | Show |
| Factor | Fact or consideration | Function (verb) | Work |
| Inform | Tell | Initiate | Begin |
| Locality | Place | Locate | Find |
| Major | Important | Practically | Nearly |
| Proceed | Go | Purchase | Buy |
| Question (noun) | Subject or topic | Render | Make |
| Require | Need | Reside | Live |
| State | Say | Sufficient | Enough |
| Terminate | End | Transmit | Send |

Source: The Complete Plain Words, Sir Ernest Gower

## Headings

Use headings throughout your bid response to define document structure as they help the evaluators find the sections they want to focus on. They break up masses of text. Title your headings correctly. This is especially important if the RFT prescribes the headings of the bid response. Do not use alternatives; if the RFT states 'project implementation' do not use 'project delivery'.

What are called telegraphic headings should be used for the main sections; 'Executive Summary' is a telegraphic heading whereas the title of this section, 'Headings', is an information heading. Do not use long headings; try to keep the heading to six words maximum. If appropriate, and certainly if requested in the RFT, use numbered headings. Do not underline words in headings.

Select the size of your headings and be consistent throughout the document. All headings should be in bold. For example, a telegraphic heading could be point 24; an information heading point 16; and a sub-heading point 14. If you are using colour, then your headings should be in colour, with the telegraphic heading using a deeper colour than a sub-heading.

## Other Tips

Spell numbers under a hundred as words unless they are followed by a unit of measure, e.g. 1m² or 5 per cent.

Dates should be given as a numbered day, then month (avoid abbreviating if at all possible), then the year; for example, 1 January 2015 – not Jan 1st '15.

## Bad Language – Risky Words

In writing your bid response, remember what you promise is in reply to a contract offer in the form of a RFT. So if your offer is accepted, the buyer will hold you to what you have contracted to do.

Which of the following sentences promises too much?

'We *guarantee* to deliver every week at 9 a.m.'

'In responding to your questions we will *constantly* provide *expert* opinion.'

'We will *never* submit the goods behind schedule.'

'*At each and every opportunity*, we will rectify all errors or omissions.'

'We will *always* deliver a quality product.'

By all means, write in a convincing and compelling manner but shop short of over-promising on what might be construed as contractual terms.

### The Seven Deadly Sins in Writing Tenders

1. You use generic brochure material and fail to focus on the buyer's specific requirements.
2. The document becomes an information dump with no structure.
3. Your USPs are not clearly spelled out.
4. Key points are buried in numerous appendices.
5. The document is full of jargon.
6. Multiple misspellings, grammar and punctuation mistakes remain unchecked.
7. You use the incorrect name for the buyer.

# Bad Grammar

The worst example of poor grammar is a sentence without a verb. Do not be lazy - rectify any grammatical mistakes that are highlighted on your computer. So always proofread the iterations of the bid response document not just for spelling mistakes (usually highlighted in red) but also for bad grammar (usually highlighted in green).

# Copywriting

If you continue to struggle with your writing and/or if the contributions you receive from colleagues are below expectations, consider using a copywriter and/or hire in a professional wordsmith. These professionals will take your penultimate draft bid response and return it to you within one or two days fully marked up with proposed stylistic, grammatical or spelling changes.

Share the recommended changes with the other members of the bid team or, better still, ask the copywriter to facilitate a workshop on better writing.

---

### TENDER TIP

Investing in writing a compelling bid response is as important as investing in the service or good you are trying to sell.

---

# 16

# The Executive Summary

## Introduction

An executive summary – included as the first page of a tender bid document – should set the quality standard for the entire bid response document. An evaluator who gets a clear and quick impression from reading the executive summary that you have a bespoke, cost-effective and fit for purpose solution will be more engaged.

Anything you can do that has the potential to score extra marks is a priority; a carefully crafted executive summary certainly falls into that category. Thus when the technical sections are being scored, the overview provided in the executive summary will give the evaluators a context within which to mark the bid response. Imagine you are an evaluator; having read a short, pithy and sales-focused page, you are now ready to go through the detail of what might be a 100+ page bid response.

There are no government guidelines about the use of executive summaries. However, the clear advice from buyers is that an executive summary helps them get a quick overview of what is proposed. So arguably the executive summary is the single most important part of your proposal.

Buyers often use an executive summary as a preliminary screening technique. So an ideal executive summary should set out the major strengths of your proposed solution and its unique features and benefits. Being able to give a 'heads-up' about the key features of the proposal in less than a minute does not win you marks, but it certainly gives the evaluators a much better appreciation of the detailed bid response that follows. In reading and allocating marks, they will have a much better understanding of the bid response than going 'cold' into a critical review of the document.

Writing an executive summary for a RFT that centres on a detailed technical solution is especially important as it gives you the opportunity to communicate with the non-technical evaluators who will be deciding on the allocation of marks. In summary, the executive summary is a sales and marketing pitch that should be written in a manner intended to convince the reader of the merits of your tender.

This chapter is designed to help you write an executive summary that will win you business.

# When Should an Executive Summary Be Written?

At the outset of work on a bid response, you will have carried out a Bid/No Bid session, which will have identified all the key messages that need to be included in the bid response document. As the drafting of these elements takes time, it is best to postpone the drafting of an executive summary until later in the bid response production cycle. On the other hand, writing an executive summary before the bid kick-off meeting is a useful way to brief the bid team about the main proposed themes of the bid response.

In practical terms, the first draft of the executive summary should be commissioned for delivery and review as part of the draft final bid response, i.e. at least a week before the final document is signed off. If you are using an executive summary that was included in a previous tender, make sure it is edited to reflect carefully the unique requirements of the current buyer.

Some suppliers prefer to write an executive summary from the start as it serves to focus the bid team on the identification of the core benefits and features of the proposed solution.

On balance, it is probably better to produce the executive summary once the key elements of the bid response have been thoroughly discussed and written up.

## Who Reads the Executive Summary?

As we have emphasised, the most important people in a tender competition are the evaluation team that assess the bid response and allocate marks under the award criteria. You are writing to them with a view to making it easier for them to evaluate your bid document.

A buyer's Chief Executive and the senior management team may also read the executive summary, but often this happens after the buyer's evaluation team has allocated marks to your bid. Therefore the primary audience is the handful of evaluators. Write to grab their attention so that they are excited to read what you have to offer.

## What Should be in an Executive Summary?

You need to communicate five messages:

1. Your understanding of the client's specific requirements. Not just those stated in the RFT but your interpretation of the real issue(s) that led to the publication of the tender. Demonstrate that you have a clear grasp of the client's problem(s) with reference to previous work.

2. How you intend to respond to the brief; in particular, the unique solutions and benefits your proposition will grant to the buyer.

3. How these solutions will be delivered and the robust approach and methodology that will be deployed based on global best practice. Also set out why your approach is better than that of your competitors.

4. Why your company/consortium is best equipped to deliver

the client's requirements. Educate the client about your key USPs and reinforce the message that you will bring measurable benefits if appointed. The buyer should also be provided with a clear understanding of your company's capacity and capability and where the project will be managed within your company.

5.  The price. If appropriate, also mention any (free) value-added proposals that you can deliver.

6.  For more complex bids, it may be appropriate to add material about issues such as the technical design, delivery dynamics, project management and quality control.

7.  If space permits, incorporate a graphic or two; for example a critical path roadmap.

8.  If the RFT expressly requests that one version of the bid response document should omit details about pricing, remember to drop this section from the executive summary.

# What Should Not Be in an Executive Summary

Many suppliers misunderstand the opportunity that an executive summary presents. So instead of addressing the client and his requirements, many executive summaries set out the company's history, profile, list of clients, capabilities, the generic products and services that are provided, the names of the senior management team and general sales and marketing material. Towards the end, the client may be mentioned.

In reading such an executive summary, tender evaluators may get the (correct) impression that you are promoting your credentials and that their needs are secondary. Also avoid the temptation to use hyperbole (exaggerated statements) such as 'very supportive'; 'fantastic achievements'; and 'wonderful credentials'. Write for a non-technical audience; so do not use industry jargon, avoid acronyms, and stay away from long-winded explanations of the proposed technical solutions.

Always write in a positive manner; any negative, vague or generic material should be avoided at all costs. Set out what will be gained if you win the contract as distinct from what they will lose if you are unsuccessful. Leave the details to the sections of the document that follows. There is no need to cross-reference sections in the bid or to cite appendices; keep it simple.

## Client Focus Is As Easy As ABCD

**Show your awareness** ('A') of the customer's requirements. Fundamental to a successful tender (indeed, selling in general) is demonstrating your clear understanding of your target client's requirements. When writing your executive summary, be sure to include a narrative of the wider client context, the nature of their current requirement and how this fits into and is influenced by their wider operating context.

**Highlight the benefits** ('B') of your offer. Another basic sales technique is to prioritise benefits over features when describing your offer to the target client. Sometimes, however, best-practice selling is forgotten when suppliers are writing their tenders – or 'selling on paper'. A benefit is a feature of your offer that in the buyer's opinion has value to them, so it makes sense to highlight these benefits both in the executive summary and throughout your submission.

**Craft** ('C') a solution around the customer. Other than a poorly structured tender, nothing frustrates a buyer more than a generic document which does not address their specific needs. In crafting a solution around the buyer's needs, you have the opportunity to reinforce your understanding of their requirements and show how the benefits will be realised. Perhaps in the past a brochure and price list was sufficient to win business, but nowadays greater effort and client-focused tailoring is required for success.

**Demonstrate** ('D') your ability. Nothing reassures a buyer more than evidence that you have successfully delivered similar contracts in the past. Demonstrate your ability to the buyer by providing case studies and testimonials from previous client success stories. In the absence of directly referenceable projects, include similar project references and draw parallels between these and the current proposed project, explaining their relevance to the buyer.

When writing your executive summary, follow the ABCD sequence in order to generate a client-focused executive summary that engages the reader and gives them a comprehensive picture of your offer and why you are the best supplier for the job.

# Sample Executive Summary

Hereunder is a sample executive summary for a tender issued by a university for the preparation of a masterplan. All the tips above-mentioned have been incorporated into the text.

### Sample Executive Summary – Master Plan

The successful, phased and timely development and completion of new faculty and associated facilities at a university is a high-priority project as it is a key element of the university's Campus Development Plan.

The university's integrated design team will need to consider the site's capacities and constraints, mobility in and around the site, landscapes, flexibilities, planning considerations, buildability, sustainable development design techniques, energy efficiency, campus integration, high-quality design and architecture, process and design innovation and deliver a value-for-money solution.

The team will in the first instance prepare a master plan and outline building design strategy that not only reflects the brief but which is consistent with the university's vision: to design to the highest architectural standards and construct new student residential accommodation and associated facilities that are vibrant, sensitive to the site, based on the principles of sustainability within its broadest meaning, integrated with and contributing to the campus as a place to live, work and learn.

The master plan will become the key reference document for securing planning permission for the project in the shortest timescale possible.

The design and engineering brief for the construction phase will reflect a robust analysis of project risks, a detailed cost-control plan and the strict procurement rules determined by the Capital Works Management Framework.

The university's advisors will need to start work from the 'get-go' as there is limited margin for project slippage. The advisors will need to demonstrate their ability to work as a team; to be creative, efficient, productive and innovative. Smart procurement, clear communications both internally to stakeholders, cost-effective design, robust cost control and expert project management skills are all essential attributes.

So too is full familiarity with the site; with the university's modus operandi and a proven track record of having delivered similar projects on time, on budget and to the highest design and architectural standards. The consortium submits that we meet all of these core requirements.

We have put in place a team of advisors that is not only highly experienced in addressing every aspect of the brief but is committed in continuing partnership with the university to drive the project through all its phases. Our deep knowledge of and experience with the site gives us unique insights into the project. In leveraging our current experience we will work with the university to identify savings and potential productivity gains and efficiencies.

We will deploy best-practice project-management techniques. At the outset we will conclude an agreed Project Implementation Plan with you; a detailed Risk Register will be developed; a Procurement Plan will also be prepared; BREEAM technologies will be built into the design; BC(A)R regulations will be implemented; a secure Extranet will be used to enable the university and the integrated design team to view and manage all project documents, reports, drawings, etc., in real time. In addition, we are also recommending that a dedicated website be used. Finally, every aspect of the project will comply, where appropriate, with the Capital Works Management Framework.

The university is also aware of our total commitment to quality; an approach that will be embedded through all activities from brief evaluation to final certification.

The consortium is fully resourced at all levels and has confirmed capacity to begin work from contract award and for the full duration of the project.

The proposed lump sum fixed price is €1.25m.

## Length of the Executive Summary

The length of the executive summary depends on the complexity and length of the RFT bid response. So try to keep it to a page for short bid responses. If a more complex bid response is involved, a two-page or even a three-page executive summary would be appropriate.

## Who Should Write the Executive Summary?

The best person to write the executive summary is the person in the company closest to the opportunity and the client. The bid manager should also be given the opportunity to contribute and review the final version to ensure it is consistent with the rest of the bid response document and executive summaries used in previous bids.

### Checklist for Writing an Executive Summary

The buyer's requirements are clearly stated  and understood  ✓

Your solution delivers measurable benefits and outcomes  ✓

You have a proven and relevant track record and credentials  ✓

Your expertise and methodology will deliver results  ✓

The fee proposal and value-added propositions are clear  ✓

### TENDER TIP

The executive summary should set the tone for the bid response and as such it is probably the most important page you will write. It is also the most important page the evaluators will read.

## 17

# Producing and Submitting the Bid Response Document

## Introduction

A final task for the bid manager is to design and produce the bid response document in full compliance with the buyer's instructions. The minimum requirement is that the bid response document needs to be easy to navigate. Furthermore all documents, regardless of their length, should use the maximum amount of white space and be formatted professionally. The quality of your bid response is a reflection of the quality of what you are offering. If you cannot deliver a document that looks and reads well, how can you be expected to satisfy the buyer's quality standards?

In this chapter, we provide some ideas (such as the preparation of a bid library and a bid production schedule) that will save you time and effort in assembling a bid document. In addition, we also cover the use of design, graphics, photography and colour to enhance the quality of the document. The chapter also contains practical information about, for example, setting out a table of contents, including a confidentiality statement. The final section deals with e-submissions.

## Bid Library

Suppliers who bid on a frequent basis are well advised to assemble a bid library comprising documents and materials that will be included in most standard bid response documents. Having a library of easy accessible templates will make it much easier for the bid manager to assemble the core materials and therefore allow him/her and the bid team to concentrate on what matters; addressing the award criteria. It is our experience that having a complete online bid library can reduce the time it takes in preparing a bid by at least a third.

## Table 17.1 – Content of Bid Library – Checklist

| | | |
|---|---|---|
| Audited accounts for past three years | Tax Clearance Certificate | Insurance certificates |
| Bank reference | Auditor's statement about turnover/solvency | Reference sites |
| Health and safety statement | CVs (short and long) | Bid Management Plan templates |
| Executive summary templates | ISO and other certificates | Awards and testimony |
| Project Implementation Plan template | Product samples | Graphics |
| Photography | Electronic signatures | Tender Declarations |

Source: Bid Management Services (2016)

So the minor investment needed to assemble a bid library will pay a dividend.

# Proposal Production Schedule

Whatever about the challenge of writing a bid response, many bid managers get spooked about the task of sourcing, co-ordinating and producing the bid response document. One way to address this task is to prepare a proposal production schedule. Hereunder is a schedule based on a RFT requiring a seven week response.

## Table 17.2 – Proposal Production Schedule

| TASK | 1 | 2 | 3 | 4 | 5 | 6 | 7 | RESPONSIBILITIES |
|---|---|---|---|---|---|---|---|---|
| First Draft | | | | | | | | |
| Source supporting documents | | ✓ | | | | | | Bid manager |
| Source material for appendices | ✓ | | | | | | | Bid manager with inputs from bid team |
| Edit sections | | | ✓ | | | | | Functional managers/ directors |

| Draft graphics | | | ✓ | | | | | Bid manager |
|---|---|---|---|---|---|---|---|---|
| Source photography | | | | ✓ | | | | Bid manager |
| Edit executive summary | | | | ✓ | | | | Bid manager |
| Complete first review | | | | ✓ | | | | Bid director |
| Second Draft | | | | | | | | |
| Edit sections to final | | | | ✓ | | | | Functional managers/ directors |
| Complete executive summary | | | | | ✓ | | | Bid director |
| Incorporate graphics and photography | | | | | ✓ | | | Bid manager |
| Final review | | | | | ✓ | | | Bid director |
| Production | | | | | | | | Bid manager responsible |
| Approve design of folders | | | ✓ | | | | | Bid team approves |
| Source folders | | | | ✓ | | | | External provider contracted |
| Printing | | | | | | ✓ | | External provider booked |
| Delivery | | | | | | ✓ | | Bid manager hand delivers to buyer |

Source: Bid Management Services (2016)

This schedule should be incorporated into the bid management plan for the opportunity.

## The Bid Cover

First impressions count, so your cover page sets the quality standard for the rest of the bid. The cover page should contain the precise language used in the RFT to identify the bid, the reference number of the RFT (if provided) and the correct full name of the buyer. Do not use the buyer's logo unless permission is granted. In addition, the cover page should indicate the name of the supplier (and main sub-contractors) and their logos. It should be dated.

## Buyer's Format

If the buyer specifies a particular format, with defined boxes and forms to complete, then adhere completely to this requirement. Quite frequently buyers will state in the RFT that tender documentation that does not comply strictly with the RFT may be deemed non-compliant; so beware of such an instruction.

If there is no set format then consider the following.

# Structure of Bid Response Document

Cover Page
Table of Contents
Executive Summary
Introduction
Selection Criteria
Award Criteria
Statutory Declarations
Appendices

# Table of Contents

A table of contents should be included in all bids as this will help the evaluators find specific information quickly. As some evaluators will not want to read many parts of the bid, being able to find, for example, the cost proposal will be of great assistance.

For short bid response documents, a simplified format could be used, as follows.

| Table of Contents – short form | |
|---|---|
| Executive Summary | page 1 |
| Introduction | page 2 |
| Understanding of the Requirements | page 4 |
| Selection Criteria | page 13 |
| Award Criteria | page 24 |
| Cost Proposal | page 37 |
| Declarations | page 41 |
| Appendix 1  CVs | |
| Appendix 2  Health and Safety Statement | |

More complex bid response documents will require a more detailed Table of Contents, as the following example illustrates. Note that sub-sections are used to identify the award sub-criteria.

It is also advisable to use dividers when a hard copy is submitted to make it easy for the evaluators to access the material they want to read.

# Word or Page Count Limitations

It is common to have a word count limit imposed, especially in tenders for works. If you are asked to limit text to three pages or a thousand words, do just that. The buyer is likely to stop marking your response at the point where the page/word count limit applies. If limits are placed on what you can include, only include graphics and photos where these are absolutely necessary. Do not be tempted to use a small font size to meet a page-limit requirement. It is difficult to read small print.

# Design

If you decide to avail of professional design services, you need to start the design process as soon as a decision is made to bid. The imagery to be used, the graphics and the photos all have to be agreed, produced and approved and, unless you have in-house capacity, this work will have to be outsourced. You have several options. You can do the very minimum in terms of design and presentation. In such a scenario – for low-value bids, for example – you just send the final document to the local printer to be bound or indeed print and bind it yourself.

As an alternative approach, you can up your game and embrace design. You will need to prepare a bespoke folder with dividers that reflects the buyer's service or goods and includes your logo and stock photography. Binding and printing should be done professionally.

Finally, if you decide this is a must-win tender and want to create the right impression, you should consider the use of professional photography, a designer, the use of graphics and a professional copy writer. In addition, you might decide to present the documents in a specially designed case or file cabinet depending on the number of folders that have to be submitted. Design is equally important in e-submission documents.

# Use Colour Wisely

Colour certainly adds impact when used properly. So throughout your bid response use colour. For example, colour can be used in the shading of your tables; in photos obviously; in graphics; and in your footer and header. Ideally, use the dominant colour of the buyer's logo.

For more complicated bid responses, take the advice of a professional advisor who will probably introduce you to a colour wheel as below. Note that complementary colours are opposite on the colour wheel and harmonious colours are adjacent. Where possible, try to limit the use of 'hot' colours, such as red and magenta, in text formatting and be conscious that the use of some colours can have significance in certain cultures. For instance, green has religious significance in Islamic countries.

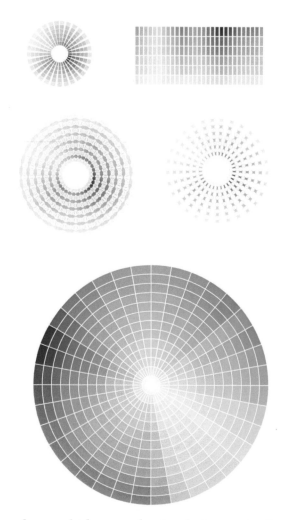

As more and more bids are submitted electronically, the option of using colour will increase as buyers will not need to print out the final version of the bid submissions they are evaluating.

## Graphics

The effective use of graphics can transform a mediocre bid into one that conveys facts, trends, quality, understanding and data in images that an evaluator will find easy to digest and interpret. It is thinking made visual. Images are an essential element of persuasion. Graphics have an impact that words cannot always attain.

**Types of Bid Graphics**

- Flow charts (to convey the logic and structure of a work programme)
- Gantt charts (that set out a Project Implementation Plan and its interdependencies)
- Matrices (indicating skills and experiences)
- Diagrams (of systems, processes or procedures)
- Maps (and plans and layouts)
- Organisation charts (showing team structures, management hierarchies)
- Drawings (or artist impressions or sketches)

Your first task is to imagine the graphics that best support your bid strategy at the outset. Evaluators need to visualise what they are buying, so a clever graphic makes this task easier. Using infographics is a prerequisite in any bid of strategic importance to the business.

Graphics are especially helpful in explaining proposed processes; in showing relationships; in highlighting trends; and in illustrating comparisons. With professional support, design the graphics and adapt them as necessary. Never overcomplicate a graphic; the rule is one idea, one graphic. A graphic, for instance, is the best way to compare and emphasise alternative solutions; yours, of course, and that of your major competitor. While graphics should be standalone aids to the evaluator, always introduce the graphic and explain what it is trying to communicate.

One important point to remember is to insert a clear description of every graphic you use in the title. All graphics and tables should be properly labelled and numbered. In addition, cite the source of your data under the graphic. An initial investment in graphics will entail some costs, but most graphics can be easily adapted for inclusion in subsequent bid response documents, so the payback time is short.

Hereunder, you can find examples of fairly basic graphics that could be used in most bids. As you will see, certain kinds of information can be better, more powerfully and more directly communicated by graphics than words.

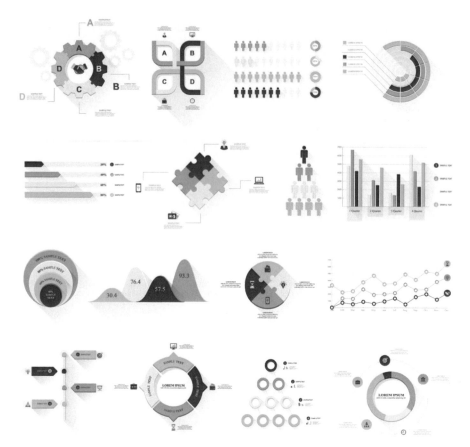

# Photography

If a buyer can see what you are offering, be it a physical good or an image of what your solution might look like on completion, this makes it easier for them to conceptualise your offer.

Professional photography should be used throughout the bid response document to assist the evaluators visualise what words might struggle to communicate. If you are selling 4X4 off-road vehicles to the army, would it help if the bid contained photographs of the finished product? Or would a 1,500-word description be better?

Most businesses have a library of photography that are used in annual reports, brochures or presentations, but rarely do suppliers employ the use of stock photography as an essential element of their bid strategy.

For example, if you are bidding for a works contract, photographs of the stages of construction of a comparable project can communicate your understanding of the brief. When using photography make sure that the resolution of the digital photograph is such that it can be printed easily. It is also important that you comply with copyright restrictions and licensing agreements when using stock photography, scanned photos or images from the internet.

# Confidentiality Statement

You need to protect your business secrets and intellectual property and indeed those of the other members of your bid consortium where appropriate. In any event, you need to ensure the buyer does not release your bid response or parts of it on foot of a request for disclosure under the Freedom of Information Acts (see chapter 18).

Therefore we recommend that all bids should include a Confidentiality Statement (usually positioned under the list of contents or as a footer) and it could be modelled on the following template.

> **Confidentiality Statement**
> This document is provided for the exclusive use of [Contracting Authority Name] and may not be disclosed to any third party without the prior consent in writing of [Company Name]. This entire document is commercially sensitive as it is a competitive tender by a private entity. It would not be provided in the absence of this restriction on disclosure and requirement of confidentiality.

# CVs

One of the ways you can differentiate your bid is by highlighting your team and what attributes and unique experiences they will bring to the buyer. Almost every RFT requires you to submit details about these key personnel. Therefore presenting Curriculum Vitae (CVs, also known as resumes) to catch the attention of the evaluator is important.

Follow these guidelines.

- Always name the individuals you are nominating; do not use the formula 'senior manager' or another generic title.

- Use the person's title as it relates to the RFT, e.g. bid director.

- Present all CVs in a consistent format.

- If you use photographs, make sure they have a consistent format/background.

- Explain why individuals have been selected to fill the most important roles, e.g. 'Peter will be the bid director as he has fifteen years experience on projects of a comparable scale.'

- Include the key personnel from all your sub-contractors.

- Put summary CVs in the body of the bid response and keep the material to twenty lines or so.

- If requested in the RFT, put long CVs into an appendix.

- It is not necessary to include head-and-shoulder photos. However, if to hand, a team photo can demonstrate your commitment to collaboration.

- Tailor each CV to the specific opportunity.

- CVs are not usually required for supporting positions.

- If a large team is being assembled, provide an organisation chart to show the key relationships.

- Use a capability and skills matrix if you are proposing a large team.

- Keep all CVs in your bid library.

# Appendices

Evaluators look on appendices as a source of evidentiary documentation. They will not bother to read detailed enclosures for insights. So you should use appendices to add detailed material that supports the narrative in the body of the bid document. Never put material that could attract marks into an appendix. For example, it is much better that your Quality Assurance Certificate appear as part of the narrative in the RFT section on Quality Control (especially if it attracts 20 per cent of the marks) than being buried as Appendix 16A on page 237.

Also, limit the number of appendices you enclose to the minimum necessary; again, think of the evaluation team members reading numerous bids. Do not be tempted to bulk up your bid response with superfluous material.

# ESPD

A significant addition to the suite of OGP templates is the European Single Procurement Document (ESPD) that appears in Appendix 4 of the standard contracts.

The ESPD is effectively a self-declaration by a supplier that it:

- Does not fall within any of the situations which would exclude it from participating in a public procurement competition ('the exclusion grounds').

- Meets the selection criteria for the competition, i.e. it has the necessary economic and financial standing and technical and professional ability.

The Public Contracts Directive allows buyers to seek supporting documents at any point where it is considered necessary to do so. A completed ESPD is required for the prime contractor and any sub-contractors or other consortium members. The main advantage of the ESPD is that suppliers may re-use it for subsequent tender competitions; just make sure the information is up to date. If buyers can obtain supporting documents (such as a tax clearance certificate) by accessing a national database they should not require suppliers to source these documents.

# Tender Response Documents

The OGP is now using standard Template Response Documents (TRD), including statutory declarations, for its framework competitions. Suppliers are required to edit in their material in the sections provided. It is not permitted to re-format the TRD or to delete the instructions. A determined font style and size is a requirement. Word-count limits have been set for responses to the award criteria.

# Assembling the Bid Document

All the documents that need to be sourced, generated or written should be clearly set out in the bid management plan. As a bid manager, you should have access to all reusable documents in your bid library. Knowing that a significant portion of the total bid response document is already to hand will allow you to concentrate on getting the other parts of the bid into order. Another advantage of the bid library material is that it has already been signed off by senior management and does not have to be reviewed for content or quality.

So one of your first tasks is to cut and paste this standard material into the bid response in line with the buyer's instructions about formatting and positioning. Get this job out of the way as soon as is practicable, so if there are missing documents you will be alerted in good time.

If there are, for example, ten sections under the award criteria being written by separate authors, it is best to keep this material in unique folders until the material has been signed off by the designated senior reviewer (as confirmed in the bid management plan). Once that is done, you can easily cut and paste the material into the selection and award sections as appropriate.

At this stage the totality of the draft bid response is ready for final review and critique. Version control was an issue in past but Dropbox and other such software make it much easier for multiple parties to work on a document at the same time and to edit and track change on an ongoing basis. Once the final draft is approved, make sure to remove all comments and tags from the document and to convert it into a read-only PDF format.

# Producing the Final Bid Document

The first thing you need to do is to check what the buyer wants. Never delegate the job of producing the final bid response document. Given the importance of the document, you as the bid manager should keep a close watch as it moves from a final approved draft into production and then is packaged, ready for submission.

If you are outsourcing the printing and binding, make sure the job is booked. When you get the pages back, make sure they have been collated correctly and insert them into the relevant sections of your bid folder. Also make sure that specialist (environmentally friendly) paper is in stock if you have decided to prove your sustainability credentials by using recycled paper or if the buyer requires the use of this type of paper. There is an increasing trend for e-submissions only (see below). If hard copies are required provide the exact number specified.

If a CD is needed, then burn a copy of the bid response onto a disk. Make sure you or a colleague has done this before and do not leave what might be a task you are going to do for the first time to the last minute. If copies are required on a memory stick, then transfer the document in read-only PDF format. If you have opted for a high-design approach, the CD and memory stick should be branded using the agreed design and ideally inserted into a specially designed pocket as part of the bid document folder. Some buyers require that two envelopes are used when packaging the document, with the inner envelope clearly referenced as a reply to a tender competition with a particular reference number.

It may also be the case that the buyer wants the bid response documents with and without the pricing information.

## Submitting the Bid Document

If at all possible, deliver the document yourself. Get a signed, time- and date-stamped receipt. If you decide to use a courier, make sure the company gets the document from you in good time; for example, at least twenty-four hours before the bid is due.

Most RFTs make it crystal clear that bids submitted after the published submission date and time will be deemed non-compliant. With such a rule, the buyer has no discretion. If a bid response was delivered late and was accepted, this could be grounds for appealing that the process was flawed and that the competition should be rerun. Nobody wants that to happen.

# E-Submissions – Ireland

Gradually, many buyers in Ireland are requiring that bid responses should be submitted on eTenders in electronic format only. From 2018, it is likely that all bids will have to be submitted via eTenders. Submitting a bid response document is quite straightforward. To manage and make your submission, you need to complete the dialogue. You can upload your fee/price proposal and supporting documents, such as the declarations that have to be signed and/or witnessed separately.

Once your bid response is submitted eTenders will send an acknowledgement to you by email. To access documents, price schedule data, etc., click on the links provided. In certain circumstances, it may be necessary to add your price proposal in a specified format. To fill out the different sections of the response form, click the appropriate button for each section. Typically, just the entire bid document needs to be uploaded. You can do this by searching for your document on your PC and once clicked it will be uploaded onto eTenders. Allow plenty of time, especially if the documents are large.

To submit your offer to the buyer, click 'Submit Response'. You will be asked to verify your username and password. After submitting, you can still modify and re-send your response until the response deadline. You will get an email acknowledgement once the bid response is uploaded. One word of caution: eTenders imposes a size limit for uploading tender documents. If you miss the deadline, it is your fault. So beware and submit as far ahead of the deadline as is feasible.

# E-Submissions – NI

E-submissions only are accepted in Northern Ireland, so when you have all your documentation to hand proceed to the 'Submission' section and complete the questions that you are prompted to answer. If you forget a question, you will be alerted. The e-submission facility will allow you to upload the required documents from your browser. When everything is ready and complete, press the 'Submit' button.

Be aware that in order to submit a tender response on eTendersNI you will need Java Runtime Environment (version 1.7 or higher); Internet Explorer (version 7 or higher or Mozilla Firefox (version 3.5 or higher); and Javascript must be enabled. eTendersNI does not work with Google Chrome. Guidance has been published about these software requirements.

# Final Checklist

Use this checklist to prevent errors when submitting your final bid response document.

> Has the document been proof read and spell checked carefully? ✓
> Is the numbering of pages and sequencing of tables correct?   ✓
> Have the final version of all sections been included?          ✓
> Are there missing pages?                                       ✓
> If the printing quality acceptable?                            ✓
> Is the binding holding the document securely?                  ✓

---

### TENDER TIP

Above all else, comply with the buyer instructions about packaging and submitting the bid response document on time.

---

# Presentations, Debriefings and Appeals

## Introduction

In this chapter, we cover how you as a shortlisted supplier should prepare for and speak at presentations. Suppliers are also entitled to a full debriefing where the contract value exceeds the EU thresholds and we set out how you can best approach the opportunity of a debriefing. If you are not successful with a bid and have issues with the procurement process, you can appeal using the EU Remedies Directive, which is explained in some detail hereunder. Finally, we explain how you can access documents and records using the Freedom of Information Acts.

## Presentations

Most RFTs will state that the buyer reserves the right to call shortlisted suppliers to a presentation. However, in practice, and based on the legal advice they get, buyers are most reluctant to engage with suppliers at the final stages of the evaluation process for fear that this could trigger a legal challenge. The exceptions are large-scale, complex contracts.

If you are called for a meeting 'to clarify aspects of your response', beware that this decision was based on the score awarded to your bid response. The buyer typically will only call two or maybe three of the highest-marked tenders and often less than two percentage points might separate these potential candidates.

It is also the case that in the course of your presentation the buyer under the procurement rules should not alter your marks as a consequence of your performance at the meeting. This rule is more honoured in the breach than the observance, let it be said.

The buyer may call you in for a meeting because they cannot decide between you and at least one other supplier or they need to clarify particular aspects of your bid. It has been determined by the evaluation panel that the companies brought in for a meeting can fulfil the contract. Therefore it is essential that you come across as more convincing; more attuned to the buyer's requirements; and as a partner who will collaborate to fulfil the contract.

The buyer will expect to get considered responses at a presentation; expert views; and knowledge and insights clearly communicated. If you fall short on your presentation, the buyer may get the impression that you will fall short when it comes to contract delivery.

When preparing for a pitch presentation, bear the following in mind:

- Confidence stems from preparedness – ensure that the entire pitch team knows their material, their place in the running order and that everyone is sufficiently familiar with the proposed project to answer questions on the fly.

- Audiences enjoy hearing relevant anecdotes and stories from experience – have examples to hand of previous similar projects and success stories.

- Rehearse all aspects of the pitch, both individually and as a team – including walking into the room and taking up positions in turn.

- Warm up your voice beforehand – do not have the presentation as the first words you utter on the day.

- Follow the audience's lead and speak at the pace they find most comfortable, using pauses carefully to help them digest your message and to create drama.

■ Listen carefully to any questions, making sure to answer each element of the question asked. If necessary, take a note of any unanswered questions to follow up promptly afterwards.

■ Be aware of how much time is available for the presentation – keep up an appropriate pace and do not speak for too long. Be flexible enough to read audience boredom or interest cues and modify the level of detail accordingly.

So ahead of any presentation take the following guidelines into account.

### Presentations – Guidelines

1. Rehearse, rehearse and rehearse your presentation.
2. Arrive in good time.
3. If you are using a computer, make sure that it is working and that you have all the required connections to the buyer's PC or projector.
4. Check in advance how your slide presentation can up uploaded; often sending the presentation in advance by way of an attachment to an email is sufficient.
5. Use the graphics and supporting visual materials that appeared in your bid response document.
6. Clarify with the buyer what exactly they expect from you. Have they issued you with a list of items to be addressed?
7. Also clarify the format; for example, whether a presentation will be followed by a Q&A session, the duration of the meeting, and the time available for the initial presentation.
8. Focus on the award criteria only as this is where the marks are won and lost; do not waste time on the selection criteria, including your company's profile.
9. Find out who will be on the interview panel and their titles and whether they evaluated your bid response.
10. Only include as members of the presentation team those who have operational responsibilities in your bid response; leave passengers out of your team, including the CEO if he/she has no role in delivering the bid's requirements.
11. The designated project director should introduce other members of the presentation team and act as chairman.
12. Try to limit the number of speakers on your side during the initial presentation to two or a maximum of three.
13. All your team should speak on designated topics during the Q&A session.
14. If appropriate, provide sample materials during the presentation.
15. Use powerpoint if you are presenting to more than five persons; otherwise prepare the slides and hand them out.
16. Eyeball the person you are talking to.

17. Use humour, but do not be flippant; stay focused – do not waffle.
18. Always use positive language.
19. Diffuse any potentially difficult exchanges as soon as possible.
20. When one person is speaking, all the other team members should look at him/her in a supportive manner. Do not fidget. Keep your iPhone out of sight.
21. Put a nameplate in front of you.
22. After the presentation, leave a hard copy of your slides and a page showing the photos and titles of the presentation team with the interview panel.
23. Carry out a debriefing after the presentation and record and share your findings.

Remember: luck favours the prepared.

For large-scale opportunities, it would be essential to go through a series of dress rehearsals with two/three facilitators playing the role of the buyer interview panel. The constructive feedback from the first full presentation rehearsal session should be used to improve the content and delivery of the second and subsequent rehearsal sessions to the stage that the bid presentation team is fully confident in their handling of the presentation. As a consequence of these iterations, your team's delivery will become smoother, more measured, more confident and less off-the-cuff.

You will need to anticipate troublesome questions so listen carefully. Expect to be probed in detail about aspects of your proposed solution. While you may be challenged about your cost proposals – unless the negotiated procurement procedure applies – you should not attempt to change your costs just because the buyer remarks they might be too high. Once the presentations are over, the evaluation panel will submit its recommendation for decision. These guidelines also apply to situations where you are asked to pitch for a private sector opportunity. The main difference in the private sector is that you may win or lose the tender based on your presentation.

## Slide Presentations

Everyone uses slides, but not everyone applies best practice in the use of slide presentations.

Consider the following guidelines.

# Use of Slides – Guidelines

1. Slides are a device to support your message and should not become the message.

2. Do not clutter the slide; use a maximum of four bullet points, with a maximum of six words per line.

3. Do not use the buyer's logo unless you have their permission.

4. Do not write out long sentences and, worse still, do not read out your slides.

5. Use graphics or infographics whenever possible.

6. Assume it will take a minute to deliver a slide, so if you have a twenty-minute presentation to deliver, generate no more than twenty slides.

7. Use large print size; at least 28 point. Be consistent.

8. Make sure the presentation flows logically.

9. Include an introduction slide.

10. Add a contact name on the last slide.

# EU Remedies Directive and the Standstill Period

The OGP has issued clear guidance as what is expected from buyers once a preferred bidder has been chosen.Unsuccessful suppliers for any public contract should be informed by the buyer of the results of their candidature or a tendering process without delay. Case law of the European Court of Justice (ECJ) has interpreted the EU Remedies Directives as requiring that unsuccessful suppliers must have the opportunity to have a contract award decision rescinded if their rights have been infringed or an award decision is deemed unlawful.

This means that unsuccessful suppliers for above-EU threshold contracts should be notified promptly of the outcome of a tendering procedure and that a contract should not be formally awarded before a standstill period during which an unsuccessful supplier can seek a review of the decision if it feels that the process has been unfair or unlawful.

This implies that any notification to the supplier deemed successful during this interval must be provisional and not constitute a contractual arrangement. The OGP advises that tender documentation should include a statement indicating the need for an appropriate interval (the 'standstill period') after the award decision is notified and before a formal contract is put in place.

Buyers are required to provide certain information on contracts above the EU thresholds. Thus an unsuccessful supplier who requests it must be informed promptly of the reasons for rejection and of the characteristics and relative advantages of the successful supplier, as well as the name of the successful supplier. The OGP recommends that the following template letter is sent to the preferred bidder.

## Figure 18.1 - Template Letter to Preferred Bidder

Date
Name
Title
Address

Re: Tender competition for the provision of XXXX services

Dear X,
I refer to your company's tender submitted by the due closing date in respect of the above-mentioned competition and I am pleased to inform you that your tender has been identified by [the contracting authority] as the most economically advantageous tender.
The [contracting authority] will not conclude a contract with your company until on or after insert date [fourteen days from issue date of letter if sent by email or sixteen days if sent by post]. This standstill notice is issued as required by the Remedies Directive (2007/66/EC) and the implementing Irish Regulations (SI 130 of 2010).
Please note that no commitment of any kind, contractual or otherwise will exist unless and until a formal written contract has been executed for and on behalf of [the contracting authority]. The identification of your tender as the most economically advantageous does not and will not give rise to any enforceable rights.
[The contracting authority] may cancel this public procurement competition at any time prior to a formal written contract being executed for and on its behalf.
Yours sincerely,
Name
Title

Source: OGP (2016)

In NI the situation is far more transparent (and helpful) as buyers release the full breakdown of the marks against each criteria and sub-criteria and support the marks with a bespoke narrative explaining the main reasons for the tender response's strengths and weaknesses.

The Irish courts can declare a tender competition 'ineffective', i.e. it cannot be granted. In such an event, the buyer has the option of re-advertising, i.e. re-running the tender competition. A severe breach of procurement law would need to be proven before the remedy of ineffectiveness could apply. Thus a supplier cannot rely on the Remedies Directive if he is unhappy with the marks awarded to his bid. A serious flaw in the procurement process needs to be proven; for example, the direct award of a contract without tendering.

Non-compliance with standstill period rule is a substantive breach of procurement law.

Importantly, the OGP advises that buyers should not enter into a contract from the point at which legal proceedings are commenced.

Hence suppliers should be aware of the following time limits:

■ The standstill period begins on the day after the day on which each candidate is sent a standstill notice.

■ A fourteen-day standstill period applies if the notice is sent by e-mail or fax.

■ In Ireland, judicial review proceedings must be brought within thirty calendar days of receipt of the standstill notice.

A standstill period may not be required for a Light Touch Regime procurement (see chapter 5). It is common for buyers to sign contracts once the standstill period ends, so if you have issues with the procurement process, consult a procurement lawyer at the earliest possible opportunity.

The standstill notice must be sufficient to enable the recipient supplier to make an informed decision whether or not to seek a review of the buyer's decision. The notice should contain a summary of the reasons for the rejection and a statement of the characteristics and relative advantages of the tender selected. The scores obtained by the preferred bidder under all the award criteria should be provided.

In Northern Ireland, the Remedies Directive was implemented in November 2009 under the Public Contracts (Amendment) Regulations and the Utilities Contracts (Amendment) Regulations. There are subtle differences between the two jurisdictions. For example, in Northern Ireland it is a requirement that the reasons for the decision be communicated, but in Ireland only a summary of the reasons are required to be issued and the standstill notice period is ten days.Note that a separate Remedies Directive applies to the utilities sector.

## The Results Letter

In order to help SMEs prepare for future bids, the OGP has advised buyers that it is helpful for an unsuccessful supplier to see which aspects of its bid were considered strong by a buyer and which aspects were considered weak. For contracts above EU thresholds, for which advertising of contracts in the OJEU is obligatory, buyers are required to give appropriate feedback to suppliers who have participated in a public procurement competition. For all other contracts, buyers are strongly encouraged to provide written feedback as a matter of good practice.

Once the tender competition is concluded, the buyer is required to issue a letter to the preferred bidder and all unsuccessful suppliers, giving them not only their marks but those of the winning supplier and the main reasons why the preferred bidder won. If a buyer fails to send you a letter in compliance with OGP guidance, then raise the issue direct with the OGP (see chapter 1).

You may spend a lot of time corresponding with a buyer who may have no intention of providing you with adequate feedback. If you are not making any headway, then send a solicitor's letter to the buyer. Once a solicitor's letter is received, this escalates the process and the buyer (through the Chief State Solicitor's Office in some cases) will be required to respond.

# Debriefings for Unsuccessful Suppliers

Apart from observing the legal obligations where the provisions of the EU Procurement Directives apply, in a situation in which contracts are awarded on the basis of MEAT/BQPR, the OGP suggests it is good practice for buyers to adopt a voluntary constructive policy on debriefing unsuccessful suppliers.

Specifically, it is recommended that unsuccessful suppliers be given an objective assessment of the comparative strengths and weaknesses of their tenders, with due regard to commercial sensitivity and the need to avoid compromising the rights or competitive situation of other suppliers. There are important benefits from giving constructive feedback to unsuccessful suppliers.

For buyers it can:

■ Identify ways of improving the process for the future.

■ Encourage better bids in the future.

■ Help establish the public sector as a fair, open and ethical buyer.

■ Encourage continued participation by suppliers which promotes competition.

For suppliers it can:

■ Generate confidence and reassurance about the integrity of the process.

■ Help improve future performance.

■ Help them understand and operate the different procedures and practices that might apply in the public sector.

The OGP points out that voluntary disclosure of information can avoid the need for recourse to formal measures such as the Freedom of Information (FOI) Acts (see below) or the EU Remedies Directive.

In relation to low-value tender competitions, at a minimum unsuccessful suppliers should be informed of the outcome of their application or tender. It is good practice (but not a legal requirement) to give suppliers the reason for the unsuccessful bid by reference to their relative performance under the relevant evaluation criteria used in the tender competition. Feedback by telephone should normally be sufficient for such procurements.

For larger contracts – for example, contracts above €25,000 for services or supplies (the value above which a more formal process is required) – buyers are encouraged to offer unsuccessful suppliers the opportunity to have a debriefing meeting. The time and resources to be devoted to debriefing is likely to be reduced if buyers provide as much information as possible in the written notification of the award decision. The notification should include the name and details of the person to be contacted about the debriefing. In practice, many requests for clarifications may be satisfied by telephone feedback.

## Debriefing Obligations – High Court Decision

A decision by the High Court (February 2016) will have significant implications for buyers in relation to their obligations to provide debriefings to unsuccessful bidders in respect of tenders over the EU thresholds. The case involved a challenge by RPS Consulting Engineering Limited about the adequacy of the reasons given by Kildare County Council in a standstill letter.

In summary, the following is the situation.

1. Where price only determines the award, it may be sufficient for buyers to supply the score of the preferred bidder and that of the unsuccessful supplier.

2. Buyers are required to give unsuccessful suppliers a comparable assessment (and not just scores) about the relative advantages and characteristics of the preferred bidder, in particular if their price was lower. The Irish Remedies Regulations will need to be amended to reflect this part of the High Court's decision.

3. Bespoke and not generic 'vague and general' reasons should be provided in sufficient detail to allow the supplier to ascertain matters of fact and law. The High Court ruled that formulaic statements that a tender is 'good' or 'very good' are insufficient.

4. Buyers must mention issues that should have been included in the unsuccessful tender and how the preferred tender was advantageous by reference to matters of fact.

5. On receipt of the standstill letter, unsuccessful suppliers may request additional information about the reasons for their rejection in writing.

6. Unsuccessful suppliers are entitled to a post-award dialogue which cannot be shut down by virtue of the fact that a standstill letter was issued. Buyers must reply within fifteen days upon receipt of a written request for additional information.

7. The standstill period runs from the date the notification is issued and this may imply that the thirty-day statutory time limit also runs from that date. The High Court commented that the Irish Remedies Regulations should be amended such that the standstill period should expire after thirty days, i.e. at the same time as the challenge period.

Therefore standstill letters must use clear and unequivocal language and the level of detail provided and the quality of information must be of a high standard. As a result of this decision, buyers will have to pay careful attention to the content of standstill letters to ensure they are meaningful to unsuccessful suppliers. If comprehensive feedback is provided in relation to every award sub-criteria in line with the High Court's decision, then suppliers may not need to seek a debriefing meeting.

Where a more formal or personal debriefing is required, a structured approach for the debriefing should be adopted by the buyer. It would be prudent to have at least two officers from the buyer in attendance and a note of the proceedings kept for the record. The process should address the supplier's RFT response against each of the award criteria. It should focus on the relevant strengths and weaknesses of the tender without being an explicit comparison between the supplier's offer and the successful offer or any other offer.

Care will be taken by buyers to ensure that information, such as the identity of other suppliers, the prices or pricing strategies of other suppliers, or information that could compromise the competitive situation or infringe the intellectual property rights of others, is not disclosed. However, it should be borne in mind that certain information about the successful tender – the price, for example – should be published in due course in a CAN.

The debriefing should not be a forum to debate the process as to how tenders were evaluated or discuss the merits of the award decision. Constructive and effective debriefing will be very much assisted if clear, objective criteria for qualification and award of the contract have been pre-established and applied objectively. In general, if there has been an objective and properly conducted tendering process, an open constructive debriefing should provide reassurance to unsuccessful suppliers.

# How to Challenge Public Contract Decisions

The EU Remedies Directive governs how suppliers might challenge buyers' decisions on the award of contract after a tender competition. Mounting a challenge is not easy as the time limits are strict and the grounds on which challenges can be taken are relatively restricted.

The Remedies Directive, which applies to tender competitions above the EU thresholds, established a special form of judicial review applying to contracts governed by the EU Public Procurement Directives. If a buyer (contracting authority) refuses to accept an unsuccessful supplier's objections to the result then High Court litigation is unfortunately the only serious option for disgruntled bidders. There is no Irish procurement authority with powers to investigate complaints and resolve disputes outside legislation.

Challenges to the award of tender contracts with a value below the EU threshold are subject to general principles of judicial review and contract law. For these contacts, buyers have to respect the overriding procurement principles of transparency, proportionality, non-discrimination, equal treatment and the observance of fair procedures.

The following circumstances might constitute grounds for a challenge:

■ Failure to advertise the contract.

■ The wrong procurement procedure was used; the buyer uses the negotiated procedure despite the fact that the competition was run using the open procedure.

■ Wrongly determining that a supplier does not meet the pre-qualification criteria.

■ One tenderer is given important information that is not shared with other bidders.

■ Bias in favour of one party, including the incumbent.

■ Incorrect application of the award criteria.

■ Changing the award criteria, or their relative weightings, after the receipt of bids.

It is important to note that a challenge cannot be made because you are not happy with the award marks allocated to your bid response. The aggrieved bidder has thirty days only after it learns of the decision, usually from the date of the standstill letter, within which to issue proceedings. This time limit may be extended at the discretion of the High Court.

If you decide to initiate High Court litigation, you are required to notify the buyer in writing, informing them of the matters that constitute an infringement. Sometimes the buyer may reply with a view to settling the case. More often than not, the High Court will transfer the case to the Commercial Court and in such an event you should expect that the case will be heard within twenty-four weeks.

The remedies available include an application to have a signed contract declared ineffective (i.e. void). There is also the option of seeking damages to compensate for any loss caused by the breach of procurement rules. If a contract has not been signed, an application can be sought to suspend contract award.

The application of the Remedies Directive has been interpreted by the Supreme Court, which found that if an eligible plaintiff sought to challenge the award of a public contract by issuing proceedings under the Regulation that transposed the Directive into Irish law, the procedure for the award of the contract concerned or the implementation of any decision taken by the contracting entity would be automatically suspended. The Supreme Court also found that the fact that the proceedings had issued outside the standstill period, during which the public contract cannot proceed irrespective of challenge, did not prevent the suspension coming into effect as soon as proceedings had issued.

If you believe you have solid legal grounds to challenge a buyer's decision, get the advices of a procurement lawyer at the earliest opportunity.

(Source: William Fry Briefing Note)

# How to Make a Complaint to the European Commission

If you cannot afford to mount a High Court challenge, you might consider making a complaint to the European Commission. It is a straightforward process. The Commission uses an online form that you should complete.

If the Commission considers the case has merit in terms of potential breaches to EU procurement law, a case officer will be assigned to your complaint. This lawyer will carry out research based on the evidence you submit. The RFT will be assessed, as will your RFT bid response and the content of the standstill letter providing the reasons why the bid was not successful.

If the Commission considers that there may be an infringement of EU law which warrants the opening of proceedings, it will send a 'Letter of Formal Notice' to the Irish Government/NI administration, requesting it to submit its comments on points of fact and law by a specified date. If the Commission concludes that the procurement rules were not respected, a 'Reasoned Opinion' will be sent to the government, setting out why it considers there to have been an infringement of European law and that action be taken, usually within two months.

For example, a buyer found in breach of EU procurement rules may be required to re-tender.

While this process may take a year or so, it costs nothing.

# Freedom of Information

FOI legislation applies to a wide range of buyers (with the notable exception of some semi-state commercial bodies) and information may be requested on records relating to a tendering procedure of a buyer covered by the scope of the FOI Acts. Certain records may be exempt from the provisions of the Acts on grounds of confidentiality or commercial sensitivity. Suppliers are normally requested to indicate, with supporting reasons, any information included in their tender bids that they wish to be regarded as confidential; see chapter 17 for a sample confidentiality statement. A buyer's deciding officer will normally consult with a supplier before deciding on whether to disclose such information on foot of an FOI request. However, no category of tender-related records is subject to either release or exemption as a class. Therefore each record must be examined on its own merits. The Information Commissioner has published a Guidance Note (February 2016) on commercially sensitive information.

**Ruling of the Information Commissioner on Tender Bids**

First, public bodies are obliged to treat all tenders as confidential at least until the time that the contract is awarded.

Second, tender prices may be trade secrets during the currency of a tender competition, but only in exceptional circumstances, would historic prices remain trade secrets, As a general proposition, however, tender documents which 'would reveal detailed information about a company's current pricing strategy', or about otherwise unavailable product information, could fall within the scope of the FOI Act even following the conclusion of a tender competition.

Third, tender prices generally qualify as commercially sensitive information for the purposes of the FOI Act. Depending on the circumstances, product information can also be considered commercially sensitive.

Fourth, when a contract is awarded, successful tender information loses confidentiality with respect to price and the type and quantity of the goods supplied. The public interest also favours the release of such information, but exceptions may arise.

Fifth, other successful tender information which is commercially sensitive (for example, details of the internal organisation of a supplier's business, analysis of the requirements of the buyer, or detailed explanations as to how the supplier proposed to meet these requirements) may remain confidential. Disclosure in the public interest ordinarily would not be required, unless it were necessary to explain the nature of goods or services purchased by the public body.

Sixth, unsuccessful tender information which is commercially sensitive generally remains confidential after the award of a contract, and the public interest lies in protecting that information from disclosure.

Source: OGP guidance (2014)

In summary, there is no appetite in Ireland to release tender documents other than PQQs. However, suppliers could request the procurement audit report that all buyers are now required to complete.

## TENDER TIP

Win or lose, you should seek feedback in the form of debriefing. If you won, find out why; rinse and repeat!

# PART V
# Additional
# Insights

**(19)**

# Contract Management

## Introduction

Winning a tender is one thing. Managing the contract in line with the buyer's expectations is quite a different issue. Bid teams usually put all their effort into the tender document and leave it to others to deal with the contract negotiations and subsequent contract delivery. While this may reflect a correct use of resources, it is important for the entire company that once a tender is won that it is delivered professionally, on time and on budget. Managing a contract in such a manner will enhance your business credentials and improve your reputation. Such a positive reference can be put to good use the next time you bid.

The importance of contract management is acknowledged in the Public Contracts Directive as it allows Member States to exclude suppliers who fail to fulfil a contract from subsequent tender competitions. This chapter covers the entire range of contract management issues from project inception to final sign-off.

## What is Contract Management?

From a buyer's point of view, it involves a process that:

1. Enables a supplier to deliver on the RFT requirements in a transparent and professional manner based on a full mutual understanding of the legal contract signed by both parties.

2. Encourages a supplier to be innovative and to deliver value for money.

3. Involves active intervention in terms of the supervision of contract fulfilment.

4. Manages expectations.

5. Secures the required outputs.

## The Problems with Contract Management

There are many reasons why buyers and suppliers end up at odds over their respective interpretations of whether a contract was delivered in line with the RFT's requirements.

1. The supplier discovers that the low-price strategy to secure the contract was a false economy. For example, buying poor-quality goods will inevitably result in below-standard outcomes.

2. Under-resourcing the delivery team is another frequent problem and this happens primarily because the supplier and buyer do not set contract KPIs at the outset.

3. The buyer, having reviewed unsuccessful bids, decides to revise the technical specifications and/or desired outputs but does not allow the preferred supplier to adapt the budget necessary to cope with these new requirements.

4. The supplier is overwhelmed by the new contract as his resources are fully deployed working for other clients.

5. The buyer adopts too relaxed an approach to contract management and allows problems to persist until it is too late to remedy them.

6. The supplier lacks project management skills and does not spot key problems with service delivery until it is too late.

# OGP Contracts

The standard OGP template supplies and services contracts (which are usually attached to OGP RFTs as Appendix 6) leaves quite a degree of discretion to the buyer (the 'Client') in terms of contract management.

Specifically, the contract states (Section 10):

A. *The Client's Contact and the Contractor's Client shall liaise on a regular basis to address any issues arising which may impact on the performance of this Agreement and to agree milestones, compliance schedules and operational protocols as required by the Client from time to time. If requested in writing by the Client the Contractor shall meet formally with the Client to report on progress and shall comply with all written direction from the Client.*

B. *The Contractor agrees to:*

1. *Liaise with and keep the Client's Contact fully informed of any matter which might affect the observance and performance of the Contractor's obligations under this Agreement;*

2. *Maintain suchrecords and comply with such reporting arrangements and protocols as required by the Client from time to time;*

3. *Comply with all reasonable directions of the Client; and*

4. *Comply with the service levels and performance indicators set out in Schedule D.*

C. *The Client or its authorised representative may inspect the Contractor's premises, lands and facilities (or such part or parts thereof relating solely to this Agreement) with due access to relevant personnel and records upon reasonable notice in writing to ensure compliance with the terms of this Agreement. The Contractor shall comply with all reasonable directions of the Client thereby arising. The cost of the inspection shall be borne by the Client.*

As can be seen, the primary obligation that suppliers must comply with is to liaise with the buyer and to address any issues which the buyer has and, at his/her discretion, agree project milestones and KPIs.

In contrast to the approach adopted in the UK and Northern Ireland, this is contract management 'lite'.

## Contract Management – Best Practice

In the UK and NI, specific guidance has been issued about the principles of contract management that must be implemented across the public service. The background is that in December 2013 the UK Cabinet Office published a review of contracts held by G4S and Serco across all departments. The review highlighted themes such as performance management, change management processes and incentives for service improvements.

Following this publication, the Crown Commercial Service (CCS) developed:

- Contract management principles: a set of cross-government principles that underpin the approach to contract management and complement departmental contract management manuals/ guidance.

- A contract management framework summary, based on the National Audit Office (NAO) Good Practice Contract Management Framework, December 2008.

- Contract management operating model overview: a generic model of the main functions required in contract and supplier management.

In addition, the contract, supplier and innovation management team at the CCS has developed a suite of contract management standards and templates which are being rolled out across the UK's public sector. The contract management standards are based on NAO contract management guidance and address recommendations in their latest related reports. Their design enables the guidance to be used by government departments and wider public-sector organisations.

While a similar set of instructions does not exist in Ireland, suppliers could be mindful of these principles when fulfilling contracts for Irish buyers.

## UK/NI Principles of Contract Management

1. Ensure that contracts are known and understood by all those who will be involved in their management. Make sure that adequate resources are identified and appointed well before the award of contracts and that there is an effective handover or transition from the sourcing team to their counterparts responsible for contract management.
2. Be clear about accountability, roles and responsibilities. Ensure contract ownership, management processes and governance mechanisms are clear, with defined roles and responsibilities at appropriate levels of seniority. Make sure contracts have a documented Contract Management Plan.
3. Establish and use strong governance arrangements to manage risk and enable strategic oversight; ensure that governance structures are proportionate to the size and risk of contracts and are suitably empowered and support the business outcomes and objectives. Understand and use contractual options such as appointment of a remedial advisor, rectification plans and step-in rights. Ensure appropriate business continuity and contingency plans are in place.
4. Adopt a differentiated approach based on risk; distinguish between tactical and strategic contracts, direct the most/strongest resources to contracts where the risks and rewards are highest. Consider a 'self-managing' approach with exception reporting for lower risk contracts.
5. Manage contracts for business/public-service outcomes; the owners of the required outcomes should be accountable for successful contract performance and should work closely with commercial staff to manage contracts. Focus on successful outcomes and take account of public-service and accountability obligations and risks.
6. Accept that change will happen and plan for it; develop flexible approaches to change through joint working with suppliers; accept that change will affect both parties during the contract life, but control costs with robust change control mechanisms. Ensure that senior-level quality assurance and controls are in place to prevent changes from altering the strategic intent of the contract.
7. Measure and report on performance and use KPIs and data efficiently to incentivise good performance; administer contracts proactively and efficiently, making maximum use of benchmarking and performance measurement data. Use a balanced scorecard to measure 'hard' data, such as KPI performance, alongside 'soft' measures, e.g. customer satisfaction and relationship management, with a focus on achievement of outcomes. React quickly to issues when they arise. Ensure KPIs and incentives are appropriate and proportionate to the contract. Challenge KPIs and incentives regularly and ensure a mechanism to change and evolve them through the life of the contract.
8. Drive continuous improvement, value for money and capture innovation; actively use contract tools and provisions to leverage the relationship, continually drive value for money and seek out and implement innovative ideas for improvement.

> 9. Accept that successful delivery of major projects is best achieved throug
> a single fully integrated team where the supplier and the client work as a
> single team with one focus; the delivery of the successful outcomes.
> 10. Adopt and encourage mature commercial behaviours; understand what
> drives suppliers' behaviour and know how to assess profit versus excess
> profit; be open and receptive to ideas, explore and use appropriate
> commercial structures (e.g. alliances), but remain competent and robust in
> protecting the Crown's commercial position and driving value for money.
> Use open book and audit provisions with confidence.

Source: Crown Commercial Service (2015)

Where appropriate, suppliers could capture the most relevant features of these principles when writing their proposals under the award criteria 'approach and methodology'. Providing a fit-for-purpose narrative about contract management may score some extra marks.

# Project Implementation Plan (PIP)

You win a tender and the first thing you do is to meet the client and get started on delivery once the preliminary 'inception' meeting is out of the way. Sounds familiar? Such an approach will work with low-risk/value contract fulfilment. However, for larger and more complex contracts, especially if a bid consortium is involved, then consider preparing a Project Implementation Plan (PIP) in close collaboration with the buyer's appointed project director. There is no standard template for a PIP as each contract is quite different.

The PIP is, in effect, a non-contractual Service Level Agreement (SLA) with the buyer. A typical PIP will translate your proposed solutions into agreed work packages, with defined milestones and deliverables. The PIP also stress-tests your capacity to deliver, in particular how best to marshal your resources and (if relevant) those of your sub-contractors. If you do not have the correct level and number of personnel to hand at the start of the contract as you proposed in the bid response, face this dilemma once the problem becomes apparent. Buyers are usually quite flexible when it comes to approving the substitution of additional personnel provided you prove they have equivalent skills and experience.

In drawing up the PIP, it is not at all unusual to discover that the buyer has a different set of priorities having assessed the bid responses of your competitors, so your proposals may need to be tweaked and perhaps re-costed.

Preparing a PIP prior to the start of project implementation therefore eliminates surprises later on. You and the buyer start with a mutually agreed set of common objectives.

### Key Elements of a PIP

1. Project scope (which is often different from what was published in the RFT)
2. Definition of work packages/activities (a Gantt chart can help define the interdependencies)
3. Confirmation of prices for all aspects of the contract (especially important if the buyer sets new specifications that are materially different from those that appeared in the RFT)
4. Transition arrangements with an incumbent (where relevant)
5. Appointment of buyer and supplier project managers
6. Roles and responsibilities (who does what, to whom and when)
7. Definition of milestones, deliverables and KPIs
8. Performance measurement
9. Managing TUPE
10. Review of the risk register
11. Change clause requests and approval protocols
12. Delivery of value-added services (where approriate)
13. Operational protocols (for every significant work package)
14. Reporting protocols
15. Communication protocols
16. Financial management and audit requirements
17. Payment terms and conditions
18. Quality control and use of certificates and standards
19. Dispute resolution
20. Contract sign-off
21. Report on lessons learned

It is also very helpful, where it is appropriate, to capture all the features of project management in a Gantt chart proportionate in detail to the RFT's requirements.

Buyers are risk-averse. Knowing that a potential supplier has a proven, workable and well-tested PIP will give them comfort that the project will be delivered by a professional team in a professional manner. As this is quite an agenda, the negotiation of the PIP should be conducted by persons who are delegated to make decisions. The sections below address aspects of the most important parts of the PIP in more detail.

# Service Level Agreement

Some buyers have asked for proposals from suppliers in their bid response document about the type of Service Level Agreement (SLA) that they would provide. For example, in a recent HSE tender 10 per cent of the marks were awarded for the design of a SLA. A sample SLA was also requested.

While the emphasis on contract management is to be welcomed, many suppliers have not had experience of concluding SLAs with buyers, so what is recommended? A SLA is a contract between a service provider and a customer. It details the nature, quality and scope of the service to be provided. As it is a legal document, it is quite different from a PIP, which does not bind the parties.

There are four main principles that should be observed when agreeing SLAs. Service levels should be:

1. Reasonable, since unnecessarily high service levels may entail higher charges and result in the focus being on these KPIs at the expense of other KPIs.

2. Prioritised by the buyer; a ranking ('critical', 'major', 'urgent', important' and 'minor') should be used.

3. Easily monitored and therefore measured and capable of quantification.

4. Readily understood by the staff of both parties.

A SLA allows the buyer to monitor and control the performance of the service provider against mutually agreed standards.

The main advantages of a SLA from the buyer's perspective are: minimum acceptable service levels are agreed; there is a clear emphasis on what the service will do; possible changes to the service can be anticipated; KPIs are included; and buyers have a heightened awareness of the cost of service delivery.

# Main Components of a SLA

1. **Recitals ('Whereas' and 'Therefore' Statements):** This section describes the mandates or capabilities of the parties involved and the overall goal of the agreement.

2. **Commencement and Duration:** This section outlines the start and end dates of the agreement. It should be reviewed at regular intervals by both parties to ensure its effectiveness and appropriateness and to make adjustments as required.

3. **Definitions:** This section includes any definitions that may be required to ensure the language of the agreement is understood and meaningful to the parties to the agreement.

4. **Scope:** This section defines the details of the service being requested and the business objectives being sought. This section should include:

   ■ Service(s): Identify the service covered by this agreement.

   ■ Service Scope: Describe the scope of the service in terms that are clear and unambiguous to both service recipient and service provider.

   ■ Resource Requirements: Identify the resources (training, for example) to be provided by the parties to the agreement to enable the service to be executed.

   ■ Service Assumptions: Identify any planning or delivery assumptions made by either party.

   ■ Relative Roles and Responsibilities: Identify the specific roles and responsibilities to be assumed by each party.

   ■ Scope Amendments and Authorities: Identify individuals who may authorise changes to the scope of service defined in the SLA and the process to effect such changes, as well as any associated changes to the financial arrangements.

5. **Service Levels and Performance Targets:** This section describes specific service levels or performance targets to be achieved by the service provider once the service has been clearly defined. There may be multiple service level targets per service. Typically, service level targets focus on service availability, cost effectiveness, end-user response time, accessibility, accuracy, and client satisfaction measurements.

6. **Operational Considerations:** This deals with key operational considerations related to the service in question.

7. **Performance Tracking and Reporting:** This section describes how the services will be measured and reported and processes that will be enacted based on a comparison of results with service level objectives.

8. **Financial Arrangements:** This section describes all aspects of the financial arrangement between the client and provider. The items typically covered include the fee structures, any incentive pricing, investments in-service enhancements, cost transparency, variances and adjustments, and settlement arrangements. Any financial consequences resulting from performance deficiencies should be clearly described.

9. **Implementation:** This section identifies the approach and timeframes for the phases and stages of the implementation process, including detailed planning, service management, service delivery, and when the parties expect the service to become operational.

10. **Security/Access to Information and Privacy:** This section identifies the service provider's requirements regarding privacy and security of data, information, and access with respect to any and all services identified in the SLA, and also covers the service provider's compliance in meeting, or exceeding, these requirements.

11. **Dispute Management:** This section describes the dispute-resolution process and procedures to be applied for each service identified in the SLA. The process that will be used to define a problem or incident should be identified. The escalation process should also be identified, as well as all responsible personnel.

12. **Designated Officials:** This section identifies who in each party will be accountable for the implementation and for the operation of the service. It may also establish committees and decision-making bodies if necessary.

## Why SLAs Fail

SLAs will fail if the buyer:

- Seeks to include everything possible.

- Sets out the requirements in too much detail.

- Includes things that are not measurable.

- Sets unrealistic KPIs.

- Does not hold proposed review meetings.

## Sample SLAs

The Institute of Public Administration (IPA) has published a report on the use of SLAs by local authorities and this provides a useful point of reference for any supplier faced with a RFT requirement to submit a SLA. The following sample SLAs could be considered by either buyers or suppliers:

- Irish Water and local authorities

- Enterprise Ireland and local authorities

- Higher Education Authority and the Department of Education and Skills

- EPA and the Department of the Environment, Community and Local Government

## Conclusion

While a PIP may be the best solution for many contracts, concluding a SLA will provide both parties with an essential degree of certainty and clarity that is especially important in larger-valued contracts, including the outsourcing of services.

SLAs are most successful when they are embedded in an agreed approach by both parties to the continuous improvement of levels of service delivery.

# Project Management

From the outset, both parties need to assign a nominated individual to act as project manager. Both project managers should have their respective role and responsibilities defined in the PIP/SLA.

For instance, the buyer's project manager might be required to fulfil the following tasks:

1. Contract award negotiations.

2. Agreeing the PIP/SLA with the supplier.

3. Day-to-day management from the buyer's perspective.

4. Performance setting and monitoring of KPIs.

5. Convening of all project meetings and attending same.

6. Internal communications.

7. Communications to/from the supplier's project manager (at intervals to be agreed).

8. Financial management and approval of invoices.

9. Ability to take decisions within set limits; for example, to approve expenditure below an agreed threshold.

10. Initial contact point for any disputes.

11. Presentation of progress reports to internal management.

12. Managing the project's risks from the buyer's point of view.

13. Managing any requests for changes to the contract.

14. Preparing the technical specifications for a re-bid.

15. Project sign-off.

The supplier's project manager would have counterpart responsibilities. It is not unusual in more complex contracts to have two layers of project management with a steering group directing the project team from a strategic perspective and a project implementation team responsible for day-to-day delivery.

The buyer's project manager cannot be expected to work in isolation. Internal procedures should be put in place that will allow him to report to the buyer's management team at intervals that are reasonable considering the nature of the contract, especially its risk profile. Equally, a supplier's project manager should have clear and direct lines of communication to the company's senior management team.

# Risk Management

A detailed Risk Register should be prepared post-award in consultation with the buyer as it is the buyer who will have to make decisions on the proposed mitigation measures identified and these decisions will have implications for the budget.

The Risk Register should list all the identified risks and the results of your analysis and evaluation. Information on the status of the risk should also be included.

| | |
|---|---|
| Assess all the risks on a scale | ✓ |
| Prioritise impacts | ✓ |
| Determine the causes | ✓ |
| Cost the alternatives | ✓ |
| Propose mitigation measures | ✓ |
| Monitor high risks | ✓ |
| Update the Risk Register | ✓ |

The Risk Register should underpin all your activities. Knowing in advance the probability of an occurrence and  adhering to the recommended mitigation action(s) should prevent unforeseen incidents that have the potential to delay the project, for example, and add costs as a consequence.

If large risks loom, consider appointing an experienced Risk Control Manager as part of your project implementation team. The Risk Register, which is very much a 'live' document, should be reviewed at monthly project team meetings and adjustments made as and when necessary.

The status or profile of a risk should be presented graphically to increase the visibility of risks. This methodology is in line with the guidelines for project management under the Capital Works Management Framework.

A simple 'heat diagram' below can be used to help illustrate this. Your project risk-management strategy should ensure that there are no 'reds' by the time the implementation phase of the project starts.

### TABLE 19.1 – OUTLINE RISK REGISTER

| Likelihood | | | | | |
|---|---|---|---|---|---|
| Very high | | | | | |
| High | | | | | |
| Medium | | | | | |
| Low | | | | | |
| Very Low | | | | | |
| | Very Low | Low | Medium | High | Very High |

**Impact**

Source: CWMF (2016)

# TUPE

## Introduction

The European Communities (Protection of Employees on Transfer of Undertakings) Regulations, 2003 (the TUPE Regulations), protect employees' rights when the organisation for which they work, or the service they contribute to the delivery of, transfers to a new employer. It applies to organisations of all sizes, both in the public and private sector.

More specifically, TUPE applies where:

■ A business or undertaking, or part of one, is transferred to a new employer; or

■ There is a service provision change involving:

1. The initial outsourcing of a service, or
2. A subsequent transfer (second-stage contracting), or
3. A service being brought back in-house.

TUPE has implications for both the employer/buyer who is making the transfer (the transferor) and the employer/supplier who is taking on the transfer (the transferee). TUPE transfers all of the transferor's rights, powers, duties and liabilities under or in connection with the employment contracts of transferring employees (and anyone automatically unfairly dismissed in connection with the transfer) to the transferee. As well as protecting transferring employees' terms and conditions of employment, TUPE preserves their continuity of employment. Any collective agreements in place before the date of the transfer will also apply post-transfer. Employees' company pension rights earned up to the time of the transfer are protected, but the new employer does not have to continue an identical pension.

It is not possible to contract out of TUPE, but the commercial risks and liabilities relating to a transfer can, and should, be managed. Despite the huge importance of TUPE, there are no detailed OGP guidelines about this important issue.

## Procurement – Suppliers' Questions

It is important that suppliers are fully aware of the any associated TUPE employment liability to allow them to factor this into their bid strategy/pricing. If this information is not fully and accurately disclosed then this may result in tenders that take insufficient account of costs, resulting in the supplier being liable for additional costs post-contract award.

As buyers rarely provide adequate information about TUPE implications in RFTs, suppliers should ask some or all of the following clarification questions:

1. Total number of staff, their grades, pay costs, and redundancy exposure.
2. Staff profiles (age, qualification, status of employment contract, contracted hours, benefits, remuneration structures, etc.).
3. General employment conditions.
4. Special terms and conditions for individuals or groups.

The names of individuals will not be provided.

## Pre-Procurement Stage – Buyers' Duties

For buyers it is important to consider at least a year ahead of the expiry of the contract whether the re-tender of any existing contracts will have any TUPE implications.

At the pre-procurement stage, where the procurement strategy is being developed, the following details should be established and information collated:

1. Lists of employees potentially affected by the transfer, and the names and contact details of relevant union officials or employee representatives.
2. Precisely what is being transferred/contracted out.
3. Who will be transferring the service (the transferor).
4. Which employees will likely be employed by the transferor in the service immediately before it is transferred (or, where the transfer is effected by a series of two or more transactions, employees who immediately before the transfer are employed by the transferor and assigned to the organised grouping of resources or employees).
5. All affected employees — any employees of the transferor or transferee (whether or not employed in the undertaking or the part of the undertaking to be transferred) who may be affected by the transfer or may be affected by measures taken in connection with it.
6. Any independent trade unions that are recognised by the transferor/transferee in respect of the affected employees.
7. Any existing employee representatives elected by the affected employees whose remit gives them sufficient authority to act as 'appropriate representatives' or any employee representatives elected specifically for the purposes of consultation and receiving information.
8. Any measures we envisage taking in connection with the transfer in relation to the affected employees and the likely

effect of such measures. Measures include plans or proposals that we foresee, and have in mind to implement, including any material change in existing work practice or working conditions or redundancies (whether voluntary or compulsory).

9. The pension schemes that any employees are in, together with contact details of the relevant pension administrators.

## Where an Incumbent Exists

Where a buyer wishes to invite tenders for a service that is already being delivered by an external provider, it will need to obtain and disclose to potential tenderers a list of all of the incumbent's employees (exit employees) that would be subject to a TUPE transfer should a new supplier be appointed. Following the completion of the tendering process, if the contract is awarded to a new supplier then formal notification with full details of the employees to be transferred must be provided to a new supplier twenty-eight days before the transfer takes place.

## Initial Outsourcing

Where a buyer wishes to undertake a tendering process to appoint an external supplier to deliver a service which is currently delivered in-house, this may, depending on the exact circumstances, result in some of the buyer's employees being transferred to the external supplier under the TUPE Regulations. The buyer will need to formulate, and disclose to potential tenderers, the provisional staff list. It will also be responsible for producing the final staff list to be issued to the new supplier on contract award.

## Contract Conditions

The OGP template contracts for services and supplies (Section 1.H) require suppliers to comply with all applicable obligations arising pursuant to the TUPE Regulations, noting that failure to so comply 'shall constitute a serious breach of this Agreement'. Buyers have to be indemnified against all liabilities from, or incurred, by reason of any claims made against the buyer under the TUPE Regulations by any affected employee. Given these severe provisions, the OGP might be mindful to instruct buyers to provide details of all personnel that are likely to be affected should a new supplier win the re-tendered/ tendered competition as well as their terms and conditions.

## PIP/SLA

Coming to an agreement on the implementation of the TUPE Regulations is often one of the most important issues that arise in the course of negotiations on a PIP/SLA.

# Setting KPIs

Contract Key Performance Indicators are a win-win option for suppliers and buyers on the condition that both sides approach the setting of KPIs in a realistic manner. KPIs allow both parties to assess the success or otherwise of contract delivery. The RFT will have required a supplier to deliver goods or services. The buyer will have determined the desired outputs but may have left open the precise definition of quantitative targets.

Some buyers will not be mindful to agree KPIs as part of the PIP/ SLA, but agreeing KPIs from the supplier's perspective means that agreed metrics are the focus of contract delivery. Agreed metrics are much more preferable to vague outputs. The first task is to discuss the desired KPIs in an open manner. Each KPI must be capable of measurement. For example, there is little point in agreeing a 15 per cent energy efficiency improvement if the buyer and supplier are odds as to what measures need to be used to drive this target.

Each KPI must be realistic. The buyer may want to set challenging KPIs. That would be in order provided the RFT was crystal clear that suppliers had to resource their bid team to meet stretch targets. Suppliers should be wary of agreeing demanding KPIs set after contract award if the buyer is not prepared to increase the budget to facilitate the achievement of the KPI.

Each KPI should be time-limited. For example, the start and end dates for all KPIs should be determined at the outset and set down in writing in the PIP/SLA. KPIs should be flexible. In some circumstance, perhaps on foot of a mid-term review, it may be necessary, indeed essential, to agree revised KPIs that reflect, for instance, changed market conditions.

EU contracts require the use of SMART indicators (as follows) to assess the extent to which project/programme objectives are being met.

- **Specific** (an observable action or achievement is described)

- **Measurable** (a reliable system is in place to measure progress towards the achievement of the objective)

- **Achievable** (can be reached/achieved within the framework of the action)

- **Relevant** (is important/relevant for the achievement of the main objectives)

- **Time-bound** (can be measured within the framework of the action)

# Measuring Contract Performance

Buyers are required to sign off a contract when it is completed. While some contracts have a single delivery point, many will have been completed in phases, perhaps over several years.

The buyer needs therefore to:

1. Be sure that the delivery of the desired outputs has been done to the standard set in the RFT.
2. Be satisfied that the supplier has met his contractual obligations.
3. Have regular reports to hand that address all key aspects of contract delivery.
4. Be alert to actual or potential problems.
5. Be capable of verifying contract performance.
6. Determine a payment schedule aligned to the achievement of agreed milestones and KPIs.

7.  Be in a position to evaluate if the contract has met all expectations and has delivered value for money.
8.  Hold back a final payment until all outstanding matters have been resolved to the buyer's satisfaction.

Against this background, suppliers and buyers should not only include a schedule of reports that need to be prepared but, as importantly, agree the outline content of such reports.

For the majority of contracts, monthly meetings are not necessary, provided the supplier's project manager and the buyer's counterpart have a mandate in the PIP to communicate on an 'as-needed' basis. A monthly written progress report would be a sensible approach on condition that precise inputs are agreed in the PIP/SLA. Ideally, the PIP/SLA should enclose reporting templates.

The supplier may feel this level of reporting is excessive. However, if problems arise – for example, if the buyer does not deliver a part of the contract – the supplier has an opportunity to flag such an issue in a timely manner.

Face-to-face meetings every quarter would be best practice. The agenda should include the following:

1.  Matters outstanding since last meeting.
2.  Review of progress report.
3.  Confirmation of delivery requirements for next period/phase.
4.  Possible variations to the contract.
5.  Financial performance (expenditure against budget and forecast spending to end of contract).

# Reporting

Most contracts are managed at meetings between the parties. It is quite surprising therefore that some buyers can be quite lax when it comes to recording the decisions taken. This is even more worrisome when the buyer at some stage later in the contract period argues that the supplier is in breach of contract, or is not meeting a KPI, on foot of a decision made earlier.

The PIP/SLA should therefore set out quite precise requirements about reporting arrangements, which should be proportionate to the value of the contract. At a very minimum, the following should be agreed:

1. The types of meetings that are needed; for example, progress reports every six months and monthly operational meetings.
2. The frequency of these buyer-supplier meetings.
3. Who will chair and convene these meetings.
4. Who is expected to attend from both sides.
5. How the meetings will be organised (setting agendas, providing documentation).
6. The option of using conference calls and Skype.
7. The appointment of note-takers and the format of the minutes, which should record decisions only and significant statements for the record.
8. The maintenance of a meeting log.
9. The preparation of an Issues Tracker that monitors every aspect of the operational aspects of contract fulfilment.
10. All contract changes.
11. How matters outstanding are to be addressed where these have not been dealt with to the satisfaction of the buyer.
12. How the reporting protocols fit with the supplier's quality control procedures.

# Contract Changes

It is not at all unusual in the course of contract delivery that the buyer decides they need additional services, supplies or works.

So much so that there are important precedent cases at EU level (including the Pressetext ECJ ruling) which found that where material changes are envisaged the contract must be re-advertised in the OJEU. Otherwise the contract will be treated as an illegal direct award.

The above-mentioned OGP template contracts allow for such an eventuality (in Section 24) and describe a change control procedure that can be triggered by either party. Basically, a change control notice has to be submitted, setting out the description of the proposed changes, the rationale and the effect of the change (where known) and an estimate of the effort and cost required to prepare an impact statement. Either party has up to twenty days to accept or reject the request and/or the impact assessment.

Suppliers may be tempted to accept variations in the contract terms, especially if this generates additional and unforeseen business. However, the buyer must comply with strict rules, as follows, if changes to a contract are being contemplated.

## When are Contract Amendments Allowed?

A contract (including a framework) may be changed without re-advertising in the OJEU where:

1. The change is not 'substantial' and this option is provided for in the RFT (and service contract) in a clear, precise and unequivocal review clause, which specifies the conditions of use and the scope and nature of the change and the overall nature of the contract is not altered.

2. Additional works, services or supplies have become necessary and a change of supplier is not practicable (for example, for operational or technical reasons), or would involve substantial inconvenience and/or duplication of costs. In such a scenario, the additional quantum should not exceed 50 per cent of the original contract price.

3. The need for change could not have been foreseen by a diligent buyer, again provided that the changes do not affect the nature of the contract or exceed 50 per cent of the price of the original contract.

4. (In examples 2 and 3 above, the buyer is required to publish a 'Notice of modification of a contract during its term' in the OJEU before any changes are made.)

5. The change does not affect the nature of the contract; it does not exceed the relevant threshold; and does not exceed in aggregate 10 per cent of the initial value for goods and services and 15 per cent for works. Subsequent adjustments to price resulting from an inflation index for instance are not to be taken into account in the calculation.

6. Where certain corporate changes have occurred – for example, the supplier has merged, is the subject of a takeover or insolvency – provided the new supplier meets the RFT's selection criteria and other substantial modifications are not made to the contract.

As a consequence of these provisions, the 'Change Clause' sections in the OGP RFT template and other contracts will have to be adapted.

Buyers and suppliers need to be extremely careful when it comes to contract changes where there is 'substantial change', i.e. it materially alters the character of the original contract; or introduces conditions which would have allowed for the admission or acceptance of a different tender; or extends the scope of the contract considerably; or changes the economic balance of the contract in favour of the contractor.

Where more than one substantial change is made, the 50 per cent limit applies each time provided the change is not aimed at avoiding the procurement rules.

The buyer should terminate the contract (as is permitted under Section 10 of the OGP's template services contract) should a substantial change be quantified that has to be re-advertise in the OJEU. Other grounds for termination include a situation where it is discovered after contract award that a supplier failed to meet the mandatory exclusion conditions or where the ECJ declares a serious infringement of the procurement rules has taken place.

Incumbent suppliers in particular should bear these rules in mind.

# Managing Sub-Contractors from Contract Award

The starting point is that the primary contractor is responsible for ensuring all the sub-contractors and/or members of the bid consortium deliver what is promised in the RFT response.

The procurement documents will usually ask the primary contractor to indicate in the bid response any share of the contract it may intend to sub-contract to third parties and any proposed sub-contractors. Sub-contractors may be asked to complete self-declaration forms. After contract award, buyers will be asked to verify the details of their proposed sub-contractors.

When the primary contractor is notified of his preferred bidder status, he should alert all the members of the consortium as in some cases they, as well as the primary contractor, will be required to provide the evidence listed in their self-declarations.

Once all this material is checked by the buyer, the preferred bidder will either be sent a contract to sign or the buyer will enter into negotiations. For routine contracts, the OGP's templates will be used. Either way, the primary contractor should keep all members of the bid consortium aware of what is a happening. In particular, he should ensure that their economic and financial situation has not changed materially since the tender was submitted.

Once the contract is signed by the primary contractor, all members of the consortium are jointly and severally responsible for contract performance. Under joint and several liability a buyer may pursue an obligation against any one party as if they were jointly liable and it becomes the responsibility of the defendants (i.e. members of the bid consortium) to sort out their respective proportion of liability and payment. The Teaming Agreement concluded prior to the submission of the tender should have dealt with this important issue.

Once the contract is signed, the buyer and supplier should proceed to conclude a PIP/SLA that will define in detail who does what, when and to what standards. Therefore it is critical that the primary contractor brings his key contractors to the meetings that will lead to the signing of an agreed PIP/SLA. In that way, all parties will have a clear and unambiguous definition about everyone's roles and responsibilities under all work packages.

To ensure that all sub-contractors perform, it would be prudent to convene a steering group of these partners to assist the primary contractor's project manager to monitor performance. This steering group should have a remit to provide the project manager will inputs for the agreed reports to be submitted to the buyer.

The PIP/SLA will also determine payment terms and conditions. If not reflected in the Teaming Agreement, the primary contractor should communicate clearly to his sub-contractors when they will be paid; for example, within four working days of him getting paid (less the withholding tax that will be refunded at a later stage). In addition, all sub-contractors should be instructed about the form of valid invoices and the level of detail required by the buyer.

If a sub-contractor under-performs or is unwilling to remain in the bid consortium, it is the responsibility of the primary contractor to find a replacement. The buyer usually has to approve all changes to sub-contractors but will not object if it can be demonstrated that a person or company of similar expertise/experience will step in.

Finally, either informally or by way of a formal notice, the primary contractor should agree on a communications plan so as to keep all members of the consortium fully briefed for the duration of the contract. This is important as the buyer may want to provide feedback to a particular sub-contractor. Furthermore, if proposed changes to the scope of the contract are mooted, all members of the consortium should be involved before a contract extension is agreed with the buyer.

# Communications

The glue of a good consortium is trust. Trust thrives when there is open communications between all parties.

Contract management needs to factor in two types of communication: internal communications (between the project team and their respective organisations) and external communications (media, social media, etc.). Obviously, the degree to which a communications strategy needs to be agreed between the parties depends on the nature, scale and complexity of the contract. For example, clear communications protocols have been agreed about media enquiries in relation to the operation of the safety cameras and the LUAS city centre works, with the buyer in each case handling all media enquiries due to the sensitive nature of the contracts.

Yet few buyers request suppliers to set out their ideas on communication as part of the 'approach and methodology' award criteria. This is perhaps surprising as poor internal communications is often the primary reason for disputes.

Suppliers should therefore consider the following menu of options when making recommendations about internal communications.

1. A project website or app should be used; for example, where multiple bookings for events are part of the contract requirements or where deliveries have to be tracked.

2. This website should be enabled to take payments if fees have to be collected.

3. An internal (secure, password-protected) extranet should be used for all internal communications.

4. The extranet should be designed to present data and financial information in the manner preferred by the buyer.

5. All users are allocated project-specific email addresses.

6. All key personnel are accessible out-of-hours and their mobile numbers are made available to key decision-makers, with a single point of contact notified for urgent matters.

7. Conference call facilities are sourced and supporting protocols put in place.

8. The use of Sykpe for non-confidential communications is allowed.

In relation to external communications, it would be quite unusual for a supplier to be allowed to have direct access to the media. On the other hand, the supplier may be required to support the buyer's communications or digital media strategy. In such an event, budget and other resources may need to be provided for and submitted in the contract price. If you have an inkling that the contract you are bidding for is likely to attract media attention, ask a clarification question about the level and type of support you may be expected to provide.

# Incumbents

Under 30 per cent of incumbents win their re-bids. Why is this? Some suppliers decide not to re-bid because – over time – the projected profit margin they had estimated has been significantly eroded. There is also the issue of the opportunity costs of having a qualified delivery team working for the public sector when they can command much higher margins in the private sector.

Fatigue is also an issue; some suppliers just want change and to move on. Buyers, too, become fatigued (and lose patience) with their suppliers. They want change for change's sake. If an incumbent decides to bid, the default position is quite often 'business as usual'. This is a big mistake in most circumstances as your competitors have no inhibitions about proposing innovative solutions, which often demonstrate better value for money.

Incumbents are often shy about cutting their costs, assuming (correctly in some cases) that the buyer may conclude they have been overcharged. The contract will have specified the duration of the assignment and the option of extending the term. Therefore it is important that suppliers have discussions with their client buyers well in advance of the dates that may trigger a decision for contract extension, or termination, as is often the case.

Also be aware that the decision to extend or terminate may not be in the control of the person who you deal with on a daily basis.

We are aware of cases where incumbents found out about the re-tendering of their services/supplies not on publication of the RFT but on contract award. They were in such a comfort zone that they missed the advertisement in e-Tenders.

Remember the buyer is under no obligation to tip you off that your contract is being re-tendered.

So as part of proactive contract management, incumbent suppliers should always keep as close as possible to the buyer's key decision-makers; and not just the buyer's project manager. To this end, it is critical to have a formal annual review as this will flush out any issues which, if left in abeyance, could cause contract fulfilment problems later on. Interim reviews are also important, especially where multiple sub-contractors have a key role in terms of service delivery.

It would also be wise to start making suggestions for process and other improvements ahead of a re-tender and ideally press the buyer to test your solution before going to the market.

You should expect that your competitors will be monitoring your performance and can get some documentation (such as the minutes of meetings) under the FOI Act prior to the re-tender. The buyer will be approached by these suppliers who will probe any apparent weaknesses and suggest alternatives where savings will be offered. As it is quite commonplace for your employees to be approached by your competitors just prior to a re-tender you should take precautions if you are developing a re-bid strategy; such insights should be kept tight.

## Payment Terms and Conditions

Again the OGP template contracts (Section 3) deals with this critical issue.

## OGP Payment Terms and Conditions

1. Buyers are required to complete a schedule ('C') setting out how payments will be made and discharged. Where this schedule is left blank in the RFT (which the supplier must accept in submitting a bid) the supplier has not agreed to specific payment arrangements prior to contract award.
2. Invoicing arrangements shall be on such terms as may be agreed between the Parties.
3. If a supplier sets out payment terms and conditions in his RFT response these are expressly disallowed.
4. The discharge of payments is conditional on the supplier complying with KPIs, milestones or other compliance provisions (where such provisions are expressly set out in the RFT: and they are frequently not).
5. Valid invoices with supporting documentation (including timesheets for example) must be furnished.
6. If there are queries on the invoice, the buyer must address these within 14 calendar days otherwise the invoice is deemed to be accepted.
7. Prices may only be increased or decreased on the first anniversary of the contract's effective date and annually thereafter and usually by the percentage by which the Consumer Price Index for the service/supply category subject to the contract has increased or decreased.
8. Suppliers must have a valid Tax Clearance Certificate.
9. The provisions of the Prompt Payment of Accounts Act 1997, as amended or revised, and the European Communities (Late Payment in Commercial Transaction Regulations, 2012 apply. This means that all buyers (apart from commercial semi-state companies) must pay suppliers within 15 days of receipt of a valid invoice.
10. Buyers will make a deduction for withholding taxes (under clause 523 of the Taxes Consolidation Act, 1997). It is important therefore to get a copy of Form 45 from the buyer and to submit it for a refund to the Revenue Commissioners at regular intervals.

Source: OGP (2015)

One critical aspect of a Bid/No Bid decision is the cash flow implications of winning a tender. If you win a €500,000 contract only to discover that you will be paid at the end of the contract and only when the buyer is fully satisfied with the outcome, this is a major risk. So ask some of the following clarification questions about payment terms and conditions:

1. What are the proposed payment terms and conditions?
2. Will the buyer accept monthly invoices?
3. Will the buyer accept phased payments in line with the work packages set out in the RFT?
4. What level of detail will have to be submitted on presentation of an invoice?
5. Is it necessary to submit detailed timesheets for a fixed priced contract?

Another issue is the need for the buyer to have an approved Purchase Order (PO). Suppliers should request a PO number at the earliest opportunity in order to facilitate prompt payment and the reconciliation of invoices under the contract.

The Public Contracts Directive allows Member States to provide in contract documentation that buyers may pay sub-contractors directly.

In summary, one of the most critical issues to agree with a buyer as part of the PIP/SLA are payment terms and conditions. Indeed, it would be a foolish supplier who signed a contract not knowing what these terms are.

Assuming the]s, then it is necessary for all suppliers who have sub-contractors to reach an agreement as to when they will be paid. Best practice suggests that the Teaming Agreement should expressly state that on receipt of a payment the supplier should settle with his sub-contractors within four working days. If the buyer makes a deduction for withholding tax then sub-contractors should have an equivalent amount deducted until such time as the supplier receives the refund from the Revenue Commissioners.

# Financial Management and Audit

For large contracts (i.e. any contract above the EU threshold) it would be prudent to clarify with the buyer from the outset (and as part of the PIP/SLA) the level and frequency of financial reporting that is needed for audit purposes and, where relevant, for project/programme evaluation.

It is necessary to set up your financial management and monitoring arrangements from the start and to secure clear guidance from the buyer as to the format of the data that needs to be presented with each invoice. Assume, for example, that all expenses will need to be supported with original statements of expenditure. Linked to this requirement is the tracking of budgets against agreed KPIs and the identification of potential savings where such a commitment was made in the RFT response.

The task of financial management and monitoring should not be under-estimated and the costs of the time spend on this should be calculated as precisely as possible in the determination of the tender price/costs. Where a supplier is working with several sub-contractors, the Teaming Agreement should provide for a proportionate deduction to cover the supplier's costs in managing the financial elements of the contract.

Beware that the European Institutions have particularly demanding conditions when it comes to financial reporting and it would not be at all unusual to set aside five to seven per cent of total costs to meet EU audit requirements.

# Dispute Resolution

Despite everyone's best intentions disputes do arise. The trick is to anticipate problems and to manage expectations.

The main reasons why disputes can arise and often escalate are as follows:

1. There is a growing divergence between the buyer's expectations and the supplier's delivery of the contract. This situation arises all too frequently as neither the buyer nor the supplier invest time after contract award to sit down, discuss and agree a PIP, whose primary purpose is to define the parameters of the contract requirements in fine detail.

2. Ill will builds up between the parties and is allowed to fester. In such a scenario, the regular scheduled meetings are bypassed and as a consequence quite minor issues can get out of control.

3. Personality clashes are another reason. If there are significant issues, a supplier would be well advised to remove personnel who are causing friction with the buyer and his team. Not removing a person who is at odds with the buyer is a significant risk.

4. The buyer interferes with contract delivery; for example, by second guessing what the supplier is doing.

5. Disagreement over proposals for contract changes. Despite quite rigid legal provisions, many buyers and suppliers do not adhere to what is recommended when contract variations are proposed.

6. Frequently there is miscommunication, such as a decision by the buyer to do one thing which the supplier misinterprets. This is another reason to stick rigidly to agreed reporting protocols and to require all communications/decisions involving contract fulfilment to be issued in writing and in a manner that is understood by both sides.

7. Infrequently, suppliers may try to attempt to default deliberately on the contract because they have concluded they are losing money or that the relationship with the buyer is putting too much of a strain on other parts of the business.

8. Attempts at resolving a dispute fail and the buyer insists on a business-as-usual approach.

Against this background, the OGP template contracts (Section 11) cover contractual disputes.

There are two types of alternative dispute resolution: mediation and arbitration.

**Mediation:** Both parties involved in the dispute agree to use a neutral third party to help solve the dispute. The terms of the agreement are decided between the parties with the help of the mediator (or alternative dispute resolution body). Generally, decisions made in mediation are not legally binding but they can be made so if both parties agree to it.

**Arbitration:** Both parties involved in the dispute agree to go to an arbitrator to resolve issues. The decision of the arbitrator is legally binding and the process is governed by law (Arbitration Act 2010). You can represent yourself but you may benefit from legal representation if a dispute is taken to an arbitrator.

---

TENDER TIP

Pay far more attention to the issue of contract management in your tender response and on contract award conclude a PIP/SLA.

---

# 20

# Dynamic Purchasing Systems

## Introduction

A Dynamic Purchasing System (DPS) is a procedure available under the Public Contracts Directive for contracts for works, services and supplies commonly available on the market. As a procurement tool, it has some aspects that are similar to a framework agreement. However, it has its own specific set of requirements. For example, it is to be run as a completely electronic process and should be set up using the restricted procedure and under some other conditions as will be explained hereunder.

The DPS can streamline procurement for both suppliers and buyers; suppliers do not have to demonstrate suitability and capability every time they wish to compete for a public sector contract and the award of individual tenders can be quicker than under some other procurement procedures.

The DPS is more flexible in some respects than frameworks, in particular as suppliers may join it at any time during its period of validity, meaning that suppliers are not locked out, as they are with traditional frameworks. As of now (July 2016) there are four DPSs in Ireland.

All buyers, including central purchasing bodies such as the OGP, may set up a DPS. In anticipation that the OGP will set up several DPSs over time, and as this option is already in use in NI and in the UK, this chapter looks at this innovative and highly efficient method of procurement and to this end draws on the CCS guidance on DPS.

## Basic Rules

The DPS is suitable for largely 'off-the-shelf' requirements which can be closely specified in advance. One-off, or heavily bespoke and / or highly complex requirements are unlikely to be suitable. The DPS is a two-stage process with some distinctive features that are attractive to suppliers, especially small businesses.

Firstly, in the initial set-up stage, all suppliers who meet the selection criteria and are not excluded must be admitted to the DPS. Buyers must not impose any limit on the number of suppliers that may join a DPS. Unlike framework agreements, suppliers can also apply to join the DPS at any point during its lifetime.

Individual contracts are awarded during the second stage. In this stage, the buyer invites all the suppliers on the DPS (or the relevant category within the DPS) to bid for a specific contract.

## Establishing the DPS and Adding Additional Suppliers

To set up a DPS, a buyer must place a call for competition in the OJEU to make known the intention to establish a DPS, and suppliers must be allowed at least thirty days to respond. As with other procurement procedures, some buyers may use a PIN to make known their intention. This initial DPS set-up phase only covers the exclusion and selection criteria as used in other procurement procedures. The OJEU contract notice should specify the nature of the requirements and the approximate quantities or values envisaged.

The documents provided should be made freely available electronically from the date of the advertisement. These documents must remain available electronically throughout the duration of the DPS.

A DPS can be divided into categories of works, services or supplies, which are objectively defined on the basis of characteristics of the procurement to be undertaken under the chosen category. The characteristics used to define a group may include size of contract or geographical area of contract delivery.

If the DPS is divided into categories, the selection requirements for each category should be appropriate to that category and may vary between categories. Suppliers should be asked to 'self-certify' their compliance with the selection requirements and confirm that none of the grounds for exclusion apply in order to gain admittance to the DPS. Normally only suppliers who win contracts under the DPS should be expected to provide documentary evidence of their economic and financial standing.

Buyers should not request supporting documents where they already hold them or can obtain relevant information from a national database. Where a supplier has already submitted documents under a previous contract (DPS or indeed otherwise), it should be asked to confirm these are still applicable and only provide new documents as preceding ones expire, or circumstances change. Where, for example, the OGP set up a DPS it would be sensible for the OGP to hold information about the evidence submitted and make this available to its own customers.

All suppliers who meet and pass the exclusion and selection criteria must be admitted to the DPS and/or the relevant categories within it.

The selection criteria and pass marks should be proportionate and objectively justifiable according to the requirements to be delivered in the DPS/category. Unnecessary or overly onerous requirements meant to limit the number of suppliers would breach the EU Treaty principles of proportionality and equal treatment; would be likely to discourage SMEs; and would tend to reduce competition.

Suppliers may join the DPS at any point during its validity if they satisfy the selection requirements and none of the grounds for exclusion apply. The buyer is required to evaluate these suppliers' requests within ten working days of receipt; this may be extended to fifteen days if justified, for example, by the need to examine documents or to verify whether the selection criteria have been met. The ten-day-minimum period for the return of tenders (including, if applicable, completion of a catalogue) in a competition under a DPS is substantially shorter than the time allowed for the other procedures under the EU Procurement Directives.

Buyers may provide for award of contracts under a DPS on the basis of updated electronic catalogues, provided that the buyer establishes the technical specification and format for the catalogue; supplier's requests to participate should be accompanied by a catalogue.

# Awarding Specific Contracts Using the DPS

Once the DPS is set up, the buyer may award specific contracts by inviting all suppliers admitted to the relevant category to bid. As with a framework, the award criteria to be used for the award of individual contracts should be set out in the original contract notice. These criteria may be formulated more precisely for specific contracts, as set out in the ITT for the specific contract.

The award process and permissible award criteria are consistent with those for other procurement procedures; the minimum timescale for return of tenders is ten days. Where the buyer is not a department, this time limit can be reduced by mutual agreement between the buyer and all suppliers in the relevant DPS category.

A supplier's initial admission to the DPS should normally be based on self-certification that it passes the exclusion criteria and meets the selection requirements. In a similar manner to other procurement procedures, the winning bidder for a contract under a DPS should be asked to provide confirmatory evidence before award of contract. If a supplier ceases to meet the original exclusion or selection criteria during the course of the DPS, it is likely that it could be excluded (indeed if it fails one of the mandatory exclusion grounds the buyer will be required to remove the supplier).

It is not permissible to remove or exclude a supplier from a DPS because the supplier had not chosen to bid for any contracts under the DPS or because the supplier had bid but was unsuccessful in all its bids. Buyers may require suppliers to confirm that their exclusion and selection status is not changed before the award of each contract.

There is no obligation to undertake a standstill period, although there may be some benefits in doing so.

The DPS is to be undertaken as a wholly electronic procedure. However, where a buyer already uses an e-procurement solution, it may well be that this can be used or adapted for a DPS. The requirement for an electronic procedure does not prevent human evaluation of tenders received under a DPS.

There is no requirement to submit any form of award notice to the OJEU following the setting up of the DPS, or when new suppliers are added to the DPS. There is a requirement to publish contract award notices within thirty days for specific contracts awarded under the DPS. However, buyers can choose to group DPS contract award notices on a quarterly basis, which must be sent within thirty days after the end of each quarter.

# Other Issues

There are no restrictions on the number or type of category into which a DPS may be divided. Buyers will have to make decisions based on the specifics of their requirements. Early market engagement may be helpful in identifying suitable categories.

The period of validity of the DPS must be stated on the original OJEU notice; but that period can be later amended (extended, shortened or terminated) subject to notification on the relevant OJEU standard form. This provides useful flexibility if the buyer's circumstances change, or developments in technology, markets, etc., mean the DPS as originally set up outlives its usefulness. Unlike a framework agreement, there is no specific maximum duration of a DPS. Buyers must make decisions based on their needs and understanding of the market. Early market engagement should help provide insights. A long-running DPS will reduce the need to re-compete, but if it is too long the DPS may become obsolete.

The EU procurement rules do not govern the terms and conditions of the contracts awarded under a DPS. So these will be set by the buyer. It would not be contrary to the rules to have different terms and conditions for contracts awarded under different categories of a DPS provided these complied with the Treaty principles of transparency, equal treatment and proportionality. There should be objective reasons why different terms and conditions are appropriate for different categories. The terms and conditions should be appropriate to contracts for commonly used purchases available on the market. In all cases, the intended terms and conditions should be included within the procurement documents made available when the DPS is first advertised.

Poor performance by suppliers on prior public or utilities contracts which have led to contract termination, damages or other comparable sanctions are grounds for discretionary exclusion. Therefore poor performance on previous contracts under the DPS which had led to sanctions could be used to exclude the supplier from the same, and other, DPSs in future. However, if a supplier had evinced poor performance in contracts under some categories but not others, although it would be permissible to exclude the supplier from the whole DPS, depending on the case, it might be more proportionate and appropriate to only remove the supplier from the problematic categories. Buyers will need to make their own case-specific judgements, and treat all suppliers equally. As with any other exclusion for poor performance, this must be based on objective failings which led to sanctions; a subjective assessment of a supplier's attitude, aptitude, etc., must not be used.

If a supplier breaches a mandatory exclusion ground during the course of the DPS, he must be excluded from the whole DPS. Most of the discretionary exclusion grounds are unlikely to be category-specific.

All suppliers under the DPS (or the relevant category) must be invited to bid every time a requirement arises; there can be no direct awards. There is no derogation for low-value contracts. This reflects the nature of the DPS; admission to the system only requires suppliers to demonstrate their suitability, ability and capability to deliver the type of requirement in the DPS or category. There is no requirement to submit any type of tender as part of the application for admission. Therefore the decision on the best value-for-money offering can only be decided at the tender stage for each individual requirement. Equal treatment requires that all suppliers on the DPS have the opportunity to bid. The European Commission regards direct awards as the worst type of breach of the procurement rules and Treaty principles.

Aggrieved suppliers can take action under the EU Remedies Directive. There is no legal requirement to provide feedback to unsuccessful suppliers.

Buyers may choose to allow or require the submission of electronic catalogues. In such an event, suppliers should not simply submit their general catalogues but should adapt the format and content to the specific requirements of the DPS. In addition, buyers may require suppliers to submit an electronic catalogue as part of tender for a specific contract under a DPS or ask for the submission of a catalogue with the initial request to participate. While there is no guidance for what the catalogue should contain, it should comply with the technical specifications and format specified by the buyer and the format and content are likely to depend on the nature of the works, goods or services to be procured. As it is not an indicative tender it is unlikely that it would need to contain detailed pricing information. Specific details of works, services or supplies and prices for each specific requirement will be completed at tender stage. Each supplier will be advised every time a buyer wishes to award a tender and invited to update its catalogue and confirm whether it wishes to participate. In practice, in some cases, it may be that the supplier will be able to simply confirm that a previous catalogue still stands unchanged.

Electronic auctions can be used for the award of contracts under a DPS provided that the subject matter is suitable, including a requirement that the technical specification can be established with precision.

# Is the DPS a SME-Friendly Procurement?

The DPS has some features which can potentially encourage SMEs to tender. The selection stage is potentially less onerous as the supplier only has to complete this stage on entry to the DPS (and thereafter periodically reconfirm its status) instead of having to do so separately for all procurements. As the DPS is open to suppliers throughout its duration, new start-ups, or businesses that wish to expand into new public sector markets, will not be frozen out of the market, as is the case with frameworks.

The division of DPS into categories by type of requirement, size of contract or geographical place of delivery could be arranged to ensure that niche suppliers and SMEs have maximum opportunity to compete. A supplier may apply for as many categories as it wishes. Any and all suppliers who pass the exclusion criteria and meet the selection criteria must be admitted to the DPS.

Where a DPS is divided into categories, the buyer should apply selection criteria that are proportionate and relevant to the characteristics of the category concerned.

If a supplier fails the exclusion or selection stage, it can reapply subsequently. Thus if a supplier failed the exclusion stage, it could reapply if the mandatory or discretionary exclusionary periods had ended or if the supplier had self-cleaned. If the supplier did not meet selection criteria, it could reapply if its circumstances changed; for example, if it had newly available skills, experience or if something else which would change its answers to the selection criteria had occurred.

## CASE STUDY

### Solar Panels

Public Power Solutions has developed a DPS which enables public sector bodies to procure solar projects whilst meeting the UK's Public Contract Regulations 2015. This DPS is a completely electronic system; it does not operate in the same way as a traditional contract/framework in that it is an 'open market' product designed to provide access to a pool of suppliers which can be constantly refreshed. Establishing a DPS with multiple providers creates an environment which encourages fair competition and allows suppliers to join at any time and choose whether to compete for all or any of the projects advertised through the DPS. A DPS model is more flexible than a traditional framework; it enables best value to be achieved and is more effective for the renewables market than using a traditional OJEU procurement. The DPS arrangement has been set up to avoid the need for individual public sector bodies to separately procure contracts which will have a financial benefit to the client both in terms of money and time. With Public Power Solution's expertise in this market and its direct links to the public sector, Public Power Solutions acts as a conventional developer within the model to ensure the solar projects are taken from inception through to completion. A Contract Notice has been published through the OJEU giving potential providers the opportunity to join the DPS.

## CASE STUDY

### Training

Portsmouth City Council invited expressions of interest from suitably qualified and experienced providers to tender for the provision of core essential training for all staff whose job roles involve working with children. The Council appointed a number of trainers that are suitably qualified and have experience delivering the courses that are key areas of underpinning knowledge and skills. The Council did this by implementing a DPS to deliver these requirements. By putting in place formal processes, the Council aims to achieve efficiencies and reduce the time taken to procure each course(s). Suppliers admitted to the DPS will be invited to submit quotes via a mini-competition for the training courses they have identified they can deliver. Estimates of the expenditure under the DPS are in the region of £250,000 to £400,000. The initial contract period will be for four years, extendable in increments to a maximum of seven years subject to performance and agreement of all parties.

# Conclusion

The DPS is no more onerous than the open procedure for individual contracts. In fact, it will be easier, as buyers will only have to examine tenders and not assess supplier's exclusion and selection status for every contract. Buyers will also know how many suppliers are on the DPS/category at any given point so they will know the maximum number of potential responses in advance.

As the DPS is for works, supplies and services commonly available on the market, it may be possible in many cases to run relatively straightforward award evaluation criteria, which will not be onerous on buyer's time. Focused categories may help limit the number of suppliers that apply for each category.

Given that the EU's rules for setting up a DPS are now much more flexible, Irish buyers should consider the relative merits of DPSs, frameworks and individual separate procurements before deciding which has the potential to deliver the best value for money.

## TENDER TIP

In anticipation that Irish buyers will start to use DPS procurement more frequently, compete for comparable NI and UK opportunities to prove your credentials.

# 21

# Private Sector Pitches

## Introduction

Many companies in the private sector adopt a formal approach to procurement of goods and services, recognising the merits of competitive tendering. It not only identifies the supplier with the lowest price, but also those who can provide the best all-round response to their needs.

Competitive tendering offers an equitable basis for selecting suppliers; access to innovative solutions; an opportunity to learn how well suppliers understand the buyer's requirements; and an insight into the supplier's approach to the working relationship proposed. In effect, the tendering process offers to both public and private buyers the most effective mechanism to establish which supplier can deliver the best value for money. In this chapter, we discuss the unique features of private-sector procurement.

## Private Sector vs Public Sector Proposals

The principal difference between private and public sector procurement processes stems from the difference between the nature of each entity.

Public procurement is undertaken to support government in providing public services to citizens, with the procurement rules governed by the EU Procurement Directives. This legislation, as transposed into law in all EU Member States, sets out how public procurement must be run – covering such aspects as tender competition run times, the thresholds applying to different areas of government, as well as permissible procurement procedures.

Private procurement, on the other hand, is driven by the business imperative to generate returns for company shareholders. There is far less focus on compliance with prescriptive processes and legislation; procurement legislation does not apply to private enterprise. Therefore companies are free to set their own procurement processes to suit their own business needs, structure and the complexity of their requirements.

While public buyers are required to follow a standard process and approach, their private sector counterparts are generally less rigid about the structure of bids, giving suppliers more scope to devise a tailored approach to their requirements. They are also generally more forthcoming about meeting prospective suppliers both before and during the tendering process to discuss the proposed project; seeing supply-chain relationships in more of a partnership view over a longer period than public buyers who are required by law to re-tender their contracts at defined intervals.

During the evaluation process, private buyers consider many of the same questions as buyers in the public sector. In a similar way to public buyers evaluating bids on the basis of MEAT/BQPR (see chapter 6) rather than lowest cost, private sector buyers appreciate that they get what they pay for and know that the lowest-priced supplier may not offer the best quality or customer service, which could lead to a higher whole-life cost of the purchase.

The business buyer's primary concern will be to identify the bid that offers the best overall value for money; one that displays the greatest understanding of their requirements and proposes the most suitable solution to the tender specification. Like their colleagues in the public sector, they will look for prices that are realistic in relation to the scale and scope of the contract; expect quality in the resources proposed for the work; insist on clearly defined outcomes; and they will seek evidence of distinctive added value and reliable performance.

In practice, private buyers are more likely to skim through bids quickly to gain an overall idea of their suitability before subjecting them to a more thorough analysis. First impressions can be decisive, which is a further reason why bidders need to make sure their bids are efficiently organised, logically structured and presented in a competent, professional manner.

# Public vs Private – Key Differentiators

|  | PRIVATE SECTOR | PUBLIC SECTOR |
|---|---|---|
| Deadlines | In a private sector bid context, the deadline is set by the buyer to suit their own business needs and their opinion of how long it should take suppliers to respond. Private sector buyers may be open to modify the deadline if requested and may look leniently on a late tender at their own discretion. | In public sector bids, the deadline is non-negotiable and timelines are enshrined in legislation. With the advent of electronic tendering platforms in the public sector, deadlines are enforced electronically to the last second and late tenders will be rejected. |
| Negotiation | It is commonplace in private sector procurement for negotiation to take place between the buyer and a number of preferred suppliers to arrive at a final contract price and offering. | Other than in the context of a negotiated procedure competition, negotiation in public sector tendering is strictly forbidden. Buying decisions are made solely on the basis of the proposal document. |

| | **PRIVATE SECTOR** | **PUBLIC SECTOR** |
|---|---|---|
| Communication | As there is no specific legislation governing private sector procurement, the degree to which a private buyer chooses to communicate with suppliers during the tendering process is left to their own discretion. This may range from zero communication to telephone calls or meetings and open discussion of their needs and the project specifications. | Communication during the public tendering process is restricted by legislation and in practice is tightly controlled to ensure that any and all communications are shared uniformly with all bidders. Thus, all communication is in writing and all clarification questions posed by suppliers are shared with all interested parties, together with the buyer's answers. |
| Regulation | In the private sector, there is no legislation specific to procurement, other than general law of contract relating to offers and invitations to treat. As such, the approach to procurement will vary from one company to another, depending on their specific processes. | Every element of public procurement from thresholds to timelines and permissible procedures is set out in the EU Procurement Directives. Public buyers in all EU Member States must follow this standard approach. Public buyers are also affected by other legislation such as Freedom of Information and Data Protection. |
| Process | Private sector procurement varies from company to company, with buyers following best practice from organisations such as the Chartered Institute of Purchasing and Supply (CIPS) and the Irish Institute of Purchasing and Material Management (IIPMM), as well as internal company policies and procedures. | The public procurement process is uniform across all public bodies, with all organisations from local authorities to central government departments being subject to the EU Procurement Directives. |

| | PRIVATE SECTOR | PUBLIC SECTOR |
|---|---|---|
| Format | Given the variety of approaches to procurement among private buyers, the format and structure of private tenders varies hugely. There is no standard approach, with everything from video submissions to reverse auctions and multi-volume paper submissions the norm. | Although the public procurement process itself is uniform, the approach to the format and content of individual tender competitions can vary between public buyers. In the main, however, a standard template-driven approach is followed, with tender request documents following a standard structure and electronic upload of tenders being most common. |
| Evaluation | Evaluation in the private sector can often be time-constrained by business pressures, with tenders evaluated by one or more personnel as business needs and resourcing requires. | Public procurement follows a strict evaluation process, necessitating multiple evaluators and sign-offs throughout the process to ensure transparency and audit after the fact. |
| Debriefing | Approaches to debriefing in the private sector vary in line with individual companies' procurement processes. Depending on the openness of the buyer company to long-term partnership and continuous improvement, they may provide detailed face-to-face debriefing to both successful and unsuccessful tenderers. | Best practice in public procurement is to provide written feedback to suppliers setting out the supplier's scores under each of the award criteria as well as a narrative describing the merits of the supplier's tender relative to the winning tenderer. |

| | PRIVATE SECTOR CONTD. | PUBLIC SECTOR CONTD. |
|---|---|---|
| Duration | Private enterprise tends to adopt a longer-term, partnership view in relation to its supply-chain arrangements and is under no external obligation to re-tender its contracts following the passage of time. Procurement projects will be driven by business imperatives and a business case made for re-tender of all contracts based on business need or market changes. | Public contract duration is restricted in time; for instance, to a maximum of four years in the case of a framework agreement. Such restrictions on contract durations are imposed in the interest of fairness to the supply market and without any regard to building long-term supply-chain partnerships, which would be inappropriate in a public sector context. |

# Pitch Presentations

In many private-sector tender competitions, shortlisted suppliers are invited to make a formal pitch presentation. The presentation gives the buyer and other executives an opportunity to ask questions and make a judgement on how they could work with the supplier and it also affords the supplier an opportunity to reinforce its key selling messages face-to-face.

In some cases, such pitch presentations are used by evaluation teams to affirm the marks which they have allocated to a supplier's tender bid on the basis of a desktop review of the submission. Thus a supplier's final tender score may depend on their pitch performance, affording them the opportunity to both lose marks and, more importantly, gain additional marks.

The focus of the pitch presentation should be largely on demonstrating an understanding of the client's needs, detailing the proposed offer and clarifying any questions the buyer may have about the proposed solutions, methodology and approach or the fee proposal.

From the supplier's side, the person responsible for implementation

– usually the project manager or client services manager – should always be present. This person's attendance is actually more important than having a CEO take part if the CEO does not have direct responsibility for ultimate delivery. In addition, there should be a clear leader acting as master of ceremonies to introduce speakers and provide continuity, but it is important to avoid having one person do all the talking. Each attendee should have a role in the pitch presentation and speak about their relevant specialist area, being in a position to answer questions if asked.

Whether a slideshow presentation or similar is appropriate will depend on the nature of the pitch, but if a slideshow presentation is used, it should be both professional in appearance and tailored in content to the specifics of the proposed contract. In every presentation there are two resources: the speaker and the slideshow. To use each to your best advantage, the speaker should deliver information and engage with the audience. The slideshow is best used for graphics and visual communication of data and concepts; certainly not for countless bullet points of text which the presenter simply reads off the screen and uses as a 'crutch' or speaker's notes. Best practice in slideshow design should pique the audience's curiosity and allow them to remember information visually.

Chapter 18 provides additional insights about pitch presentations.

TENDER TIP

Recognise the differences between public and private sector tendering competitions and adjust your approach accordingly to make best advantage of both.

## 22

# Top Tender Tips

## Introduction

We have endeavoured to explain in plain language how to bid to win. Tendering, and in particular writing a compelling bid proposal, is not an easy job, as you have probably gathered by now.

The constant imperative throughout this book is 'bid to win'.

In this final chapter, we bring together the 'Top Tips' that we present to clients who want to cut to the chase.

## Top Tender Tips

| | TIP | COMMENT |
|---|---|---|
| 1 | Put the buyer's needs at the centre of your proposal/ solution. | This means that a 'generic response' is useless. |
| 2 | Address the buyer's 'underlying needs' by going beyond mere compliance with the RFT. | A compliant bid scores 80 per cent; a winning bid gets 85 per cent or more and wins. |
| 3 | Use clear, jargon-free language so that you avoid confusion. | Remember that the buyer does not necessarily speak 'your' language. |

| | TIP | COMMENT |
|---|---|---|
| 4 | Propose a compelling solution that captures the client's attention and sets your bid apart from the competition. | What are your key differentiators? |
| 5 | Communicate your solution to the client in terms of benefits, not generic features. | If you can generate savings or productivity gains, then quantify them. |
| 6 | Demonstrate your capability to deliver better than anything else. | Buyers are always seeking to reassure themselves that the supplier can deliver what they propose, so give them practical examples. |
| 7 | Be open to the concept of partnership/consortium bidding in order to deliver on every aspect of the client's requirements. | Be sure that you choose your partners carefully! |
| 8 | Be strategic in your pricing model – think what is going to be important to the client | Look carefully at sub-criteria for pricing. Also determine your price 'profit' point. |
| 9 | Be sure to use relevant, high-quality reference sites in your bid. | Buyers view past performance as one of the best indicators of future performance. So pick 'fit-for-purpose' references and explain why they were selected. |
| 10 | Read and re-read the tender documentation, keep ahead of legislation and know what you can and cannot do within the tendering process. | Attention to detail and knowledge of the evaluation process will score you more marks. |
| 11 | Keep the buyer 'on side' by making your bid easy to navigate. | Consider using tabbed dividers to split your document into logical sections. |
| 12 | Prepare an engaging document that commands attention and presents a professional image. | Creating a positive impression improves your chances. |

| TIP CONTD. | COMMENT CONTD. |
|---|---|
| 13 Write a powerful but concise Executive Summary. | Decision-makers usually start with this section of the bid response and it forms an early impression of you and your proposal, which should summarise your bid from the buyer's perspective. |

# Your Win Rate

When we work with clients on live bids there is only one possible outcome: we win.

We hope the insights, know-how and practical advices peppered throughout this book help you win more often and more profitably.

---

TENDER TIP

Decide which Tender Tip is the most relevant to you and your business.

---